Better Homes and Gardens®

rose
gardening

WILEY

John Wiley & Sons, Inc.

Better Homes and Gardens® Rose Gardening

Contributing Writer: Jeff Wyckoff, president, American Rose Society
Project Editor: Deb Wiley
Contributing Designers: Sundie Ruppert, Lori Gould
Editor, Garden Books: Denny Schrock
Editorial Assistant: Heather Knowles
Contributing Copy Editor: Fran Gardner
Contributing Proofreaders: Terri Fredrickson, Peg Smith
Contributing Indexer: Don Glassman
Contributing Photographers: Scott Little, Dean Schoeppner,
    Denny Schrock, Deb Wiley, Jeff Wyckoff
Contributing Photo Researcher: Susan Ferguson

Meredith® Books
Editorial Director: Gregory H. Kayko
Editor in Chief, Garden: Doug Jimerson
Editorial Manager: David Speer
Art Director: Tim Alexander
Managing Editor: Doug Kouma
Executive Director, Sales: Ken Zagor
Director, Operations: George A. Susral
Business Director: Janice Croat
Imaging Center Operator: Mitchell Barlow

John Wiley & Sons, Inc.
Publisher: Natalie Chapman
Associate Publisher: Jessica Goodman
Executive Editor: Anne Ficklen
Assistant Editor: Charleen Barila
Production Director: Diana Cisek
Manufacturing Manager: Tom Hyland

This book is printed on acid-free paper.

Note to Reader: Due to differing conditions, tools, and individual skills, Meredith Corporation assumes no responsibility for any damages, injuries suffered, or losses incurred as a result of following the information published in this book. Before beginning any project, review the instructions carefully and, if any doubts or questions remain, consult local experts or authorities. Because codes and regulations vary greatly, you should always check with authorities to ensure that your project complies with all applicable local codes and regulations. Always read and observe all the safety precautions provided by manufacturers of any tools, equipment, or supplies, and follow all accepted safety procedures.

Better Homes and Gardens® Magazine
Editor in Chief: Gayle Goodson Butler

Meredith National Media Group
President: Tom Harty
Executive Vice President: Doug Olson

Meredith Corporation
Chairman of the Board: William T. Kerr
President and Chief Executive Officer: Stephen M. Lacy

In Memoriam: E.T. Meredith III (1933–2003)

Photo Credits
Photographers credited may retain copyright © to the listed photographs.

Bailey Nurseries 133BC, 113BL, 166BL; Louise Clements, Heirloom Roses 113R, 175BR, 193TL; Clemson University-USDA Cooperative Extension Slide Series, Bugwood.org 90R; Division of Plant Industry Archive, Florida Department of Agriculture & Consumer Services, Bugwood.org 92R; Sandy Lundberg 202BL, 207BR; Purdue University, Plant & Disease Diagnostic Lab 91R; Robin Rosetta, Oregon State University 89C; Star Roses/Conard-Pyle 210TR; Ward Upham, Kansas State University 89R; Carroll E. Younce, USDA Agricultural Research Service, Bugwood.org 91L

For general information on our other products and services or for technical support, please contact our Customer Care Department within the United States at (800) 762-2974, outside the United States at (317) 572-3993 or fax (317) 572-4002.

Wiley also publishes its books in a variety of electronic formats. Some content that appears in print may not be available in electronic books. For more information about Wiley products, visit our web site at www.wiley.com.

Library of Congress Cataloging-in-Publication Data
Better homes and gardens rose gardening.
   p. cm. Includes index.
   ISBN 978-0-470-87845-3 (pbk.)
   1. Rose culture--United States. 2. Roses--United States.
   I. Better homes and gardens. II. Title: Rose gardening.

SB411.B47 2010
635.9'33734--dc22
                                        2010042157
Printed in the United States of America

10 9 8 7 6 5 4 3 2

table of contents

p.4 HISTORY & DEVELOPMENT

Roses weren't always in the forms, shapes, and colors you see today. Learn how they evolved.

6   The first roses
8   Modern roses
10   Bigger & smaller blooms
12   Recent trends

p.14 SELECTING THE RIGHT ROSE

There's a rose right for every garden. Use these helpful guidelines when you buy them.

16   Rose basics
22   Flowers & bushes
26   Rose families
34   Roses by region
38   Buying roses

216 Resources
218 Index

p.44 LANDSCAPING & DESIGNING

Roses can beautify and solve problems in your yard. Be sure to cut some for bouquets!

46   Garden styles
50   Problem solvers
58   Pots & bouquets
62   Rose garden plans

p.70 ROSE CARE & MAINTENANCE

To keep roses performing at their best, they need a little tender loving care. Here's help!

72   Preparing & planting
80   Watering
82   Mulching, feeding & fertilizing
86   Dealing with pests
94   Pruning
98   Seasonal care
102 Hardiness & regional care calendars

p.110 GALLERY OF ROSES

Each of these 386 roses is rated 7.5 or higher by the American Rose Society, ensuring garden success.

114 Hybrid teas
128 Grandifloras
134 Floribundas
156 Polyanthas
158 Shrubs
174 Old Garden Roses & species
190 Miniatures & minifloras
208 Climbers & ramblers

history & development

A rose by any other name is just as fascinating. These beautiful blooms have been manipulated into a multitude of sizes, shapes, forms, and colors that continue to evolve and change.

p. 6
THE FIRST ROSES

Roses grow wild almost everywhere in the world. With just a little help from nature and rose breeders, beautiful changes began to appear over time.

p. 8
MODERN ROSES

The beautiful classic form of a hybrid tea (the type found in florist bouquets and shown above) is a blend of two types of roses.

p. 10
BIGGER & SMALLER BLOOMS

Whether you like a big bouquet formed by an entire spray of floribundas or delicate thumbnail flowers of a miniature, there's a size that's ideal.

p. 12
RECENT TRENDS

New roses arrive on the market every year. But the most exciting developments are with tough-as-nails, easy-care shrub roses that anyone can grow.

The First Roses

The earliest roses were wild. Botanists call them
the species of the genus *Rosa*, part of the family Rosaceae. Taxonomists—specialists who classify roses—debate the issue, but they generally agree that 100 to 150 are true species. How the species evolved, possibly from one or two ancestors, can only be answered by extensive DNA analysis. Since that process is quite expensive, the answer is not likely to come soon.

Species roses thrive today
Most species roses originated in Asia and Europe; about a dozen are native to North America. Many species roses do very well in gardens today, displaying excellent blooms, hips, foliage, and thorns.

Rose hybridizers still rely on species roses as part of their breeding line to improve disease resistance and cold hardiness. Virtually all species roses can still be purchased today.

Other roses appeared by about the first century, when classical writers mentioned specific roses, including three of the five old European rose families—gallicas, albas, and damasks. References to centifolias (also known as cabbage roses) emerged at the end of the 16th century.

About 100 years later, the centifolias mutated into moss roses. (The "moss" actually refers to the small growths on the sepals, the green, petal-like leaves at the base of each bud.)

Champneys' Pink Cluster, a soft pink noisette rose created in 1811 in South Carolina, is still available today. Other than wild roses, it's considered the first truly American rose.

Breeding hybrids begins

The first known rose hybridizing originated in Holland in the 18th century. Breeders planted roses close together, letting them naturally cross-pollinate, then harvested and propagated the seeds. Hybrid roses had been created this way in nature for thousands of years, but breeders used the same idea to speed up and improve the process.

By the end of the 18th century, a watershed in rose development arrived with reblooming roses from China. They were originally called Chinas and tea-scented Chinas and the latter became known as tea roses. While many of these first China roses were unsuited for gardens because they weren't cold hardy, they turned out to be significant as parents. Their desirable reblooming genes were quickly blended with species and European roses.

Chinese roses become American

In 1811, the first crosses from Chinese roses created the noisette rose family. John Champneys of South Carolina produced Champneys' Pink Cluster from a cross between *Rosa moschata* (musk rose) and Parson's Pink China. While this can be considered the first truly American rose, the most famous is surely Harison's Yellow, created in 1824 from two other species. This beloved and tough rose was carried and planted by pioneers and settlers throughout the American West, where its small, fragrant flowers still bloom today.

In 1817, Parson's Pink China again played an important role. Paired with an unknown damask rose, it created a new hybrid to found the Bourbon family of roses. These large semiclimbing plants originated on Bourbon (now called Reunion), a French island in the Indian Ocean east of Madagascar.

Beginning in the 1830s, many types of roses made their way into the bloodlines of the hybrid perpetual family. Hybrid perpetuals—strong, upright plants with double, long-lasting but sparse repeat blooms—dominated rose breeding until the end of the 19th century.

American Beauty, immensely popular as a cut flower in the United States, is a hybrid perpetual hybridized by Henri Lédéchaux of France and originally named Madame Ferdinand Jamin.

Below left: **Madame Ferdinand Jamin, a hybrid perpetual bred in France, came to the United States in 1886 and was renamed American Beauty.**

Below right: **The Apothecary's Rose, also called *Rosa gallica officinalis*, dates from before 1240 and is still a popular garden rose.**

TEST GARDEN TIP

Have no fear!

Roses have a bad reputation with some people for being hard to grow. Not true! Many of the most recent and the very oldest roses are disease resistant. Check the tag for excellent disease resistance and repeat flowering, then water and feed these tough beauties for easy-care blooms throughout the growing season.

Modern Roses

Any rose family created since the late 1800s is considered a modern rose, including the beloved hybrid tea. The name implies that it's a cross between a hybrid perpetual and a tea, but so many rose families contributed to the earliest varieties that the original hybrid tea will never be positively identified.

The American Rose Society has declared La France, a light pink rose created from a white tea and a red hybrid perpetual, to be the first.

In 1880, the Horticultural Society of Lyon, France, gave the moniker *Hybrides de Thé* (French for "hybrid tea") to roses created by English breeder Henry Bennett. The term came into general use about 10 years later.

Polyantha means "many flowers"

Polyantha (Greek for "many flowers") roses, a family of low-growing plants with a profusion of small flowers, have a more definitive history.

The first polyantha was the white Pâquerette, introduced by Guillot et Fils of Lyon, France, in 1875. Pâquerette was a seedling from a low-growing *Rosa multiflora*, but unlike its parent, had a repeat-blooming habit.

Although polyanthas were all the rage around the turn of the 20th century, they've mostly fallen out of favor. However, some beloved varieties, such as The Fairy, are still available.

Ramblers and climbers appear

In 1880, Max Wichura sent a set of Japanese species plants to Europe, where they were promptly named *Rosa wichuriana* in his honor. These roses grew near to the ground with fairly long, creeping canes. While their small white blooms were unremarkable, their potential for breeding landscape plants was apparent. Among the first to take advantage of this potential were Americans Michael Horvath and Walter Van Fleet.

Horvath introduced Pink Roamer, a cross of *R. wichuriana* with the red China Cramoisi Supérieur in 1897. A year later, Van Fleet unveiled May Queen, a cross of *R. wichuriana* with Mrs. DeGraw, a pink Bourbon. These roses, with their long, flexible canes and masses of blooms, quickly became known as ramblers.

Ramblers were widely bred during the early 20th century. Although they don't rebloom, they are still popular, and many are available from mail-order sources.

Hybridizers in the early 20th century also wanted long-caned roses with a repeat blooming habit and larger flowers. Again, they enlisted a combination of species and hybrids. Many climbers were introduced although most are now long forgotten.

The first true large-flowered climber was New Dawn, a light pink, very fragrant variety introduced in 1930. New Dawn is a sport—a genetic mutation—of the rambler Dr. W. Van Fleet. It blooms recurrently, with one flush following another, rather than just once.

New Dawn was the first rose to receive a plant patent in the United States.

Opposite: **La France is considered to be the first hybrid tea.**

Above left: **La Marne, a pink polyantha, should be protected for winter in cold areas of the country.**

Above center: **Cramoisi Supérieur, a climbing China rose works well trained on a trellis or fence.**

Above right: **The reblooming qualities of its soft pink blooms make the large-flowered climber New Dawn a good choice for arbors.**

Bigger & Smaller Blooms

Searching for roses that bloomed in clusters like polyanthas but with larger flowers,

breeders crossed polyanthas with hybrid teas and other large-flowered types to create what they initially called a hybrid polyantha. The family name for this new rose changed from hybrid polyantha to floribunda in 1950. The first floribunda (Latin for "many flowers") is generally credited to Danish hybridizer Svend Poulsen. His Rödhätte (Danish for "Little Red Riding Hood"), a cherry red cross of a polyantha and a hybrid tea, debuted in 1911.

Floribundas flourish

World's Fair, a floribunda, was one of the first four roses honored in 1940 by All-America Rose Selections (a nonprofit association of growers and introducers), but the public tended to ignore floribundas until Fashion was introduced in 1949 and Vogue in 1951.

Both were hybridized by American Gene Boerner, who became known as "Papa Floribunda" during a 45-year career of breeding roses for the Jackson & Perkins Company.

The well-named Brass Band, a floribunda, grows large sprays of luscious blooms with tones of orange, apricot, and melon.

Grandifloras arrive on the scene

Another American, Walter Lammerts, created the grandiflora—Latin for "large flowers"—family. His Queen Elizabeth, introduced in 1954, was touted as the beginning of a new type of roses.

These large, robust plants combine the spray habit of floribundas with the large, fragrant blooms of hybrid teas. Few grandifloras approach the physical stature, bloom habit, and floral production of Queen Elizabeth, the second variety inducted into the World Rose Hall of Fame, in 1979. (Peace, a hybrid tea, was the first, in 1976.)

Smaller blooms suit other purposes

Miniature roses, with blooms about 1 to 1½ inches wide, originated from a dwarf China rose sent to England in the early 1800s. The rose was apparently lost, then rediscovered more than a century later and named Rouletii after its finder, a man named Roulet. Breeding started soon after its rediscovery. One of the first miniatures was the red Tom Thumb, bred in 1936 by Holland's Jan de Vink from Rouletii and a polyantha.

The first American hybridizer of minis, Ralph Moore, became known as the "King of the Miniatures" during more than 50 years of breeding hundreds of varieties.

A little more than a decade ago, the rose world welcomed a new family called miniflora, consisting of small- to medium-size plants whose blooms boast the classic hybrid tea form and grow slightly larger than miniatures.

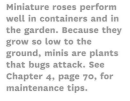

Miniature roses perform well in containers and in the garden. Because they grow so low to the ground, minis are plants that bugs attack. See Chapter 4, page 70, for maintenance tips.

ASK THE GARDEN DOCTOR

Which roses take the most work?

ANSWER: The bigger they are, the more work. Miniatures generally need less tender loving care than large-flowered climbers.

Recent Trends

The multiple petals and rich fragrance of Prospero characterize the qualities of most David Austin English roses.

Thanks to their easy-going, disease-resistant qualities,

shrub roses made the biggest splash with gardeners in the past 25 years.

Botanically, all roses are shrubs because they fit this definition: a woody plant of relatively low height with several stems arising from the base.

However, the American Rose Society calls any rose a "shrub" if it doesn't fit easily into one of the other classes.

Shrubs break down into four subfamilies: hybrid kordesii, hybrid musk, hybrid rugosa, and hybrid moyesii, but many varieties are simply generically called shrubs.

This incredibly diverse class includes large spreading plants as well as low-growing groundcover types and everything in between.

David Austin roses: Old with new

Among shrubs, the first significant development began nearly 50 years ago with the introduction of David Austin's Constance Spry. This pink cross of an Old Garden Rose with a floribunda was the first of hundreds of Austin roses that he dubbed "English Roses."

Austin roses combine the flower forms and fragrance of Old Garden Roses with the reblooming habit and wider color palette of modern roses. They're available in many plant sizes and growth habits, and in an equally large series of colors, bloom habits, and aromas.

Most Austin varieties have reasonably good disease resistance; some are exceptional.

Rugosas and other tough contenders

Rugosa shrub roses (technically, "hybrid rugosas") are super winter hardy with extremely disease-resistant foliage and very fragrant blooms. The downside is a rather sparse bloom habit. The plants, most introduced a century ago, can grow quite large, 7 to 8 feet tall.

In the mid-1980s, low-growing rugosas about 3 to 4 feet tall with a moderate spreading habit came on the market. This family of two to three dozen low-growing varieties usually carries the word "Pavement" or "Roadrunner" in the name.

In 1990, the extremely disease-resistant Flower Carpet series emerged. Touted as groundcover roses, Flower Carpets often grow more upright than spreading. They reach about 3 feet tall and wide and are available in nine color varieties. Unlike low-growing rugosas, most Flower Carpet blooms have slight aromas.

The roses in the newest groundcover family, Drift, are crosses between full-size groundcover roses and miniatures, making them ideal for small gardens. Drift roses come in seven colors.

Knock Out roses introduced

The Knock Out series, which began in 2000, represents the most significant recent addition to shrub roses. The original cherry-red Knock Out grows 4 to 5 feet tall and blooms from spring until frost. It's touted as one of the most disease resistant roses and is the most widely sold rose in North America. The series currently includes seven roses in a range of colors and flower forms. (For a list, see page 33.)

Knock Out and Rainbow Knock Out earned All-America Rose Selections awards, and the original also received an American Rose Society's Members' Choice award. They're widely available at nurseries, garden stores, and by mail order.

Exciting upgrades in the future

What will the future bring for rose development and evolution?

Hybridizers around the world seek two qualities: improved disease resistance and more fragrance—hopefully both in the same variety.

Some hope for a blue or black rose, but it remains to be seen if genetic engineering can bring either of these chimeras to reality.

Whatever happens in the next 10, 20, or 50 years, one thing is sure: There will be intriguing and thrilling additions to the millennia-long story of the world's favorite flower.

TEST GARDEN TIP

Make a tough choice

There's an apparent genetic link between fragrance and disease problems in roses. The more fragrant the blooms, the more disease-prone the plants can be. Gardeners often have to choose between fragrance and a clean, disease-resistant plant.

Below left: **Cherry red blooms and incredible disease resistance make Knock Out a garden winner.**

Below right: **Rainbow Knock Out's floral display of coral-pink blooms and yellow centers lasts the entire growing season.**

selecting the right rose

Every rose is perfect for someone, but no rose is perfect for everyone. Identify the right rose, plant it in the right spot, and you'll love the results.

p.16
ROSE BASICS

So many roses, so many decisions to make! Use a handy checklist when hunting for the perfect rose bush for your yard.

p.22
FLOWERS & BUSHES

Planting a rose means knowing more than the flower color. Some roses grow tall enough to tie onto a trellis; others are short and wide. Learn which roses meet your needs.

p.26
ROSE FAMILIES

Like people, roses have families. Learn the differences among them so you can make the best decision about which ones should join *your* family.

p.34
ROSES BY REGION

Roses can thrive in every region but perform differently from place to place. See these recommendations for your region.

p.40
BUYING ROSES

Should you buy from a mail-order company or a local nursery? Bare root or potted? Each has advantages and disadvantages.

How to Start

Success with roses begins with picking the right one. Avoid buying blooming roses on impulse in the garden center checkout lane—do some research first! Roses that perform well in southern California won't necessarily act the same in Maine or Kansas. Favorable reviews from producers don't always mean their roses will grow well everywhere.

Untold numbers of enthusiastic gardeners get discouraged with growing roses simply because they make poor choices. But with a little guidance, it's easy to make a good pick.

Become a savvy shopper

Buy your roses by following a number of critical steps that are somewhat akin to buying a new car—but without the hasslee of negotiating a price.
Decide your wants for color, shape, and use.
Calculate your needs for the garden.
Determine how much time and energy you want to devote to care; some roses are easier to maintain than others.

If possible, select a rose that's not yet blooming. That means the bush is spending most of its energy growing good roots instead of flowers.

Choose whether to use fungicides, insecticides, and miticides, or whether to take a purely organic approach.

Check the marketplace—local and mail order—to compare when shopping for varieties.

Identify your local USDA plant hardiness zone (see map, page 103) to see which rose types grow best where you live.

While this may seem like a daunting list, it's easier than it looks. As you follow each step, selecting a rose becomes an exciting and much-anticipated process that will beautify your garden.

Select your priorities

Remember: There is no perfect rose. No single variety will offer every desirable bloom quality, such as beauty, size, fragrance, long vase life, long stems, plus a bush with vigor, heavy bloom, quick repeat bloom, winter hardiness, disease and insect resistance and a neat, upright habit.

You'll need to compromise. As the song performed by the group Poison suggests, "Every Rose Has Its Thorn." It helps to make a prioritized list for bloom and bush.

Although fragrance is often a priority, remember that many very good to excellent roses carry little to no fragrance. You may have to make a tough choice between disease resistance and fragrance.

Check with a Consulting Rosarian

Free rose guidance is available through the American Rose Society's Consulting Rosarian program. An experienced, trained rose-growing consultant can offer you free advice on selection, culture, or other aspects of rose growing.

To find an e-mail address for a local expert, click on the "Need Advice?" link at www.ars.org.

Check the plant tag for notes on disease resistance, sun requirements, and other helpful information.

ASK THE GARDEN DOCTOR

Why is bloom color so variable?
ANSWER: Weather plays a significant role in rose bloom colors. Some varieties stay more colorfast in heat while others fade. Ask a local Consulting Rosarian (www.ars.org, "Need Advice?") what works best for your area.

Rose Checklist

Take a checklist when you visit a garden center, and examine a plant tag closely to see whether the rose you like fits your criteria. Answer these questions before buying:

WHAT COLOR DO I WANT?

WHAT SIZE DO I NEED?

WHAT SHAPE DO I WANT (UPRIGHT, LOW, CLIMBING)?

IS IT EASY CARE OR DOES IT NEED MORE EFFORT?

WILL I USE ORGANIC OR CHEMICAL CONTROLS?

DOES IT HAVE A FRAGRANCE?

IS IT THE BEST PLANT AT THE BEST PRICE?

WILL IT GROW WHERE I LIVE?

Color, Shape, Form

Upper left: **Angel Face, a floribunda, grows with purple-pink sprays.**

Upper right: **Scentimental, a floribunda, shows unusual red and white candy-striped petals.**

Lower left: **Octoberfest, a grandiflora, displays brilliant orange classic blooms.**

Lower right: **Black Jade, a miniature rose, is one of the darkest roses available.**

Roses grow in almost every color—other than blue, black, or green.

Even among color families, blooms appear as solids or blends, from bright to pastel. Some roses have different colors on the tops and bottoms of their petals. Others can be striped or mottled.

Choose bloom shape

Bloom shape is described by the number of petals and overall appearance. Here are petal definitions:

Single: While a "single" is often defined as a rose with five-petal blooms, the American Rose Society's definition is five to eight petals.

Semidouble: A semidouble rose has 8 to 16 petals, usually noted when the rose is at its peak and bloom stamens are visible.

Double: Doubles may contain 16 to 60 petals. Hybrid teas, grandifloras, miniatures, minifloras, and floribundas are often said to have classic form. When viewed from the top, a classic double resembles a perfect bull's-eye with a tight or pinpoint center around which the petals unfurl evenly to a nearly horizontal level. Other doubles are called informal, and includes anything that doesn't look classic.

Very double: Very double roses, including many of the Old Garden Roses and the David Austin English roses, have more than 60 petals.

Choose bloom habit

Bloom habit simply refers to the various ways the rose bush and its flowers may behave or look. Despite what the plant tag states about when and how often the plant will bloom, your climate will influence the number of flowers produced and the time between bloom cycles.

Your first major decision depends on the rose family. Some roses, such as hybrid teas, miniatures, and minifloras, generally produce one bloom per stem. Others, such as floribundas and many varieties of shrubs, climbers, and Old Garden Roses, produce sprays of roses on which clusters of small flowers grow together.

Some roses work best for specific purposes. For cutting or exhibiting at flower shows, choose a hybrid tea or a miniature, although many floribundas and other types have adequate stem lengths for cutting.

For landscape considerations, varieties with flowers that grow in sprays are good choices. Some types, such as hybrid teas, offer a combination of both spray and one-bloom-per-stem habits.

ASK THE GARDEN DOCTOR

What is a fully open or quartered rose?

ANSWER: A rose bloom can be described as fully open or quartered. A fully open rose is a double or very double bloom open to the point that the stamens are visible. A quartered rose is a very double bloom that looks divided in four sections.

Select a Bloom Shape

SINGLE BLOOM
Flower Carpet Coral

SEMIDOUBLE
Playboy

DOUBLE CLASSIC
Voluptuous!

DOUBLE INFORMAL
Livin' Easy

VERY DOUBLE
Königen van Dänemark

Select a Bloom Habit

SPRAY ROSES
Trumpeter

ONE BLOOM PER STEM
St. Patrick

FULLY OPEN
Cupcake

QUARTERED
Tournament of Roses

Fragrance Choices

If beauty is in the eye of the beholder, fragrance is in the nose of the sniffer.

Fragrance is extremely hard to quantify or qualify, and its effect can vary significantly from one person to the next.

Olfactory experts have identified about four dozen distinct rose fragrances. Rose breeder Henri Delbard says the first fragrance noticed in roses—called the head—is a citrus scent (such as lemon and mandarin) or an aromatic (such as lavender and citronella). This is followed by the heart—a longer-lasting floral scent (such as lilac), a fruit (raspberry), or a spice (nutmeg).

Sometimes fragrance relies on the cumulative presence of many blooms such as the ones covering the shrub Westerland or many of the Old Garden Roses. Because fragrance is so subjective, visit rose shows and rose gardens to find which varieties seem aromatic to you.

Which roses are most fragrant?

It's hard to find objective evaluations of rose fragrance. The aroma of any variety can vary from one geographical area to another and can depend on climate and other factors.

The All-America Rose Selections, a nonprofit association of rose growers and introducers, evaluates new roses on about a dozen criteria, including fragrance. If a rose has earned an AARS award, its background information will include details about its scent (if any).

Hybrid teas, grandifloras, and many of the David Austin English roses are quite fragrant. Nearly all purple roses are moderately to highly fragrant.

Perdita, Molineux, Sceptered Isle, and Teasing Georgia have won fragrance awards in the United Kingdom. Although many overseas rose trials make fragrance awards each year, the only one in the United States is at the Rose Hills Pageant of Roses Garden in Whittier, California.

Molineux, a shrub rose from English breeder David Austin, is highly fragrant, like many of the Austin roses.

Rose Hills Fragrance Award Winners

The only fragrance award presented in the United States is at the Rose Hills Pageant of Roses Garden in Whittier, California.

ASK THE GARDEN DOCTOR

When are roses most fragrant?

ANSWER: The fragrance of a garden rose is enhanced by mild humidity and warmth, but not excessive heat. Depending upon your climate, mornings and mid- or late afternoons are the best times to enjoy the fragrances of your roses.

Augusta Luise
Barbra Streisand (*above*)
Firefighter
Maria Shriver

Pope John Paul II
Rouge Royale
Sweet Intoxication
Wild Blue Yonder (*above*)

James Alexander Gamble Award Winners

The James Alexander Gamble Award is presented by the American Rose Society to a rose with outstanding fragrance that has been in commerce at least five years with an ARS rating of 7.5 or higher on a 10-point scale.

Angel Face (*above*)
Chrysler Imperial
Crimson Glory
Double Delight

Fragrant Cloud (*above*)
Fragrant Hour
Fragrant Plum
Granada

Mister Lincoln
Papa Meilland
Secret (*above*)
Sheila's Perfume

Sunsprite (*above*)
Sutter's Gold
Sweet Chariot
Tiffany

Picking a Plant Habit

SHRUB
Shrub roses usually grow as wide as they do tall—often 3 to 6 feet—and have an attractive bushy growth habit.

ROSES TO LOOK FOR:
Autumn Sunset (*above*)
Pink Knock Out
Chuckles

MINIATURE
Scaled-down versions of larger roses, these delicate plants range from 1 to 2 feet tall with tiny leaves and blooms.

ROSES TO LOOK FOR:
Jilly Jewel (*above*)
Giggles
Jean Kenneally

For peace of mind and the overall appearance of your garden, pick the right plant size and shape. Roses that are too tall or too wide to fit comfortably into their spaces are unattractive, hard to control, and more difficult to keep disease free. Placing a small rose into a big space can be disappointing when the proportions look wrong.

Some rose varieties can grow canes less than 1 foot long, while others' canes reach 40 to 50 feet long. If long-caned plants are not well supported, they can slump over and become almost equally wide.

Learn the differences among rose families (also called classes) to understand size differences. Some families, such as hybrid teas, generally produce bushes and flowers consistently the same size and shape. Shrub roses, on the other hand, vary widely in terms of sizes and habits; look closely at their individual characteristics before buying.

HYBRID TEA

Hybrid teas grow fairly upright and can reach 6 feet tall in the right conditions. The lower canes can appear leggy.

ROSES TO LOOK FOR:
Kardinal (*above*)
Irish Elegance
Touch of Class

GROUNDCOVER

Low-growing roses 3 feet and shorter grow with sprawling canes that extend to cover the ground.

ROSES TO LOOK FOR:
Flower Carpet (*above*)
Sea Foam
White Meidiland

RAMBLER

Ramblers, which only bloom once a year, are the giants of the rose world, sometimes reaching 30 feet tall.

ROSES TO LOOK FOR:
Lavender Lassie (*above*)
Paul's Himalayan Musk (*above*)
Albéric Barbier

STANDARD

Lollipop shape plants, sometimes called tree roses, can grow 2 to 6 feet tall but need winter protection.

ROSES TO LOOK FOR:
Almost any rose trained as a standard. In cold regions try Northern Encore, an own-root rose.

CLIMBER

Climbers come in many sizes, including miniatures that reach 6 feet and large-flowered climbers up to 30 feet.

ROSES TO LOOK FOR:
Dr. W. Van Fleet (*above*)
Dream Weaver
Don Juan

PILLAR

Any rose with moderately long canes can be trained on a structure as a pillar, making a strong vertical accent.

ROSES TO LOOK FOR:
Pierre de Ronsard (*above*)
Altissimo
American Pillar

Rose Bush Shapes

Some roses grow in very specific or unusual ways. Use these terms when selecting a plant habit.

Standard

Standards are often dubbed tree roses, and can be created from many modern rose families. To make a standard, a bud from a hybrid rose is grafted onto a wild rose cane that's 1½ to 3 feet tall, giving it the look of a small tree.

A standard can make a stunning focal point in a garden. Some nurseries offer "weeping" standards created from lax-caned varieties that give a cascading effect.

Double-budded standards offer even more drama. A double-budded standard has two different varieties grafted on opposite sides, creating a plant that can produce two colors and types of flowers.

Because standards are more susceptible to winter damage than their bush counterparts, they're recommended only for warmer climates. In cold areas, a standard can be overwintered in a pot if kept where the roots won't freeze.

Groundcover

Varieties touted as groundcover roses are usually low growing, somewhat bushy shrubs that don't actually spread and cover the ground.

Most are quite disease resistant and attractive, but they must be planted close together for a true groundcover effect.

Sea Foam, a white variety often described as a trailing climber; some of the Meidiland series; and the Blanket and Ribbon varieties are among the best groundcover roses available today.

Patio

In Europe, the term "patio rose" refers to any low-growing, floriferous rose suitable for growing in a pot on a patio. Because the term is not normally used in the United States, European patio varieties are officially classed here as miniatures, shrubs, and, occasionally, floribundas. If you get roses from Canadian mail-order sources, you may see patio roses listed because Canadian growers often acquire bud wood from England.

Pillar

Any long-caned rose that is trained to grow straight up can be called a pillar rose. Roses grown as pillars need support to keep them from collapsing.

Rambler

The now-unofficial name "rambler" is still useful when describing once-blooming roses with very long, flexible canes. This rose class was abolished by the American Rose Society in 1999. Most were reclassified as hybrid wichurianas or hybrid multifloras.

In general, ramblers are heavy bloomers perfect for training along a fence or over an outbuilding. Many are highly fragrant and widely available to buy in garden centers.

Hedge

Virtually any rose can be used as a hedge. Roses can form privacy hedges, low-to-medium border hedges, security hedges, wind reduction hedges, and so forth.

The challenge is to select a rose type or variety that is the right height and has the right characteristics (for example, very thorny plants are good for security hedges), then planting them close enough together so they present an unbroken appearance when they're mature.

ASK THE GARDEN DOCTOR

What is a rose sport?

ANSWER: In rose terminology, a "sport" is a genetic mutation. There are two kinds: color sports, in which the bloom color changes but all the characteristics of the plant remain the same; and climbing sports, from bush varieties with long canes, such as Climbing Peace. Most rose sports are unstable and revert to their original form, making them not commercially viable.

Above left: **Carpet of Color demonstrates how groundcover roses blanket the garden.**

Above center: **Ramblin' Red, a large-flowered climber, can grow massive enough to cover an entire house wall.**

Above right: **Hybrid rugosa roses planted close together make an attractive hedge.**

Opposite: **Northern Encore was created as the first own-root tree rose to survive winters in northern climates.**

Meet the Rose Families

It's good to know the differences among rose types so you know what to plant.

On the next eight pages, you'll meet the 11 main rose families designated by the American Rose Society (ARS), the international registration authority for roses. All rose families other than species and Old Garden Roses are considered modern roses.

❶ Hybrid tea

Hybrid teas come from a very uniform family. They normally grow 4 to 6 feet tall with fairly strong canes. The blooms, generally the largest of any rose family, are borne singly or in clusters. Plants rarely need support to withstand rain and wind. The foliage normally begins 1 or 2 feet above ground level, often giving hybrid teas a bare-legged look that some gardeners prefer to screen with companion plants such as catmint (*Nepeta*) or low-growing roses. Gemini and Elina are good hybrid teas for nearly every climate. Ingrid Bergman is pictured.

❷ Miniature

Miniatures grow with an upright to bushy habit, usually 1 to 2½ feet tall, although some reach as tall as 4 feet. The blooms tend to be smaller than 1½ inches in diameter and, like those of hybrid teas, are borne singly or in small clusters.

Most miniatures may be thought of as scaled-down hybrid teas. A few bear the heavy bloom habit of floribundas. Because their foliage is close to the soil, miniature roses are particularly susceptible to spider mites. Irresistible is an example of a hybrid tea type of miniature; Anytime has a floribunda style.

To see examples of miniatures, visit the Ralph Moore Rose Garden in downtown Visalia, California, featuring roses bred by the late Ralph Moore during his 60-year career. His work produced more than 300 miniatures, plus floribundas, hybrid teas, shrubs, ramblers, polyanthas, and Old Garden Roses, all registered with the ARS. Rainbow's End miniature climbing rose is pictured.

3 Floribunda

Floribundas are bred to produce an abundance of blooms. They range from about 2 to 5 feet tall, and all have a bushy habit. Their canes range from strong in some varieties to rather thin in others, such as Iceberg. While floribundas can hold themselves erect in dry weather, the canes can collapse under the weight of heavy blooms after a rain. Consider adding support for floribundas if you live in a wet climate. Europeana does well in all climates; Margaret Merril is a super-fragrant member of this family. Escapade is shown.

4 Miniflora

Most minifloras in the United States have been bred for exhibition and have a classic bloom form and are held singly on their stalks. Plants grow up to 4 feet tall with blooms as wide as 3 inches—larger than miniatures but smaller than floribundas. This is a relatively new class designated by the American Rose Society in 1999. Most miniflora varieties are available only through mail order. Dr. John Dickman is one of the best-performing minifloras. Shown here is Olympic Gold.

? ASK THE GARDEN DOCTOR

How can I get bigger blooms?

ANSWER: To get large, one-bloom-per-stem hybrid teas, remove all the buds on a stem except the one on the end, which is the first one to emerge. To get consistent, well-spaced blooms in a floribunda or other spray rose, do the opposite: Take out the terminal (end) bud and let the side buds develop into blooms.

Each of these rose families offers special qualities you may want in a garden.
The American Rose Society recognizes 37 different classes (or families) of roses; these are the most commonly grown.

⑤ Grandiflora
An idealized combination of hybrid teas and floribundas, grandifloras will sometimes grow 7 to 8 feet tall. Most have an upright plant habit, with large blooms borne either singly or in sprays. Grandifloras work well in the background of a rose bed or a mixed flower border. Grow Melody Parfumée for fragrance, although Queen Elizabeth remains the best variety in this class. Shown here is Dream Come True.

⑥ Large-flowered climber
There are two types of reblooming, large-flowered climbers that grow with long canes.

The first type has stiff canes held mostly upright that reach 8 to 12 feet tall. It has a spreading habit and can be trained onto a support when the canes are young and still somewhat flexible. Altissimo is a good example.

The second type features thin, flexible canes that reach up to 16 feet but are more easily trained due to their suppleness. Royal Sunset, the ARS's highest rated climber (8.9 on a 10-point scale), is an example.

There's little difference in habit between large-flowered climbers and large shrub roses. Sometimes all long-caned varieties are called climbers, such as Climbing Altissimo or Climbing Dortmund. The variety shown is Royal Sunset.

⑦ Polyantha
Polyanthas are low-growing plants—about 3 feet tall—bearing small blooms in very large clusters. Over time, many polyantha varieties have turned into climbing forms, bearing lax canes up to 10 feet long that can be readily trained. Although few polyanthas are hybridized today, several older varieties are still available. The Fairy remains the most popular polyantha. China Doll is pictured.

⑧ Old Garden Rose
An Old Garden Rose is a specific term used by the ARS to denote members of any rose class existing prior to 1867, when the first hybrid tea was introduced. There are

22 different kinds of Old Garden Roses, including hybrid gallicas. Since hybrid gallicas existed before 1867, any roses bred in the 20th century with a hybrid gallica parent can be registered as hybrid gallicas and be considered Old Garden Roses.

Many rosarians disagree with this definition, so there are many synonyms for 18th- and 19th-century roses: heritage roses, heirloom roses, old roses, and others. Charles de Mills (pictured) is an old gallica, while James Mason, also a hybrid gallica, was introduced in 1982.

9 Noisette

Noisette roses are truly American. Although it's not known exactly when this family originated, experts lean toward 1811 as the date when John Champneys, a Charleston, South Carolina, rice farmer, received a Parson's Pink China from Philippe Noisette, his neighbor, and crossed it with a species musk rose. His Champneys' Pink Cluster began a rose revolution that resulted in a new class of Old Garden Roses.

Noisettes became known for their vigorous and abundant repeat bloom. Although at one time there were about 250 varieties in South Carolina, only 75 to 80 still exist today. You can visit more than 55 varieties—the largest collection of noisette roses in the United States—at Edisto Memorial Gardens in Orangeburg, South Carolina, celebrating the 200th anniversary of the noisette rose in 2011. Alister Stella Gray is the variety depicted.

10 Portland

Portland roses, a relatively small Old Garden Rose classification originating in the late 1700s, were named for the English Duchess of Portland. Medium size, tidy plants can fit easily into almost any garden and produce lovely hips. The original Portland, a scarlet rose named Duchess of Portland, is still available today. Comte de Chambord is shown.

11 Hybrid wichuriana

Hybrid wichuriana is the official class for virtually all varieties formerly known as ramblers. It includes any very long-caned, once-blooming rose. Albertine (pictured) and American Pillar are good examples of this family.

Rose Family Traits
Each rose family offers advantages and drawbacks. Standards and groundcover roses don't represent families—they're forms—but they have their own issues.

HYBRID TEA
Shown: Bewitched

Blooms: Perfect flowers with reliable repeating; deadhead for repeat bloom

Fragrance: Many varieties

Hardiness: Requires heavy winter protection in Zone 5 and colder

Disease: Some varieties are susceptible to black spot

Comments: Most popular type of rose; rather bare on lower canes

GRANDIFLORA
Shown: Strike It Rich

Blooms: Reliable repeat bloomers if deadheaded

Fragrance: Many varieties

Hardiness: Winter hardiness varies by variety

Disease: Some varieties are susceptible to black spot

Comments: Smaller blooms than hybrid teas

FLORIBUNDA
Shown: French Lace

Blooms: Nonstop bloom with large trusses of many flowers; deadhead for repeat bloom

Fragrance: Many varieties

Hardiness: Winter hardiness varies by variety

Disease: Some varieties susceptible to black spot

Comments: Easy to grow; suitable for wet climates; attractively bushy; smaller blooms than hybrid teas

POLYANTHA
Shown: Lovely Fairy

Blooms: Small flowers grow in large clusters with nonstop bloom

Fragrance: Some varieties

Hardiness: Winter hardiness varies by variety

Disease: Good disease resistance but some varieties highly susceptible to black spot

Comments: Low-growing; excellent container roses; attractive foliage

SHRUB
Shown: Pink Meidiland

Blooms: Some have old-fashioned bloom shapes and many petals; most do not have a classic hybrid tea form

Fragrance: Some varieties

Hardiness: Cold hardy

Disease: Generally disease resistant

Comments: Huge variety of shapes and sizes; versatile in landscape; often used for groundcover

MINIATURE & MINIFLORA
Shown: Sun Sprinkles

Blooms: Most usually have tiny blooms, part of their charm

Fragrant: Little fragrance

Hardiness: Grown on own roots so more hardy

Disease: Susceptible to black spot and spider mites

Comments: Excellent for small-space gardens; perfect for containers

CLIMBERS & RAMBLERS
Shown: Fourth of July

Blooms: Ramblers bloom only once. Both types come in many flower forms and colors

Fragrance: Varies

Hardiness: Some not winter hardy in Zone 5 and colder

Disease: Varies, but often disease resistant

Comments: Useful for adding vertical color in the landscape or disguising unattractive structures

SPECIES & OLD GARDEN
Shown: Complicata

Blooms: Some repeat but others bloom only once

Fragrance: Varies

Hardiness: There's a type to suit nearly any hardiness zone

Disease: Some varieties are prone to mildew

Comments: Versatile landscape roses; offer a connection to the past; some spread problematically through suckering

GROUNDCOVER
Shown: Knock Out

Blooms: Small flowers provide mass color; little deadheading needed

Fragrance: Usually not much fragrance

Hardiness: Most are winter hardy

Disease: Disease resistant

Comments: Great solution for mass color in problem spots, such as slopes; when massed close together and pruned to stay short, smaller shrub roses can be used

STANDARD
Shown: Ruby Ruby

Blooms: Flowers grow on a striking form

Fragrance: Varies

Hardiness: Needs winter protection in all but the warmest climates

Disease: Disease resistance varies by variety

Comments: Perfect for containers; relatively small selection of varieties

Shrub roses

Dortmund, which grows tall enough to be a climber and ranks as one of the highest rated shrub roses, is a kordesii.

The shrub family includes roses of all shapes and sizes.

Naturally, this leads to some confusion, since rose producers sometimes come up with their own descriptive names such as groundcover, shrublet, and Flower Carpet for plants of a certain size and habit.

Rose hybridizers have different views of what constitutes a shrub, and the sizes and habits vary widely. For example, David Austin's English roses range from short floribunda-like plants such as Bredon, to virtual climbers such as Abraham Darby, but Austin has chosen to classify them all as shrubs.

To better define shrubs, mostly for exhibition purposes, the American Rose Society has designated four subfamilies of shrubs: hybrid kordesii, hybrid rugosa, hybrid musk, and hybrid moyesii.

Hybrid kordesii
These are mostly large spreading shrubs, 6 to 7 feet tall and wide, originating from the Kordes nursery of Sparrieshoop, Germany, in the 1950s and '60s. They are very disease resistant, and many of the varieties have blooms in shades of red. Dortmund, one of the highest rated shrubs at 9.1, is a hybrid kordesii.

Hybrid rugosa
This family could be considered the ideal low-maintenance rose. These shrubs are uniformly very disease resistant and hardy. Almost all rugosas have a strong fragrance. The blooms range from single to double, in colors of white, yellow, pink, red, and purple. Older varieties grow up to 6 feet tall with upright to spreading habits. Newer varieties introduced in the last 20 years tend to be short—3 to 4 feet tall—and relatively compact. Most rugosas readily form hips and should be deadheaded routinely to ensure continual bloom throughout the growing season. Hansa and Blanc Double de Coubert are time-tested hybrid rugosas.

Hybrid musk
This family was named for the first varieties, which resembled the musk rose, *Rosa moschata*, in plant habit and bloom fragrance. Most have very good disease resistance and a heavy bloom habit, and grow into tall, spreading plants. Some varieties, including Felicia and Pax, are very fragrant.

Hybrid moyesii
The fourth shrub family, not as well known as the other three, includes about two dozen varieties. The best known, Nevada, is a single white repeat bloomer reaching 7 to 12 feet tall.

Species roses
These are wild roses, the results of crosses made by nature before humans became involved in the process. Most have single (five-petal) blooms in white or light pink, and most are vigorous enough to grow into good-size plants.

Distinctive Shrub Roses

Some shrub roses become known by a specific name.

These often represent the output of a single hybridizer; many were bred for a special purpose, such as cold hardiness.

① Buck

Griffith Buck at Iowa State University in Ames, Iowa, bred nearly 100 varieties for winter hardiness during his tenure from 1948 to 1985. Most Buck roses are medium-size shrubs—up to 5 feet tall—with a wide range of bloom forms and colors. Carefree Beauty and Polonaise are both fine Buck roses. Gardeners may visit the most complete collection of Buck roses at the Helen Latch Jones Rose Garden at Reiman Gardens in Ames. The rose pictured above is Carefree Beauty.

② David Austin

This group has grown to more than 100 varieties, all bred and originally tested in England. David Austin English roses combine the bloom forms and fragrance of Old Garden Roses with the repeat blooming habit and extended color palette of modern roses. Plant habits range from climbers to low-growing floribundas. Most, though not all, are quite fragrant and disease resistant. All are classified by the American Rose Society as shrubs. The yellow Graham Thomas (pictured) and the orange-pink Abraham Darby are two of Austin's best.

③ Earth-Kind

Earth-Kind roses, tested by the Texas AgriLife Extension Service in College Station, are rated for outstanding landscape performance and minimal care in Texas. Some Earth-Kind varieties need hot weather for best performance, while others such as Knock Out, Sea Foam, and Carefree Beauty, perform well in nearly all areas. Belinda's Dream is shown. For a list and more information, see pages 56–57.

4 Easy Elegance

Hybridized by Ping Lim for Bailey Nurseries of Minnesota, the Easy Elegance series of about 20 own-root shrubs was designed for hardiness and disease resistance. Like the Bucks, these roses are mostly medium size. They're sold at independent garden centers and online specialty gardening outlets. Sunrise Sunset and Grandma's Blessing (pictured) are good examples.

5 Explorer

These medium to large shrubs, mostly in pinks or reds, originated in Canada. Many are hardy in far-north Zone 3 gardens. All are named after early Canadian explorers, such as John Cabot (pictured), Charles Albanel, and David Thompson.

6 Knock Out

Knock Out, a medium-size shrub with single red-pink blooms and outstanding disease resistance, was introduced in 1999. Since then, it has become the best-selling rose in the world. The Knock Out family includes seven varieties: Knock Out, Double Knock Out, Pink Knock Out, Pink Double Knock Out,

Rainbow Knock Out (pictured), Blushing Knock Out, and Sunny Knock Out. All Knock Outs, bred by William Radler of Wisconsin, are very disease resistant but may not be hardy in the farthest northern regions.

7 Morden

Bred at the Agriculture Canada Research Station in Morden, Manitoba, the dozen varieties in this series all bear the word Morden in their names. The plants are low to medium in height and extremely winter hardy, although some are reported to be prone to black spot. Morden Blush (pictured), probably the most popular of the series, is rated at 8.0.

8 Romantica

Boasting many petals and intense fragrances, Romantica series roses are bred in France by Meilland. Romanticas, mostly hybrid teas or floribundas plus a few climbers, have flower forms similar to the David Austin English Roses but grow on smaller plants. Examples include Jean Giono (pictured), a hybrid tea, and Polka, a large-flowered climber.

Roses by Region: Northwest

Almost all rose families and varieties grow well in the generally temperate area west of the Rockies. This a rose grower's heaven covers Northern California, Oregon, Washington, and western Idaho, generally includes USDA Zones 7 to 9.

In the Northwest, own-root and budded plants on Dr. Huey or multiflora rootstocks do well. Before buying a rose, check the rootstock.

Once-blooming "cool-weather" Old Garden Roses, including hybrid gallicas, albas, damasks, centifolias, and mosses, plus Bourbons, hybrid perpetuals, and Portlands grow especially well here. Avoid the reblooming families of teas, Chinas, and noisettes because they need more heat for best performance.

Floribundas and other spray roses do very well throughout a Northwest growing season. Black spot is a problem in rainy areas, so plant disease-resistant varieties.

Best Roses for the Northwest

BEGINNERS
Hansa hybrid rugosa

HYBRID TEA
Olympiad

FLORIBUNDA
Livin' Easy

GRANDIFLORA
Fame!

MINIATURE
Gourmet Popcorn

OLD GARDEN ROSE
Stanwell Perpetual

SHRUB
Sally Holmes

CLIMBER/RAMBLER
Compassion

Midwest & Plains

This is one of the coldest areas of the country, so choose roses that can withstand hard winters. This large territory covers Minnesota, Wisconsin, Michigan, Ohio, Indiana, Illinois, Iowa, North Dakota, South Dakota, Nebraska, Wyoming, Montana, and eastern Idaho, and generally includes USDA Zones 3 to 6.

Midwestern and Plains states gardeners growing hybrid teas and other modern roses should select plants grown on their own roots and provide extensive winter protection. During winter, roses grown in pots should be moved to a greenhouse, garage, or other space that doesn't freeze, so the roots will survive.

Cool-weather Old Garden Roses grown on their own roots, such as hybrid gallicas, albas, damasks, centifolias, mosses, Bourbons, hybrid perpetuals, and Portlands, are good choices for this area. Avoid the reblooming families of teas, Chinas, and noisettes that need more heat for best performance.

Hardy shrubs such as rugosas, Explorers, Bucks, Knock Outs, Easy Elegance, and Mordens do well in chilly Midwestern winters.

Best Roses for the Midwest

BEGINNERS
Carefree Beauty shrub rose

HYBRID TEA
Elina

FLORIBUNDA
Eyepaint

GRANDIFLORA
Earth Song

MINIATURE
Hot Tamale

OLD GARDEN ROSE
R. gallica versicolor

SHRUB
Graham Thomas

CLIMBER/RAMBLER
Royal Sunset

Northeast

While often not as cold as the upper Midwest, conditions in the Northeast still require gardeners to plant hardy varieties and provide winter protection. This region runs from Maine south through New Hampshire, Vermont, New York, Pennsylvania, West Virginia, and the Atlantic seaboard states. It generally covers USDA Zones 3 to 7.

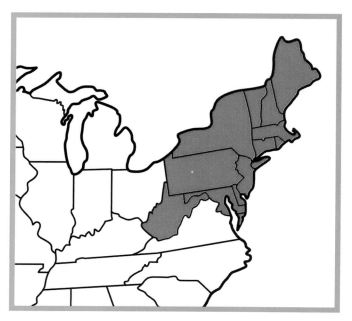

Nearly all shrub families do well in the Northeast, as do most cool-weather Old Garden Roses, including hybrid gallicas, albas, damasks, centifolias, mosses, Bourbons, hybrid perpetuals, and Portlands. Avoid the reblooming families of teas, Chinas, and noisettes because they need more heat for best performance.

Modern roses, either budded or on their own root, do best with winter protection because this region has four distinct seasons and potentially severe winters.

Roses enjoy the adequate rain and snowfall common to this region.

Best Roses for the Northeast

BEGINNERS
Double Knock Out shrub

HYBRID TEA
Gemini

FLORIBUNDA
Betty Prior

GRANDIFLORA
Queen Elizabeth

MINIATURE
Irresistible

OLD GARDEN ROSE
Mme Hardy

SHRUB
Robusta

CLIMBER/RAMBLER
New Dawn

Southeast

The warm, wet weather in most of the Southeast provides ideal growing conditions for many kinds of roses. From Alabama, Mississippi, Louisiana, Georgia, and Florida in the south and ranging north to Kentucky and Virginia, the area generally includes USDA Zones 6 to 10.

All repeat-blooming Old Garden Roses perform well in the Southeast, particularly teas, Chinas, and noisettes. The Earth-Kind roses and most shrub families are good choices. Grow minis and minifloras on their own rootstock and modern roses on Fortuniana rootstock.

Gardeners along the coastline should test their soil for salt content. Ask a local extension service which soil amendments are best for growing roses.

The moist conditions of this region are ideal for spawning black spot, so check with a Consulting Rosarian ("Need Advice?" at www.ars.org) for disease-resistant varieties.

Best Roses for the Southeast

BEGINNERS
Mlle Cécile Brünner polyantha

HYBRID TEA
Moonstone

FLORIBUNDA
Lavaglut

GRANDIFLORA
Melody Parfumée

MINIATURE
Bees Knees

OLD GARDEN ROSE
Champneys' Pink Cluster

SHRUB
Abraham Darby

CLIMBER/RAMBLER
Pierre de Ronsard

South Central & Lower Midwest

Extreme summer heat often followed by very cold winters makes this region a challenging one in which to grow roses. Covering eastern Colorado, Kansas, Missouri, Oklahoma, and heading south to the tip of Texas, this area generally covers USDA Zones 5 to 10.

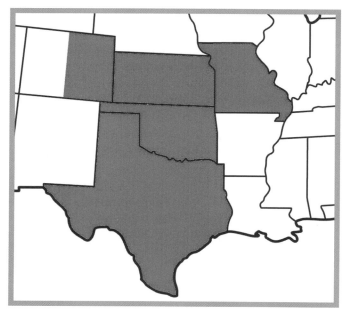

The Earth-Kind family of roses does very well in the lower Midwest and Texas, as do repeat-blooming Old Garden Roses that like more heat: noisettes, Chinas, and teas.

Modern roses growing on Fortuniana rootstock are preferred by many rosarians.

Some gardeners in this region avoid the David Austin English roses, believing they are less well suited to the heat.

Hot, humid conditions promote black spot and other fungal diseases. Water the roots, not the foliage, and plant disease-resistant varieties to win the battle.

Best Roses for the South Central & Lower Midwest

BEGINNERS
Belinda's Dream shrub rose

HYBRID TEA
St. Patrick

FLORIBUNDA
Playgirl

GRANDIFLORA
Tournament of Roses

MINIATURE
My Sunshine

OLD GARDEN ROSE
Mutabilis

SHRUB
Sea Foam

CLIMBER/RAMBLER
America

Southwest & Southern California

Often considered the prime rose-growing area of the country, the Southwest, with warm summers and temperate winters, allows nearly all rose families to flourish. From central and southern California, Nevada, and Utah to western Colorado, Arizona, and New Mexico, this area generally covers USDA Zones 5 to 10.

Modern roses growing on Dr. Huey and Fortuniana rootstocks do well. Most Old Garden Roses, miniatures, minifloras, and shrubs perform nicely. Heat may bring more saturated colors to the blooms and darker colors to leaves.

High temperatures, especially in desert regions, also mean roses will require daily or even twice-daily watering. To prevent fungal diseases always water the roots, not the foliage.

In most areas, amending the soil with plenty of organic material, such as compost, and mulching will improve water retention.

Best Roses for the Southwest & Southern California

BEGINNERS
Julia Child floribunda

HYBRID TEA
Marilyn Monroe

FLORIBUNDA
Hot Cocoa

GRANDIFLORA
Gold Medal

MINIATURE
Baby Grand

OLD GARDEN ROSE
Rose de Rescht

SHRUB
Sally Holmes

CLIMBER/RAMBLER
Fourth of July

Buying Roses

This healthy bare-root rose arrived in good condition with large canes and strong roots. Prune off any extra-long roots, and soak the rose overnight before planting.

Once you've decided what kind and color of rose you like and what

will work best in your yard, the next important choice is where to buy roses and in what form.

First, choose between a budded or an own-root rose. Each has its advantages.

Budded roses

Budding is a type of grafting that creates a stronger rose. A bud (called the scion) from a hybrid rose is inserted into a cutting of a vigorous wild or nearly wild rose (called the rootstock or understock). This gives the hybrid scion hardiness it might not get on its own roots, as the rootstock is usually stronger than the scion.

The rootstocks grow in a field for as long as a year before they are grafted (budded). The newly grafted plant stays in the field for another year before it is harvested, put into cold storage, and shipped to retailers. Most budded roses are 2-year-old plants.

Budded roses are graded by a system from the American Association of Nurserymen. A number 1 grade plant must have at least three canes, one of which must be at least ⅝ inch in diameter. A number 1½ grade plant must have two "reasonably sized" canes, while number 2 grade plants are essentially throwaways.

Own-root roses

Roses can also be started as cuttings. Because it's considerably less expensive to produce a plant on its own root than by budding, most mail-order outlets use this method. Own-root roses are generally propagated in a greenhouse and occasionally replanted outdoors.

Own-root roses are not subject to a grading system. Mail-order nurseries may send anything from a 4- to 6-month-old greenhouse plant to a field-grown rose more than a year old. It's a good idea to contact the company before you order to discover the age and size of the plants.

Which is better? You decide

Despite claims to the contrary, there is no inherent superiority of own-root over budded roses, or visa versa.

Own-root plants have the advantage of being more winter hardy than budded ones since they will grow back true to their variety if the plant is killed to the ground, while budded roses will revert back to their rootstock. You'll find a wider range of rose cultivars sold as own-root plants.

The major disadvantage of own-root roses is that they're often sold younger than budded roses. Because own-root roses need more time to reach productive maturity, they're not as good a value.

Rootstocks vary by climate

Owners of budded roses should learn what rootstock their plant has. The overwhelming majority of budded roses in the United States is grown in southern California or Arizona on a rootstock called Dr. Huey, a near-species variety. This rootstock is used primarily because it's compatible with the soil in those areas and works well with most hybrid scions.

However, Dr. Huey doesn't perform well everywhere in the United States. Gardeners in the South or Southeast should seek out roses budded on a Fortuniana rootstock. This is a near-wild species much better suited to southern soils and climate.

Likewise, gardeners in the northern United States and southern Canada will do better with budded plants on a strain of *Rosa multiflora*, suited for colder areas. Roses purchased from a Canadian company (there are no importation problems) will be budded primarily on this tougher rootstock.

Above left: **Read the plant tag carefully to determine what kind of rose you're buying and what kind of care it will take.**

Above center: **This Knock Out rose shows good form. If possible, buy plants that are not in bloom, or completely remove all blooms after planting so the rose can direct its energy into getting established.**

Above right: **You can see the bud union—the knobby scar where the grafted parts meet—just above the fingers on this bare-root rose.**

Where to Buy Roses

The next big decision is where to buy roses.

Purchase by mail or locally? From an independent garden center or a big box outlet? Each choice has its advantages and disadvantages.

Mail order

Mail-order companies offer the greatest selection of both varieties and rootstocks. Even the largest local nursery cannot begin to carry the array of roses found online or in catalogs.

Another advantage: Budding propagators ship bare-root plants with well-established root systems 1 foot long or longer, something not usually available from a local nursery or big box store.

The obvious disadvantage of mail order: not being able to inspect the plants prior to sending money.

Check the reputation of any mail-order nursery with a Consulting Rosarian ("Need Advice?" at www.ars.org) or through online reviews before placing an order. For a list of sources, see page 217.

Bagged plants

The most common way to package rose plants for sale at big retail outlets is in plastic bags, often with wax-sealed canes. Both of these features are

In recent years, online ordering has become even easier than ordering from a catalog. Check the reviews of any mail-order source before you order, or ask a Consulting Rosarian for an opinion.

designed to keep moisture in the plant during shipping and display. Despite what sellers may say, bagged plants are not bare root.

The disadvantage of bagged plants is the unknown amount of time they are out of water and the fact that they are often not number 1 grade. The advantage: They're usually inexpensive.

If you buy a bagged plant, remove the bag and submerge the entire plant in water for a couple of days to rehydrate it before planting. Many rosarians also advise cutting off the waxed canes entirely, allowing the plant to start over with new, healthy canes. All in all, bagged plants are the lowest quality.

Local nurseries and garden centers

Almost all nurseries sell roses in peat or plastic pots, a practice that also cannot be termed bare root. The reason for potting the plants is economic: Too many careless buyers seek refunds after their bare-root plants dry out and die from lack of prompt planting or rehydration by soaking. Potting provides a source of moisture and nutrients for the roots.

TEST
GARDEN
TIP

GROW OWN-ROOT ROSES IN POTS

Grow own-root roses in pots for a year. That gives them a little extra time to grow bigger and stronger before being transplanted into the garden.

Buying from Local Nurseries

Should you buy your roses locally or from a mail-order source? It depends on what your priorities are. Consider these advantages and disadvantages of buying locally.

ADVANTAGES:

BEST SELECTION OF PLANTS You can see exactly what you are purchasing.

ACCESS to rose advice from a trained nursery staff person.

EASY RETURN OR EXCHANGE of damaged or otherwise low-quality plants.

DISADVANTAGES:

LIMITED selection of varieties.

ADDED EXPENSE for the cost of the pot, the potting soil, and the labor.

SHORT ROOTS that have been trimmed to fit into the pot. The more and longer the roots, the better start a plant gets.

How Roses are Sold

Roses are generally sold in three ways: bare root, container, and bagged. Although the most attractive choice is a blooming container, starting as a bare-root plant gets the rose off to a better start.

landscaping & designing

Roses are the most flexible of flowers when it comes to landscaping, thanks to their wide variety of sizes, shapes, and colors. Use them as star attractions or supporting players.

p.**46**
GARDEN STYLES

Whether your yard has a formal or more casual look, roses fit beautifully into any garden design.

p.**50**
PROBLEM SOLVERS

Use roses to tame slopes and problem areas, spruce up a border, create a hedge, or decorate a structure. Discover varieties that require less water and maintenance.

p.**58**
POTS & BOUQUETS

Everyone loves to get roses, whether in a bouquet or a container. Follow these tips for great-looking flowers you can give to others or keep for yourself.

p.**62**
ROSE GARDEN PLANS

Need inspiration? Use these four garden plans, each with a plant list and planting design. Now you can have a garden that looks like something out of a book!

Roses for Formal Gardens

Large urns planted with miniature or miniflora roses next to columns draped with large-flowered climbers create a classic formal look.

Above left: **Neatly clipped, curved boxwood borders provide distinctive edges for a formal design.**

Above right: **Pebble pathways serve as the borders in this formal design. Massing roses in single colors packs a punch.**

TEST GARDEN TIP

Getting a uniform look

Plant roses in pairs or groups to give a sense of solidity and avoid the disorganized look of single-variety plantings.

The traditional image of a formal rose garden is one

with a geometric layout, usually containing hybrid teas or grandifloras and surrounded by a low boxwood hedge. However, any planting devoted entirely to roses can be considered a formal rose garden, whether bordered by boxwood or not. The form can be a series of simple rectangles or something more intricate.

Design considerations

When designing a layout for a formal rose garden:

Plant hybrid teas and grandifloras about 3 feet apart to give them room to grow and for easier maintenance.

Install soaker hoses or allocate space to move hoses because roses usually need extra water.

Add pathways for access to cut or smell the blooms, and to avoid walking directly on the beds, which compacts the soil and affects roots.

Create parallel lines of roses, the most efficient planting scheme for maintenance. Rows can be straight or curved, but the denser the plantings, the harder they are to maintain.

Exquisite gardens of any kind require an immense amount of work. Many large gardens have paid or volunteer staffs to keep them looking good. Consider how to allocate time, energy, and finances to maintain the garden, not just install it. Think and plan realistically.

Formal garden ideas

Enhance the geometric or linear patterns of a formal rose garden by adding focal points that draw your eye to the center or to the corners. In warm areas of the country, standards (also called tree roses) can serve as visual anchors.

Instead of edging a rose garden with boxwood, use low-growing floribundas, polyanthas, or shrubs to add color and camouflage the bare lower parts of hybrid teas and grandifloras.

Center a circular formal garden with a gazebo or other structure, training large-flowered climbers (using one or more varieties) vertically along the columns.

When planning a formal rose garden, think about the architectural maxim "form follows function." A formal garden can provide bouquets, serve as a peaceful place of repose, offer fragrance, and more. Knowing how you'll use the garden will dictate some of its design. A cutting garden may be strictly functional while a sanctuary garden might include benches.

Finally, don't be constrained by what books say a formal rose garden should look like. Be creative when conjuring up your dream garden. Do what serves your needs and makes you happy.

Roses for Mixed Gardens

The English cottage garden, a seemingly unplanned, riotous mixture of plants of all types that spill over and crowd one another in a "natural" setting, is a rose-laden landscape plan most gardeners seem to love.

Don't be fooled! The English cottage garden is as deliberately designed and planned as any other landscaping approach, and woe to the gardener who simply adds plants willy-nilly without careful consideration.

Friends or foes

Roses play well with most other plants and can add blooms and fragrance to the mixed garden that no other plant family can match.

When choosing partners for a cottage garden, remember that some plants should not be partnered directly with roses:

Tall plants that may block the sun.

Plants with invasive root systems, including most groundcover plants, that can rob a rose of food and water. Some plants formerly common in gardens, such as purple loosestrife (*Lythrum salicaria*), should be avoided entirely because of their invasive habits.

Acid-loving azaleas and hydrangeas that need a different soil pH from roses. (Roses prefer a soil pH of 6.0 to 7.0.)

Plants that require shade. Roses are sun worshippers that need at least 6 to 8 hours of sun per day.

Pink shrub roses provide height and color that balance the yellows, blues, and whites along this garden path.

Carefully consider the needs of your garden's companions: heights; widths; blooming seasons; and needs for water, food, and other cultural necessities. Unlike some landscape plants, roses need regular care such as pruning, fertilizing, watering, and winter protection in many areas.

These tasks are difficult when roses and other plants are placed close together. Plan the space needed to perform these cultural chores before installing the garden, not after.

Mixing it up

Caveats aside, a mixed garden can be a glorious display, offering opportunities well beyond what roses alone can provide. Creative gardeners can:

Produce a four-season garden, packed with plants that bloom at different times and foliage that changes colors with the passing seasons.

Use plants with a variety of textures and colors. For example, the bright pink single flowers of *Rosa rubrifolia* (also known as redleaf rose or *R. glauca*) grace the landscape for two months, and the blue-gray foliage with reddish overtones provides a unique color much of the year. It's a tough plant that can hold its own in a cottage garden.

Employ other flowers to compensate for the lack of blue (and black) in rose blooms. Most blue-flowered plants mix well with roses, including catmint (*Nepeta*), 'Rozanne' hardy geranium, and delphiniums.

Appear to paint the garden with pastel shades of blues, pinks, and whites—almost required in mixed garden plantings.

Pink Knock Out shrub roses pair beautifully with blue catmint (*Nepeta*).

ASK THE GARDEN DOCTOR

What goes in a mixed border?

ANSWER: A mixed border cries out for both horizontal and vertical accents. Add foxgloves, delphiniums, and similar spiky plants to create upright interest. Spreading groundcover roses give a horizontal dimension to the palette. For an unusual focal point, consider growing *R. sericea pteracantha* (*left*) for its huge red, translucent thorns.

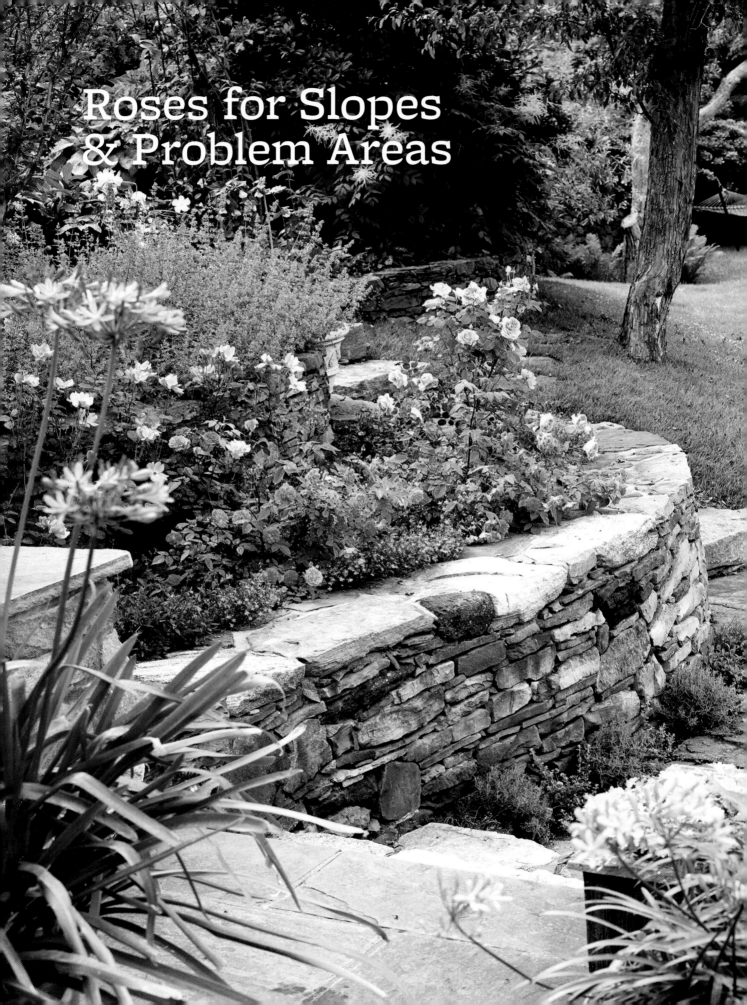

Roses for Slopes
& Problem Areas

A slope, even a moderately steep one, need not be a problem planting area.

If attractively terraced, it can be an ideal location for almost any kind of rose. A slope provides ready-made drainage, and walls or embankments are perfect places to fill with improved soil.

Some yards have spots you'd like to cover with attractive plantings—and then basically ignore. Roses can fulfill this purpose admirably with a little planning.

Groundcover roses

Most roses touted as groundcovers do not truly fit that definition. Some are are simply low-growing shrubs, others are very upright, and some grow with a slight spreading habit. To allow them to cover the ground, they must be planted very close together—1 foot apart or less.

Most of the Flower Carpet varieties fall into this category. Low-growing rugosas are even more suitable as groundcovers. If grown on their own roots, rugosas have a tendency to sucker and spread into unfilled areas, eventually presenting a mass of color on a low-maintenance plant.

A few rose varieties grow long, low-growing, relatively lax canes that can truly be considered groundcovers. These include Sea Foam, with white blooms on canes that can reach 6 feet or more, and Red Ribbons, with lax canes between 4 and 6 feet. The next best: Max Graf, a once-blooming rugosa hybrid with single pink blooms, and Nozomi, a miniature with 3- to 4-foot-long, lax canes. Many of the ramblers can also be used effectively as groundcovers.

Making more plants

To cover a larger area, gardeners can propagate more plants using a process known as layering, similar to creating new strawberry plants from runners.

About 3 feet or farther from the mother plant, pin one of the long canes to the ground with a strong piece of wire, such as a coat hanger, being careful not to cut into the bark. Cover the pinned spot with a little soil. Within a few months, new roots will form where the cane meets the soil. In a few months, once the new plant gets established, remove the pin and cut the cane between the new growth and the mother plant.

Care for groundcover roses

Although many groundcover roses are touted as carefree, they produce more flowers when spent blooms are removed (deadheading.) This is especially true for low-growing rugosas. Avoid thinking of them as plants that can thrive without any attention. They grow best with fertilizer once or twice in the spring and summer plus additional water. Many are winter hardy to Zones 4 or 5 with little to no winter protection.

Opposite: **Raised beds offer better drainage and the opportunity to amend and improve the soil.**

Above left: **Use the many heights and sizes of roses to create layers of color within sloped and terraced beds.**

Center: **Red Ribbons, a highly rated shrub rose, grows with canes long enough to let them flop and cover the ground.**

Above right: **Groundcover roses stabilize and beautify a sunny hillside.**

Roses for Mass Plantings, Hedges & Borders

Nothing catches the eye of a garden visitor like a mass planting of one rose variety.

That bright wall of color makes a focal point like no other. Mass plantings can include tight groupings of three plants, a linear hedge, or a border of dozens of plants. Generally, the more plants used, the greater the visual impact.

For best effect, choose a variety that grows no taller than about 4 feet. The best selections for mass plantings include heavy-blooming floribundas, polyanthas, and shrubs. Walls, other structures, or evergreens serve as effective backdrops to set off the brilliant colors.

Close neighbors require care

When designing a mass planting, check the plant tag to see how wide the rose bush grows. Roses in a mass display should be planted about 1 foot apart for the best blooming display. However, planting roses close together makes it more difficult to care for them.

Use these guidelines when massing roses:

Plant no more than two bushes wide when making a border or a hedge so plants can be approached from either side.

Keep tight circles of bushes no larger than 3 feet wide to allow access to all plants from the outside. A larger arrangement creates a hard-to-reach area inside.

Choose disease-resistant a varieties for mass plantings because problems will spread quicker than among wider-spaced plants. Use products that help control problems.

Above: **Plant tough shrub roses next to a see-through fence, such as split rail or ornamental iron, for an extra decorative effect.**

Opposite, above: **Use color as a mass planting opportunity. The yellow Behold miniature rose shields the leggy lower portions of the St. Patrick hybrid tea.**

Opposite, below: **Spaced close together, Martha's Vineyard shrub roses make an effective and beautiful hedge.**

Roses as hedges

An old adage claims that fences make good neighbors. Using roses to create a hedge or fill a border is a most beautiful fulfillment of this promise. A rose hedge can keep animals and people out of the yard, serve as a visual privacy hedge, or simply create a garden room.

If you want privacy, however, remember that roses drop their leaves for winter in most areas of the country.

Decide how high you want your hedge, choose an attractive variety, then determine its spreading habit to decide how closely to plant the bushes. The closer they are planted to one another, the more quickly a hedge will fill out.

Varieties touted as hedge roses often are not the best choice for this purpose. Shrubs work well, as do hybrid rugosas, which can reach up to 6 feet tall. Rugosas can be pruned lower, if needed, require no spraying and little water, and display attractive hips and varying foliage colors in autumn. Most shrubs and all rugosas are generally hardy in most areas of the country.

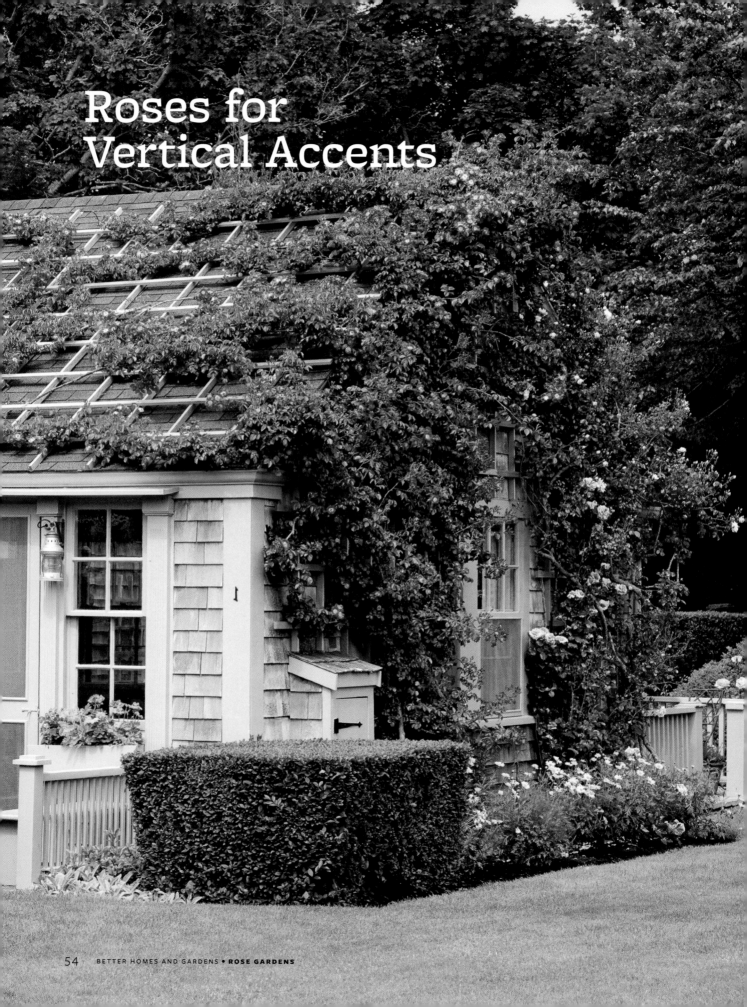

Roses for
Vertical Accents

Many rose varieties grow very tall and, if trained to do so, very wide.

In a garden, blooming roses in all their glory can grace arches, trellises, pergolas, columns, gazebos, and other structures. Roses can also screen or decorate buildings, trees, fences, and other structures.

Choose climbers with recurrent bloom for the best effect. The beautiful cascading roses in pictures of Giverny, Bagatelle, and other French rose gardens are primarily planted with once-blooming ramblers that look spectacular for about two months but less than wonderful the rest of the year.

How to train long-caned roses

Climbing, rambling, and shrub roses with long canes cannot attach themselves to supports. They must be trained in the desired direction, then manually attached to the supporting structure. Latticework is especially convenient, because the openings make it easy to attach the ties.

Training is an apt word: it happens over time. Begin by attaching growing young canes to the support with a material that will not cut into the canes when they're blown about by the wind. Avoid twist-ties with wire centers or hard plastic ties. Soft plastic or cloth ties are just as durable but gentler to the plant.

In a couple weeks, continue training. Move the canes a little farther along the structure and secure them again. Repeat this process as often as necessary. By the time the canes grow to their full lengths, they should be in their proper places.

Be gentle with tender new canes. If forced too far, they have a tendency to break. Most long-caned roses grow canes one year and bloom on them the following year.

Above: **Use cloth or soft plastic ties (shown in green) to keep climbing roses attached to pergolas and other structures.**

Opposite: **To keep climbing roses on structures, attach a trellis, then train the roses to grow in the right direction. Use a climber or rambler with the longest possible canes.**

Right: **Training rose canes horizontally forces the plant to bloom along the top of the canes by removing the plant's apical dominance, a botanical process that inhibits the growth of side shoots or buds on a stem.**

TEST GARDEN TIP

Best blooms on long canes

To get a heavy bloom from long-cane roses, train the canes as nearly horizontal as possible.

Roses for Water-Wise Gardens

Water restrictions exist in many parts of the country.
An eco-conscious gardener who wants to wisely use the earth will want to consider growing roses that need fewer resources, including water.

For best performance, most roses need moderate but dependable amounts of water, usually 1 to 2 inches per week. However, some varieties adapt nicely to arid conditions and are especially recommended for drier regions of the country.

Seek out Earth-Kind varieties
The easiest way to know which roses thrive in dry climates is to check for an Earth-Kind designation. Earth-Kind rose trials began about a decade ago at the Texas AgriLife Extension Service in College Station. Plants were given a minimum of food and water. There was no insecticidal or fungicidal

New Dawn, a rose which earned the first plant patent in 1930, is hardy in Zones 4–9a. It tolerates poor soil and partial shade. Give it strong support, such as an iron fence, for its heavy canes.

spraying. After years of scientific testing, 15 varieties earned the Earth-Kind designation for pest tolerance and outstanding landscape performance. The list has now expanded to 21.

The group includes Old Garden Roses, shrubs, polyanthas, floribundas, and climbers—but no hybrid teas.

Not all vendors label these high performers as Earth-Kind, so take a list of names when shopping for roses. Some are not hardy in northern climates; research the care requirements first.

Earth-Kind expands

The Texas program inspired six other universities (Colorado State, Iowa State, Kansas State, Louisiana State, University of Minnesota, and University of Nebraska) to institute similar research. Earth-Kind designations for other areas of the country are planned in the future.

In addition to providing water resource suggestions, the Earth-Kind website advocates other environmental practices, such as growing roses in clay or loam soils using compost and organic mulches to eliminate the need for commercial synthetic or organic fertilizers.

For more growing tips see: aggie-horticulture.tamu.edu/earthkind.

ASK THE GARDEN DOCTOR

What does my soil need?

ANSWER: Roses need a balance of aeration, drainage, and water-holding abilities. Texas AgriLife Extension Service recommends adding 3 to 6 inches of plant-based compost to sandy or loam soils. For clay soils, amend once with 3 inches of expanded shale, then compost.

Earth-Kind Cultivars These varieties have been scientifically proven to use less fertilizer, pesticide, and water. Gardeners, especially those in the South, should consider growing these environmentally friendly roses.

DWARF SHRUBS
Marie Daly
Souvenir de St. Anne's
The Fairy (*above*)

SMALL SHRUBS
Caldwell Pink
Mlle Cécile Brünner
 (*above*)
Perle d'Or

MEDIUM SHRUBS
Belinda's Dream
Carefree Beauty (*above*)
Ducher
Duchesse de Brabant
Else Poulsen
Georgetown Tea
Knock Out
La Marne
Mme Antoine Mari
Mutabilis
Spice

MANNERLY CLIMBERS
Climbing Pinkie
Sea Foam (*above*)

VIGOROUS CLIMBERS
New Dawn (*above*)
Rêve d'Or

Roses for Containers

Small shrubs or miniature roses blend well with annuals in large containers. Because containers can dry out quickly, monitor the soil—but avoid overwatering.

Far left: **A pair of standard roses in containers flanks a garden path. Begonias or other annuals are natural companions to add color at the base.**

Left: **Even if you don't have room for a full rose garden, cluster groups of containers and cut roses together to achieve this look.**

Any rose can be grown in a pot or other container.

You just need a container with enough room to allow the roots to expand. The bigger the mature plant, the bigger container it needs.

Hybrid teas, grandifloras, and floribundas can be grown in 10- to 15-gallon containers. Miniatures, minifloras, and small shrubs take 3-gallon or larger pots. Shrubs and large climbers require at least a 15-gallon container.

Selecting a container

All kinds of containers can be used for growing roses. A classic concrete urn is appropriate for a formal garden, while a pot that resembles a giant head reflects a sense of whimsy. Wooden half barrels suit rustic gardens. Southwestern-style terra-cotta pots easily house a collection of miniatures. Ceramic or metal work well almost anywhere.

While container gardens generally add beauty to a garden, some rose enthusiasts have even been known to grow entire rose gardens in trimmed plastic garbage cans mounted on dollies or casters.

Advantages of containers

Potted roses offer gardeners the best of all possible worlds, with virtually unlimited designs and a wide range of roses.

Place containers virtually anywhere in the landscape without worrying about soil conditions or drainage.

Station pots in the sunniest spots, moving them during the growing season to follow the sun's changing position.

Shoehorn a series of small to medium containers into tiny spaces, such as apartment balconies and on patios.

Place pots on tables, benches, or other elevations so you don't need to bend or kneel, making it easy for people with physical limitations to grow roses.

How to grow container roses

The basics of growing successful container roses are much the same as for any other plant: good potting soil, good drainage, and a nearly continuous supply of water during warm summer months.

Roses destined to stay in pots should be repotted periodically as their size increases. Plants that will stay in one container need to have their potting soil changed or replenished every couple years.

Other cultural considerations, such as disease and insect control, fertilizing, and pruning, are virtually the same as for roses in the ground.

TEST GARDEN TIP

Potted roses in winter

In northern climates, move container roses to a sheltered space or garage to avoid winter-kill. Avoid planting in clay pots, which crack when the soil goes through freeze-and-thaw cycles.

Roses for Bouquets

Everyone loves a bouquet of roses. While one-bloom-per-stem hybrid teas and grandifloras are usually considered best for cutting, don't overlook floribundas and other spray roses such as shrubs and climbers. Their blooms can also have a long vase life, and one floriferous stem can create an entire bouquet.

Most Old Garden Roses have a relatively short vase life compared with modern roses, which should last about a week with proper cutting and conditioning. Shrub roses can be used, but cutting lengthy stems removes the next buds; instead, float only the blossoms on water.

How to cut roses
Although taking a special cutting vase to the garden may look romantic, it's not recommended. No matter how quickly the cut stem drops into the

Use an opaque container such as galvanized metal or pottery to hide unsightly stems. To ensure freshness, strip any leaves from the stems that will be under water.

water, air hits the cut and immediately seals off the capillaries, eliminating or seriously impeding water uptake.

To ensure a reasonable cut life for roses, recut the stem underwater. Make a slanted cut about 1 inch up the stem, keep it underwater for about 5 to 10 seconds, then transfer the stem to a vase or other container. Add nothing to the water used for cutting because its sole purpose is to open the stem so water and nutrients can be freely taken up.

How to fill a vase

Once a rose is cut underwater, lift it up and place it in a vase of very warm, almost hot, water. The heat helps harden off the bloom. Vase water has two purposes: to feed the bloom just as it would be fed on the plant and to suppress any bacteria that could shut down the flow of nutrient-bearing water to the bloom.

For even longer cut-flower life, place the vase of roses in warm to hot water in the refrigerator for approximately one hour to significantly increase the life of a cut flower. Vegetables and other foods in the refrigerator will not affect the bloom in this short time period. Strip foliage off any portion of the stem that will stay underwater because the foliage naturally carries bacteria that can multiply rapidly in water.

Ways to lengthen vase life

Add a floral preservative to the vase water for best results. Brands such as Floralife, Chrysal, and other products can be bought inexpensively from a florist or floral supply house. Homemade preservatives work, although not as well as professional products.

Vase water, with new preservative added, should be changed at least every other day. If a stem works its way out and its blooms wilt, recut the stem underwater and place it back in the vase. It will usually rehydrate and freshen up.

When cut roses are not being actively admired, place them in a dark, cool area. Heat and light cause the blooms to continue to develop, hastening the eventual wilt and petal drop.

Below left: **Roses will last longer if you cut their stems underwater.**

Below right: **Consider using shrub roses, such as this assortment from the Knock Out series, as short-stemmed floating blooms. Cutting long stems from roses means the bush needs more time to rebloom because new flowers grow from the tips.**

TEST
GARDEN
TIP

Snap off thorns

Though thorns can stabilize a stem in a bud vase, they generally get in the way when arranging a group of roses in a large vase. To remove unwanted thorns, push them sideways (perpendicular to the length of the cane), and they should snap right off. This is easier and quicker than using a commercial thorn stripper and does not disturb the outer stem.

Rose Garden Plans:
An Arbor Entry

Roses love company. Their relationship with companion perennials and shrubs grows even more beautiful when planted in coordinating colors. The burgundy of Japanese barberries and the soothing greens of creeping junipers provide a calming foil for an array of easy-care New Dawn climbing roses, The Fairy polyanthas, and fragrant Constance Spry shrub roses.

Allow violet-blue Jackman clematis to twine around the climbers. Because clematis grow with sparse foliage, they don't compete with roses for sunlight. Hold off pruning in the fall; wait until spring growth begins before removing rose or clematis limbs that were injured during the winter. Clematis like to grow with their heads in the sun and their feet in the shade, but they don't like to be heavily mulched in summer.

An arbor dripping with roses surrounded by more roses and complementary perennials extends the perfect welcome.

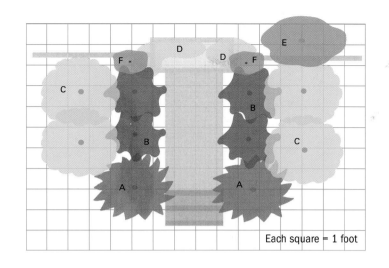

Each square = 1 foot

PLANT LIST

A. **2 Creeping junipers**
(*Juniperus horizontalis* Bar Harbor):
Zones 5–9

B. **4 Red Japanese barberries**
(*Berberis thunbergii* Atropurpurea):
Zones 5–8

C. **4 The Fairy polyantha roses:**
Zones 5–9

D. **2 New Dawn climbing roses:**
Zones 5–9

E. **1 Constance Spry shrub rose:**
Zones 5–9

F. **2 Jackman clematis**
(*Clematis* × 'Jackmanii'): Zones 4–8

ASK THE GARDEN DOCTOR

Which clematis is best?

ANSWER: Match the characteristics of a rose with a clematis. Vigorous climbers deserve rampant clematis varieties such as sweet autumn (*Clematis ternifolia*). A small shrub rose pairs well with a tiny clematis, such as *Clematis* × *durandii*.

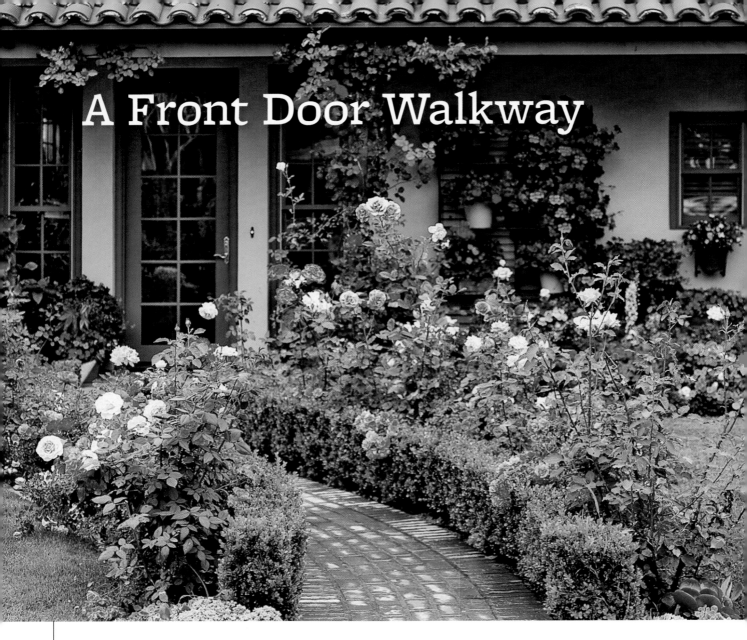

A Front Door Walkway

A gently curving sidewalk flanked with boxwood and a colorful riot of blooms beckons guests to stop and smell the roses. Hybrid teas, with their heavenly fragrance, classic bloom form, and single stems ideal for cutting, are considered the perfect rose. Here, the boxwood borders cleverly hide the gangly lower stems and provide a green background to show off the colors. In a landscape, hybrid teas require the most maintenance in the form of organic or chemical controls to keep them looking their best. They're also not very hardy in northern climates.

To get this look in a cold region, replace the hybrid teas with similar colors of hardy shrub roses, especially those in the Knock Out, Easy Elegance, or Flower Carpet series. Many of the Old Garden Roses or David Austin roses are also cold hardy.

Complete the look with climbing roses. Attach them manually to supports such as trellises near windows or doorways.

Grow fragrant roses where they'll best be enjoyed. The heights of these hybrid teas invite a sniffing of their fragrance.

TEST
GARDEN
TIP

Off with their heads!

Hybrid tea roses, like most other roses, rebloom faster when the spent blooms are trimmed off, a process called deadheading. By late summer or early autumn, however, stop deadheading and let the flowers turn into seedheads, called hips. Doing this allows the plant to cease vigorously producing more flowers and go dormant for winter.

PLANT LIST

A. **25 Boxwoods** (*Buxus* Green Gem):
Zones 5–9

B. **2 Carefree Wonder roses:**
Zones 5–9

C. **1 Gold Medal rose:**
Zones 5–9

D. **1 Perfume Delight rose:**
Zones 5–9

E. **1 Queen Elizabeth rose:**
Zones 5–9

F. **1 Royal Highness rose:**
Zones 5–9

G. **1 Rio Samba rose:**
Zones 5–9

H. **2 Blaze climbing roses:**
Zones 5–9

I. **1 Mister Lincoln rose:**
Zones 5–9

J. **1 St. Patrick rose:**
Zones 5–9

K. **1 Sexy Rexy rose:**
Zones 5–9

L. **1 Playboy rose:**
Zones 5–9

M. **1 Crystalline rose:**
Zones 5–9

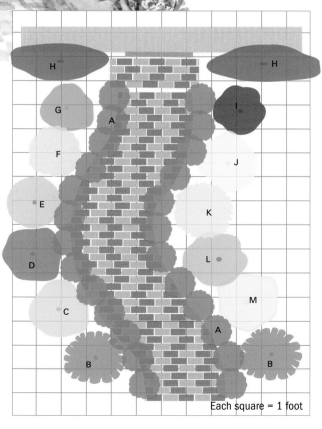

Each square = 1 foot

A Circular Bed

An easy-care circular bed with French country charm suits nearly any sunny landscape. Extend the French theme with a tuteur (which means "guardian" or "support") and a load of Romantica roses, bred in Provence by the famed House of Meilland. The Romanticas, a series of hybrid teas that resemble the many-petaled English roses, are named for famous authors, painters, and other artistic characters.

Like other hybrid teas, Romanticas must be tended with extra care for best performance, but they reward with blooms that beg to be cut and brought into the house. Shrubs or polyanthas can be substituted in northern gardens, but the effect won't be quite the same.

Fill out the rosy ring with low-maintenance perennials such as lambs' ears, sedum, perennial salvia, and chrysanthemum. Their colors will complement almost any color of rose you choose. All of the plants require a mininum of 6 hours of sun per day for best performance. Prune any spent blooms from the salvia so they will rebloom.

A vertical element that centers a circular bed adds dimension and impact. Center the bed with a wooden tuteur, *(above)* or an elegant wrought-iron structure.

PLANT LIST

A. **1 Climbing rose** such as Colette: Zones 5–9

B. **8 Chrysanthemums** (*Chrysanthemum × morifolium*): Zones 5–10

C. **10 Romantica shrub roses** such as Auguste Renoir, Comtesse de Provence, Francois Rabelais, Guy de Maupassant, Johann Strauss, Tchaikovski, Yves Piaget, and Peter Mayle: Zones 5–9

D. **6 Miniature roses** such as Alfie, Baby Paradise, and Rainbow's End: Zones 5–9

E. **6 Tall sedums** (*Sedum spectabile*) such as Autumn Fire: Zones 4–9

F. **6 Perennial salvias** (*Salvia × sylvestris* May Night): Zones 5–9

G. **3 Lady's mantles** (*Alchemilla mollis*): Zones 4–7

H. **3 Lamb's ears** (*Stachys byzantina* Silver Carpet): Zones 4–8

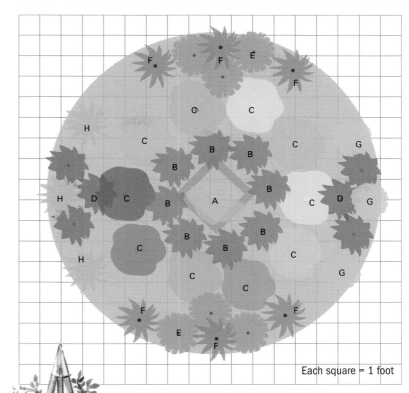

Each square = 1 foot

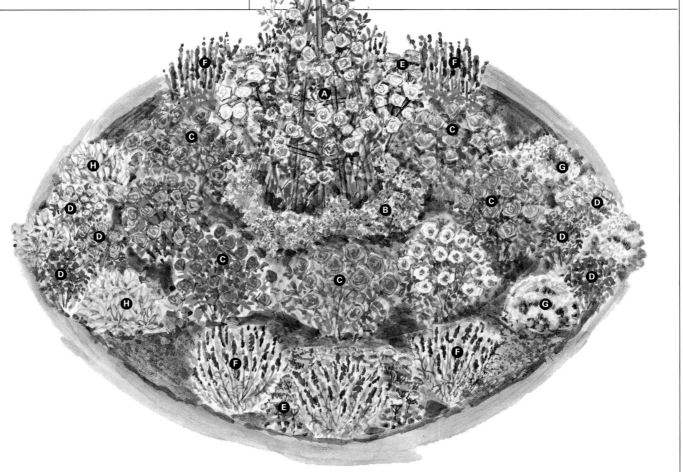

A Romantic Gateway

Imagine this picture without the roses. It just doesn't look right, does it? Roses add the romance that kicks up this garden entry from merely pretty to spectacular. Luckily, it's an easy project that can be completed in just a few hours of time and will look beautiful for years to come.

On each side of a garden gate (or welcoming arbor), plant a New Dawn climbing rose. This tough rose (it's even earned an Earth-Kind designation for being eco-friendly) will bloom once in spring and again throughout the growing season. Extend the delicate color theme with a Ballerina shrub rose, which produces fluffy pink clouds of single pink roses that resemble apple blossoms.

On the opposite side of the arbor, the Annabelle smooth hydrangea grows about the same height as Ballerina, providing balance. This easy-care hydrangea likes partial shade, but needs about the same amount of water as roses.

Low-growing, long-blooming perennials such as pinks and perennial verbenas add color throughout the growing season.

Keep roses and other perennials mulched to conserve moisture. Use plant-based organic mulches, which will break down and improve the soil.

Each square = 1 foot

PLANT LIST

A. **2 New Dawn climbing roses:**
Zones 5–9

B. **1 Ballerina rose:**
Zones 5–9

C. **8 Rose verbenas** *(Verbena canadensis):*
Zones 4–8

D. **3 Pinks** *(Dianthus* spp.):
Zones 3–10

E. **1 Annabelle smooth hydrangea**
(Hydrangea arborescens 'Annabelle'):
Zones 4–9

F. **3 Foxgloves** *(Digitalis purpurea):*
Zones 4–8

rose care & maintenance

Get your roses off to a good start with proper care: food, water, protection, and an occasional haircut. Add sunlight and you're set!

p.72
PREPARING & PLANTING

Preparing a bed for planting may be one of the least glamorous of garden chores but it's also one of the most important.

p.80
WATERING

Turn off that overhead sprinkler! Roses usually need extra water, depending on your climate and soils. Learn when, why, and how to water.

p.82
MULCHING, FEEDING & FERTILIZING

Serve your roses a balanced meal by adding materials that feed and fertilize, then protect them with mulch.

p.86
DEALING WITH PESTS

Aphids and black spot and deer, oh my! Insect, disease, and nibbling pests are facts of life, but you can prevent or fix most problems.

p.94
PRUNING

Have no fear! Although it's almost impossible to hurt a rose with pruning, the right kind of cuts make a rose behave better.

p.98
SEASONAL CARE

Spring and fall mean it's time for special chores in the garden. Done properly, these techniques enhance the survival and performance of your roses.

p.102
HARDINESS & REGIONAL CARE

Roses behave differently in New England than in the Southwest. Know your USDA Hardiness Zone and learn when to tackle tasks.

Preparing the Site

A raised bed protects roses from neighboring tree roots, and a fence or wall provides support.

You'll succeed with roses if you plant them where and how they like to grow.

Choose the right site and prepare the soil properly so roses have everything they need to grow like a weed—figuratively, of course!

Keep on the sunny side

To perform at its best, a rose needs at least six hours of sunshine a day—preferably more. Without sunlight to promote photosynthesis, the plant cannot make the food it needs to thrive. If there's a choice, place a rose where it gets morning sun to help dry overnight rain or dew off the foliage, suppressing fungal growths such as black spot.

Hybrid teas, grandifloras, and floribundas need the most sun. Miniatures also require at least a half-day of sun; when planted in pots, they can be moved to better sun locations as the growing season progresses.

Some types of roses can grow in less than a half-day of sun, though they'll thrive with more. These include large, vigorous types that can grow tall enough to find sunlight and perform well, such as shrubs, climbers, and some Old Garden Roses. If they're planted in a shady area, these roses require fertilizer and good air circulation around the plants to get them off to a good start.

Root for good roots

Roses' extensive root systems grow with thousands of hair roots to feed the plants. Once established, these roots can coexist with many annual and perennial plants. However, the invasive roots of nearby large trees and shrubs can rob a rose of water and nutrients, leading to its decline and eventual death.

Check for roots in the planting area before placing a rose near a tree or large shrub. Remember that the TLC you give a rose—good soil, water, fertilizer—may also attract other roots to the site.

Some gardeners grow roses in raised beds 6 to 12 inches deep to solve two critical needs: good soil and good drainage. The beds can contain the soil mix of your choice and drain well because excess water can easily flow beneath the walls.

You can also grow roses in large pots or other containers. Use pedestals or stumps to raise the containers a few inches off the ground to allow drainage and avoid invading roots from neighboring trees.

Below left: **Roses, especially hybrid teas, grandifloras and floribundas, grow best in full sun—at least six hours every day.**

Below right: **Raised beds are ideal for roses. You can add the right soil and amendments for good drainage and to allow roots to grow deep.**

TEST GARDEN TIP

Measure your soil drainage

To find out how well your soil drains, dig a straight-sided hole 12 inches deep. Fill the hole with water, let it drain completely, then refill with water. Wait one hour. Use a ruler to measure how far below the soil line the water dropped. Less than 1/2 inch indicates poor drainage; 1/2 to 2 inches is moderate; a 2- to 6-inch drop is good; more than 6 inches indicates rapid drainage.

Amending
the Soil

A spading fork is useful
for incorporating organic
amendments such as
compost and peat.

Roses need well-aerated, organically rich soil with a pH range of 6.2 to 6.8.

To determine soil pH, take a sample to your local extension service office or buy a home kit. If possible, prepare an entire bed rather than just a planting hole for your roses.

You can remove sod and dig up the ground to make a new bed. But there are two easier ways:

Spray the existing lawn carefully with an herbicide containing glyphosate, following label directions. Use a spray with droplets rather than a mist, which can drift and kill nearby plants. These herbicides don't leave residual chemicals in the soil, so the bed can be prepped as soon as one day later. You don't need to wait for the grass to completely die; the spray is already killing the grass tissues.

Then, place several sheets of newspapers over the bed, and cover them with compost or mulch. By the time the newspapers decompose, the grass will be dead and compost or mulch can be tilled in.

When to dig

Many home lots have been graded to remove all but a thin covering of topsoil, leaving only impenetrable clay or hardpan. In these cases, fill a raised bed with a commercial 3- or 5-way soil mix. These mixes contain variable amounts of soil, sand, sawdust, and manure. For best results, amend the soil mix with another 10 to 15 percent of organic material such as compost.

Amend soil only when it is fairly dry and loose to the touch. If you try to work with soil that's too wet, you risk ruining the soil structure. Test a handful of soil; if it clings together in a ball and won't come apart when prodded with a finger, it's too wet to work. Wait a few days for the soil to dry before working in amendments.

Traditional digging—or an easier way

There are two schools of thought about how to amend soil. The traditional method is to dig the bed at least 1½ feet deep, then work in about 25 percent compost or other organic material. Because this process raises the soil level 6 to 12 inches, it's best done a few months before planting to allow soil to settle.

A more contemporary method is to plant a rose bush in natural, nonamended soil, then topdress the planting area with about 6 inches of organic mulch—compost, manure, wood chips— every year. Nutrients from the decaying mulch leach into the soil, sustaining biotic activity and making the labor-intensive work of amending the soil unnecessary. The Earth-Kind rose trials in Texas, as well as a growing number of gardening and landscaping experts, use this approach.

Whichever method you choose, continually add organic material into the soil for healthy and vigorous rose growth and production. Buy or build a container to make your own handy source of compost, and seek local sources for well-aged animal manure or other materials.

TEST GARDEN TIP

Water, but provide good drainage

Roses need water (at least 1 inch per week) but they don't like wet feet, so avoid planting roses in a low area of your yard or garden. Heavy clay soil that doesn't drain well can cause problems. Amend the soil with compost and other organic material. Water that doesn't drain away causes roots to rot.

Above left: **Properly prepared soil should be rich and crumbly, allowing both good drainage and water retention.**

Above center: **Place several layers of newspapers on the ground and cover with mulch to make a new bed.**

Above right: **Use a soil testing kit before you plant your garden to learn which amendments to add.**

Preparing Roses
for Planting

Gently ease the rose from its pot. If needed use your foot to squeeze the rootball from its container. Prune all buds and flowers before planting.

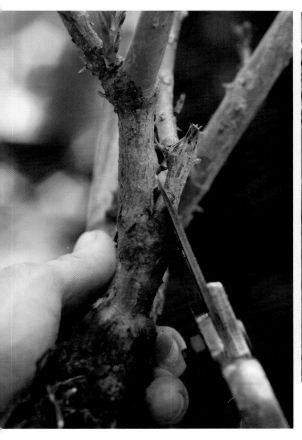

Left: **Roses often need a little pruning before planting. Remove old, dead wood. On bare-root plants, trim canes to the length of the roots.**

Right: **Before planting, prune the tips of bare-root roses to encourage the growth of root hairs, which feed the bush.**

Proper planting gives your rose a foundation

that protects against inevitable setbacks in coming years. The better health a rose bush has, the better it can ward off pests and diseases, stretch out its roots to find food and water, and produce more leaves that allow the plant to convert sunlight into food.

When to plant
A rose bush can be planted or transplanted whenever the soil is workable. The best time is late fall to early spring when plants are dormant. Although most nurseries won't ship plants in the fall, autumn-planted bushes develop roots over the winter. Local nurseries sell potted plants at the appropriate planting time for your area.

Preparing bare-root roses
Bare-root roses often arrive with longer and more canes than the roots can feed. Choose three to six of the best canes spread in all directions, then cut them back with a pruner to a length of 4 to 8 inches, snipping just above outward-facing buds.

Snip about ½ inch off the tips of the larger roots. A fresh, clean cut helps by callusing the root end, which causes the plant to form nutrient-seeking hair roots.

Some types of roses, such as hybrid teas, come grafted onto sturdier rootstocks. The roots of a rose grown on a Dr Huey rootstock tend to naturally spread horizontally, while those of multifloras twist downward. Fortuniana roots are shallow and spreading.

Preparing potted or boxed roses
Always assume a potted or boxed rose is dehydrated. Remove all packaging and soil from a boxed rose, and completely submerge it in a bucket of water for at least one day to rehydrate.

Avoid planting it encased in a box or peat pot. Although the container will eventually decompose, it severely restricts a plant's roots, resulting in a small and unhealthy root system.

Water potted roses for one or two days before planting. Remove damaged stems. Prune all buds and flowers so the plant will put its energy into establishing its roots before developing new stems and flowers.

To remove the rose, place the container sideways on the ground, then gently press your foot on the pot so you can ease the rose from its container.

TEST GARDEN TIP

Bare roots are best
Roses thrive when started as bare root plants. Because the roots of a container rose may not wish to venture out from the potting medium, shake some of the soil off or rough up the root ball before planting..

Planting Roses

Use a tool handle across the hole to see where to place the bud union of a hybrid tea. In warm areas, set it above the soil line, as shown. In colder areas, plant it 2 to 3 inches below the soil line.

Proper planting is like serving a balanced breakfast to your child. It gets your rose off to a good start.

Although it's tempting to buy a rose bush already in bloom, if a plant is growing vigorously and buds or flowers have already formed, the transplant shock can be severe. Instead of putting it into the ground right away, repot a blooming rose into a larger pot, keeping the root ball intact, and maintain it through the growing season. Plant it in the ground in the fall, when the plant is naturally beginning to go dormant.

How deep to plant

How deep to plant a rose varies according to geographical location.

In cold areas of the country, position the bud union (the swollen area where a grafted rose meets the rootstalk) 2 to 3 inches below ground level. On an own-root rose, the crown (the area where the roots fan out) should be used as the guideline. Placing the bud union or crown below the soil gives it more winter protection. In milder regions, the bud union should be planted at or slightly above the surface of the soil.

Dig the hole

When you plant roses, give the roots a firm soil base. Dig a hole about 2 feet wide by 1 foot deep, amending the soil with compost. To support bare roots, pack some soil into a small, firm cone and position the plant so it is firmly anchored. Spread out the roots in all directions. Potted roses should be positioned so the bud union is placed in the correct position.

Avoid adding any chemical fertilizer containing nitrogen to the planting hole because it burns the plant's roots. New rose bushes develop slowly from food stored in their canes and need no fertilizer at the time of planting.

The only chemical that may be placed in the planting hole is phosphorus, in either organic or chemical form. Because phosphorus moves very slowly through the soil, adding it to the hole makes it more available to the plant than if it is added on the surface. Phosphorus will not burn the tender plant roots.

Fill the hole

Once the plant is positioned, half fill the hole with soil, then add water, using a hose or watering can. Once the water has drained, completely fill the hole with soil to ground level; water well again.

Avoid firming the soil around the plant with your foot or a shovel which compacts the soil too much.

If you plant during cool weather, mound enough soil up over the canes so just about 1 inch or so of the tips are visible to protect the canes from drying out in wind and cold temperatures. Once the weather warms and the plant starts to sprout, gently wash the soil away.

ASK THE GARDEN DOCTOR

How do I move a rose?

ANSWER: When transplanting a rose bush, the guideline is to balance the length of the root system with the length of the canes the rose needs to feed. Cut canes to the length of the roots. Because it takes time for a rose's roots to get established and start feeding, any long canes left on the bush will die.

Below left: **Inspect and loosen any circling roots before planting a container rose.**

Below right: **Carefully water the entire root area of a newly planted rose.**

Watering Roses

A soaker hose allows a slow, steady application of water, sending it to the roots instead of the foliage.

While the image of a gardener watering roses with a watering can seems charming, hand watering is a labor-intensive and inefficient practice. Roses need regular, deep watering during hot weather; watering by hand is simply not very practical.

The kind of watering system you use depends upon the layout of the garden, the number of roses, and factors such as water pressure and time availability.

Water slowly
Watering slowly allows moisture to percolate down to the deep roots and prevents wasteful runoff. If you have only half a dozen plants, the most efficient method is a slow drizzle from a garden hose. To prevent runoff, build a low earthen dam around the drip line (approximately the same width as the plant's upper parts.) Let the hose run slowly for a half hour or so on each plant. Large rose gardens generally require a watering system.

Know when and how much
Some estimates say roses perform well with 1 inch of water per week. However, this doesn't take into account the temperature, soil type (water moves quicker through sandy soils), the size of the plants, and other factors.

The best way to determine how much and how often to water is to check the soil moisture. Push a hollow metal tube into the soil about 1 foot deep and check the condition of the extracted soil. The 6 inches of the soil in the bottom of the tube—representing the 6- to 12-inch levels— should be moist but not dripping wet. If this area of soil is dry, water deeply. Avoid waiting until your plants tell you they need water by wilting or dropping their leaves.

Avoid overhead watering
Some gardeners prefer to water with an overhead sprinkler. Although many plants can be covered in a short time, this method carries two big

drawbacks for roses: it encourages black spot fungus spores to germinate, and it wets and spoils the blooms. If you must water with a sprinkler, do it early in the morning so the foliage has a chance to quickly dry in the sun.

Another option is to apply a fungicidal spray shortly after overhead watering, as the water tends to open the leaf stomata (pores) that allow the spray to be readily absorbed.

Bed layouts dictate choices

If you have individual plants strategically placed in the landscape, an aboveground hose is probably the most efficient way to water. However, if you have large beds of roses or mixed plants, you'll want a watering system that can serve as large an area as possible.

It's best to water the soil of the entire bed, not just at the base of the plants, to encourage root systems to expand and give the plant better access to food and water.

When beds are linear, use a rigid plastic pipe laid above or below the ground to carry water. Emitters of various kinds can be attached to the pipe to disperse water to plants.

For an irregular layout, use flexible tubing or soaker hoses fitted with emitters to reach all areas. Leaky hoses can be used, but they should be laid out to ensure maximum coverage. The emitters—nozzles, tubes, pinholes—should deliver water in a fine spray or slow drizzle to cover the most area and to prevent runoff. To prevent black spot germination, water should not touch lower foliage.

For container gardens, use thin, flexible tubing with one or two emitters per pot.

How will it look?

Watering systems include hoses, pipes, or a combination of both, which can be located above- or belowground. Aboveground pipes are relatively easy to maintain and can be moved or removed when working in the beds, but they're visible and can look awkward among plants and flowers. Underground piping is generally more attractive but is difficult to repair if you sever it with a shovel while working in the beds.

Other considerations

The length of the tubing and emitters depends on water pressure. Emitters at the end of the run should function just as well as those at the front. If needed, add a device to increase water pressure on outside faucets. Other time- and labor-saving tools include automatic timers and liquid fertilizer dispensers.

ASK THE GARDEN DOCTOR

Why do I need to water so deeply?

ANSWER: Deep watering encourages root growth deep in the soil. Shallow watering forces the roots to grow near the surface of the soil, where they are susceptible to drought and winterkill.

Below left: **A programmable water timer automates watering chores.**

Below right: **Single watering sources can be laid below individual plants. Water deeply less frequently; avoid frequent applications of less water.**

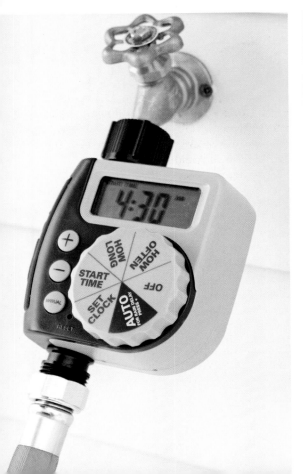

Mulching, Feeding & Fertilizing

Mulch—the material added to the planting area surface to retain water—

helps keep roses moist. Water evaporates quickly from soil in hot weather, and mulch slows this process. Unless you plan extensive planting or moving of roses, apply organic mulch every year.

Why mulch?

Mulch has many purposes. It suppresses weeds, adds organic material to the soil, hides the appearance of an aboveground watering system, gives beds a pleasing overall appearance, and serves as the base for winter protection of the crowns of budded roses.

While vegetable gardeners often use black or clear plastic mulch to boost the soil temperature around tomato plants, and landscape fabric does a great job of weed suppression, neither of these materials is recommended for mulching a rose bed. Organic mulch is preferred because it serves a variety of purposes well.

Mulch 3 to 4 inches deep

Add 3 to 4 inches of organic materials on top of the soil every year. The list of good choices includes:

Pine needles The most common rose mulch used in areas of the country with extensive pine forests, pine needles are readily available, inexpensive, do not germinate weed seeds, and add nutrients to the soil.

Hardwood chips This mulch has the same advantages as pine needles. The environmentally friendly Earth-Kind program at Texas A&M uses this material.

Shredded or chipped bark Although bark can work well, beware of the source. Logs are often moved and held in saltwater prior to milling. The retained salt in the bark is unhealthy for roses and other plants. Check the origin of the bark or have it tested for salt content before applying it to rose beds.

Manure and compost Although manure and compost feed and improve the soil, weed suppression ability is low because weeds can germinate both below and in the mulch. They also retain water somewhat less well than other materials.

Feed your soil before fertilizing

Feeding and fertilizing your roses are actually two separate but complementary practices.

Organic materials in the soil are constantly depleted and must be regularly replenished. Chemical and organic fertilizers are of little value if the soil is not teeming with beneficial microorganisms ready to convert the fertilizer into a form that can be absorbed by the plant.

So, fertilizer alone is not the solution. First, feed the soil with a regular supply of organic matter such as soil amendments when planting, followed by mulching and topdressing existing beds. Organic material nourishes the soil bacteria and other microorganisms that break down minerals and other nutrients into forms that can be used by plants.

What is fertilizer?

A fertilizer contains the minerals or elements necessary for plant growth and development. The three most important macronutrients are nitrogen, phosphorus, and potassium.

Micronutrients—elements needed in small amounts—include calcium, sulfur, magnesium, boron, chlorine, manganese, iron, zinc, copper, molybdenum, and selenium.

Fertilizers must be labeled with the percentage of the three macronutrients. The numbers 6-4-8 on a label mean the product contains 6 percent nitrogen, 4 percent phosphorous, and 8 percent potassium. The letters are also referred to as N-P-K, the scientific abbreviations for those elements.

The remaining 82 percent of the fertilizer is filler or carrier material. While micronutrients, sometimes called trace elements, may be present in the product, the percentage is not required to be listed on the label.

When to fertilize

Organic fertilizers are best applied early in the season, since they remain in the soil for longer periods than inorganic products. However, they can be applied at any time. More is not better— apply as recommended on the label.

Inorganic fertilizers are best applied later in the spring when the soil warms up. Depending upon the length of your growing season, two to three applications of dry inorganic fertilizer should be enough. Many gardeners add small amounts of liquid or water-soluble fertilizer to their fungicidal spray.

TEST GARDEN TIP

All the news that's fit to mulch

To suppress weeds, lay a couple layers of newspaper over the soil before applying organic mulch. The newspapers allow air and water to pass through to the soil, they keep weed seeds from germinating, and the paper decomposes before the end of the growing season.

Opposite: **Wood chips, bark, straw, and pine needles (left to right) are all excellent organic mulch choices.**

Below: **An annual top-dressing of compost adds nutrients that roses need.**

Organic & Inorganic Fertilizers

Organic and inorganic fertilizers do the same job but have significant differences.

Organic fertilizer comes from plants or animals that contain macronutrients and micronutrients. Examples of plant-derived fertilizers are compost, alfalfa meal, seaweed meal, and cottonseed meal. Animal-derived fertilizers include manure, blood meal, bonemeal, fish meal or extract, and feather meal. Some fertilizers can be either organic or chemical. Urea, for example, can come from animal urine or synthesized urea.

Because there are no consistent standards for processing organic fertilizers, the N-P-K (nitrogen-phosphorus-potassium) analysis can differ among products. For example, bone meal, an organic source of phosphorus, may have an analysis of 4-12-0 from one supplier and 2-14-0 from another. Commercial organic products usually contain a blend of vegetable and animal components to produce a balanced fertilizer. Carefully read the label to check the contents as well as the N-P-K analysis.

Plants can't tell the difference

When choosing between an organic and an inorganic product, consider:

Roses can't tell the difference between organic or synthesized nitrogen, minerals, or elements. Once soil microorganisms convert the nitrogen into a form the plants can use, it's all the same to them.

You do not need a fertilizer specially formulated for roses. Roses need a balanced (or mostly balanced) fertilizer such as a 20-20-20 liquid or a 6-6-4 granular product.

High-nitrogen fertilizers such as a 22-2-2 lawn fertilizer are not recommended for roses unless the roses show nitrogen deficiency.

Organic benefits & drawbacks

Organic fertilizers are relatively low in nutrients when compared with inorganic fertilizers but they have several advantages. They:

Remain in the soil longer and don't leach out with rain or overwatering.

Release nutrients slowly over an extended period of time.

Help improve soil structure.

Can mobilize existing soil nutrients. For example, alfalfa meal or pellets contain the chemical triacontanol, an alcohol-based hormone that acts as a catalyst to increase nutrient uptake and promote more vigorous plant growth.

The biggest disadvantage of organic fertilizers is the high cost. You can make your own inexpensive organic meal fertilizer mix

Alfalfa pellets release an alcohol containing triacontanol, which acts as a growth stimulant for roses. You can buy alfalfa pellets in feed and grain stores as well as some well-stocked nurseries.

from bulk meals bought at a feed store. Ask a Consulting Rosarian for a recipe that works for your region ("Need Advice?" at www.ars.org). Large quantity meal mixes, such as Mills Magic Rose Mix, may be available in some areas.

Experienced rosarians depend heavily upon alfalfa meal or pellets, also available at nurseries or feed and grain stores. Spread the pellets on rose beds a couple times a year or apply an alfalfa tea to revitalize any slow-growing or problem plants.

To make alfalfa tea, fill a 33-gallon trash can or other large container nearly full of water. Wrap one or two 5-gallon amounts of alfalfa in a burlap or permeable plastic sack and submerge in the water. Let this mixture steep for five to seven days (or until you can no longer stand the odor.) Apply about 1 gallon of the tea to the roots of each big rose, a half-gallon for miniatures. The alfalfa contains a hormone that helps the plant take in more nutrients.

Inorganic benefits & drawbacks

Inorganic fertilizers, sold in granular and liquid form, are mined or synthetically manufactured. Most offer a balance of N-P-K, but some are weighted heavily to specific elements.

The advantage: they're quick acting because the nutrients are readily available to the plant. The disadvantage: if overused, or applied before the soil warms up enough to activate the microorganisms that break them down,

inorganic fertilizers can leach through the soil and foul nearby waterways.

When using inorganic fertilizers:

Wait until temperatures reach about 60°F. before applying so soil microorganisms are active enough to use the fertilizer.

Water beds well before applying.

Apply either liquid or granular fertilizer in moderation. Frequent small doses are better than one or two big ones.

Avoid getting granular fertilizer on wet foliage because it can burn the leaves.

Scratch a dry fertilizer into the soil, then water the beds again.

How to get your money's worth

When purchasing a fertilizer, whether organic or inorganic, get the greatest amount of active ingredients for your money. With different N-P-K analyses, dry weights, and prices among products, this can be hard to determine.

Here's a simple formula: Divide the price per pound of the product by the total percentage of N-P-K. For example, a 6-8-6 product selling for $9.99 for 1.8 pounds costs $5.55 per pound. Divide 5.55 by .20, the total percentage of N-P-K, for a cost of $27.75 per pound of actual fertilizer.

By comparing the true cost of macronutrients between products, you can determine which offers the best value, regardless of label names and claims.

ASK THE GARDEN DOCTOR

Does foliar feeding help?

ANSWER: Although foliar feeding is touted as a way to feed roses before the soil warms up, most liquid sprayed on the leaves will drip onto the ground. The majority of the leaves' stomata (the pores through which the leaf absorbs air and liquid) are found on the undersides of the leaves. Unless the spray has a surfactant (sticky spreader) and is directed to the undersides of the leaves, the spray actually feeds the roots.

Left: **A slow-release chemical fertilizer may only need to be applied once each growing season.**

Below: **Look for balanced N-P-K numbers on fertilizers for roses. This means that the numbers will be approximately the same value.**

6-6-4

GUARANTEED ANALYSIS

Total Nitrogen (N)................................	6.0%
3.5% ... Ammoniacal Nitrogen	
0.2% ... Other Water Soluble Nitrogen	
2.3% .... Water Insoluble Nitrogen	
Available Phosphate (P_2O_5)	6.0%
Soluble Potash (K_2O)	4.0%
Calcium (Ca).....................................	3.0%
Total Magnesium (Mg).........................	0.5%
0.3%..... Water Soluble Magnesium (Mg)	
Sulfur (S)...	5.0%
5.0% .... Combined Sulfur (S)	
Boron (B)...	0.02%
Chlorine (Cl).....................................	0.1%
Cobalt (Co).......................................	0.0005%
Total Copper (Cu)...............................	0.05%

Dealing with Pests

This rose, with a portion of the bloom chewed away, shows damage caused by a Japanese beetle.

Everyone loves roses, including a host of diseases, insects, and animals.

Although pest damage may not seriously affect plant health, it may make your rose garden look unattractive. A few pests kill plants entirely.

Take an Integrated Pest Management (IPM) approach to control these threats. Although chemical pesticides take time to apply, cost money, and carry risks to the environment, they can serve as the last resort in certain cases, such as when dealing with downy mildew.

Integrated Pest Management

IPM combines cultural, physical, biological, and chemical tools to minimize economic, environmental, and health risks. The levels, in order of use, are:

Establish acceptable pest levels.
Take preventive cultural practices.
Monitor pests.
Add physical controls.
Use biological controls.
Apply chemical controls.

Follow these steps on an individual basis with every garden pest, then proceed in order until you reach the control level that's right for you.

How IPM works with aphids

As an example, consider aphids, a common pest in nearly all rose gardens, and follow the six-step process.

Establish acceptable pest levels: What is an acceptable amount or level of aphids in your garden? Some people cannot accept any aphids on their roses while others believe they do little overall damage and tolerate them.

Take preventive cultural practices: Aphids seem less attracted to Old Garden Roses and some shrub roses than to hybrid teas, floribundas, and miniatures. Few, if any, cultural practices prevent aphids from appearing.

Monitor pests: Pay attention to your roses and look for the presence of aphids or other pests. There's no point in taking curative measures if the pest is not present.

Add physical controls: You can crush aphids with your fingers (gloves are optional) or wash them off with water.

Use biological controls: Biological controls can take a variety of forms. For aphids, this includes adding insect predators such as green lacewings or ladybugs, spraying insecticidal soaps made from plant or animal products, and applying insecticides made from jojoba oil.

Apply chemical controls: Use an insecticide.

Steps to take against disease

What is an acceptable level of disease? Like insects, some diseases are merely annoying while some pose a more serious threat to rose health. Unlike insect pests, you can take completely organic cultural and mechanical steps to lessen the impact of fungal diseases on roses:

Purchase disease-resistant varieties. No rose variety is totally free from all fungal diseases, but some are much more resistant than others. The rose varieties featured in the Gallery of Roses beginning on page 110 contain individual evaluations of disease resistance.

Avoid crowding plants to maximize air circulation. This deters the germination of disease spores.

Prune each plant enough to open it to air circulation and sunshine. Continually remove unproductive wood.

Practice good sanitation. Keep the ground free of infected leaves, and frequently spray your pruning shears with a disinfectant, using a mild bleach solution, Lysol, Citrox Natural Garden Disinfectant, or other product.

Avoid overhead watering and watering late in the evening to prevent fungal diseases.

Never increase the dilution rate of any fungicidal product; protect the environment and your personal safety.

ARS-endorsed products

The American Rose Society endorses several commercial products. All are multipurpose formulas with varying kinds of insecticides, fungicides, miticides, or fertilizers combined into one product. They have been thoroughly tested by a panel of experienced rosarians and found to be effective and safe if used according to label directions. Three of the most frequently used products and their chemical components:

Bayer Advanced All-in-One Rose & Flower Care: 0.8 percent tebuconozole (fungicide), 0.15 percent imidacloprid (insecticide), and 9-14-9 (fertilizer).

Ortho RosePride Insect, Disease & Mite Control: 0.25 percent acephate (insecticide), 0.10 percent triforine (fungicide), and 0.10 percent resmethrin (miticide).

Immunox Plus Insect & Disease Control: 0.78 percent myclobutanil (fungicide) and 1.25 percent permethrin (insecticide).

These chemical components are available individually in other commercial products. A multipurpose product may not be necessary.

Read the list of active ingredients on the label. Toxicity and other data are available from the Pesticide Action Network (PAN) Pesticide Database at www.pesticideinfo.org. This useful website indexes all pesticide chemicals with their commercial product names.

Organic insecticides include pyrethrins, a natural product produced by a chrysanthemum species, and neem oil, an extract from the fruits and seeds of the neem tree. Both are contact insecticides not absorbed into the leaves, so you can reapply them when more insects appear.

Greencure, a potassium bicarbonate-based fungicide, cures and prevents powdery mildew, black spot, downy mildew, blights, molds, and other plant diseases.

ASK THE GARDEN DOCTOR

How do I identify garden pests?

ANSWER: The first step toward control is correctly identifying the pest. Abrupt weather changes and other factors can fool beginning rose growers into a bad diagnosis. An extension agent or an ARS Consulting Rosarian ("Need Advice?" at www.ars.org) can help. Once the pest is identified, you can take steps to repel or eradicate it.

Far left: **Release ladybugs into your yard to help control the common problem of aphids on roses.**

Below: **Gardeners can choose from chemical or organic controls endorsed by the ARS to help deal with pests.**

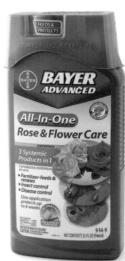

Common Insect Pests

Cane Borer
Many insects, including sawflies, carpenter bees, and some wasps, bore a hole into the end of a dead rose cane or one that's been pruned too high above a bud or leaf axil. Cane borers do not kill the cane; the cane is already dead or dying before the borers enter to lay their eggs. Canes and leaves turn brown and rot. It can be difficult to find either the original insect or its larvae.

DAMAGE: Holes appear in the pithy center of canes.

SIGNS: Difficult-to-see larvae become small caterpillars.

PREVENTION AND MANAGEMENT:
Though many sources suggest painting or coating newly pruned canes with a sealing substance, it's a waste of time. Simply prune dead or dying canes that show evidence of cane borers. Some wasps lay their eggs on cut canes. The eggs hatch into caterpillars that burrow into the cane pith. Because the wasps feed on aphids, controlling aphids may also encourage the wasps to find other nesting sites with a more reliable source of food.

Japanese Beetle
Japanese beetles are prevalent and destructive in every state east of the Mississippi River. Infestations are noted in California, Iowa, Missouri, and Nebraska. Beetle larvae appear as white soil-borne grubs. Adult beetles typically emerge in midsummer.

DAMAGE: Leaves are chewed between the veins, creating a lacy appearance.

SIGNS: Metallic green and bronze, ½-inch long beetles with a white fringe near their wings appear.

PREVENTION AND MANAGEMENT:
Grubs can be treated biologically with milky spore (*Bacillus popilliae*) or with parasitic nematodes. Insecticides containing imidacloprid can also be effective against grubs. For adult beetles, hand picking is the most popular mechanical remedy. Drop them in a bucket of soapy water, since crushing and leaving them in place emits a pheromone that attracts more beetles. Mechanical traps attract more beetles than they kill. Several chemical insecticides show effectiveness against adult beetles. Most Japanese beetles overwinter in turfgrass, so treating your lawn for grubs may help.

Leafhopper
Leafhoppers suck the sap out of leaves. The name comes from the insects' habit of hopping off leaves when the plant is touched.

DAMAGE: Foliage is white stippled or puckered.

SIGNS: Slender, wedge-shape insects about ½-inch long are usually green, yellow, or brown. Usually found on the undersides of leaves, they run sideways and jump when the plant is touched.

PREVENTION AND MANAGEMENT:
Clean up plant debris in fall to prevent leafhoppers from overwintering. Ladybugs, damselwings, and lacewings consume leafhopper eggs and larvae. Organic insecticides such as neem oil and pyrethrins can be effective against leafhoppers. Wash them off leaves with a strong spray of water directed to the undersides of leaves, but do this in the morning so leaves can dry quickly, which prevents fungal problems.

Leaf Roller
Leaf rollers, essentially caterpillars, can be spotted when you inspect curled, rolled up leaves. They feed on foliage and buds at the end of rose shoots.

DAMAGE: Leaves and buds appear chewed and curled.

SIGNS: Green caterpillars, ½- to ¾-inch long and hatched from the larvae of small moths, are found inside rolled leaves, often bound with silken webbing.

PREVENTION AND MANAGEMENT: Since leaf rollers in the United States often infest canna plants, remove cannas from rose gardens. Mechanically control leaf rollers by cutting off and disposing of infected leaves. Organic controls include neem oil, pyrethrins, and *Bacillus thuringiensis* (also called Bt). Predators, such as lacewing larvae, assassin bugs, tachinid flies, and wasp parasites will dine on leafroller larvae or eggs. Inspect plants in late winter or early spring for egg masses that are about the size of a thumprint, laid on smooth wood. Large infestations may require chemical products.

Midge
A tiny fly, *Dasineura rhodophaga*, lays its eggs on the tips of growing stems. After hatching, the larvae feed on the buds and stems then drop to the ground to pupate in loose soil inside a silken cocoon.

DAMAGE: Stem tips turn black, giving a burnt appearance.

SIGNS: Adult rose midges resemble mosquitoes in shape and appearance, growing about 1 to 2 millimeters long. Full-grown larvae, sometimes reddish, reach nearly 2 millimeters long.

PREVENTION AND MANAGEMENT: Mechanical and biological controls are generally ineffective against midges, although you can lightly cultivate the soil to destroy the cocoons. Apply the chemical Diazinon to the soil to prevent ground pupation and overwintering as a preventive approach. Most commercial insecticides are effective when applied to new foliage.

Raspberry Cane Borer
This slender, ½-inch-long beetle doesn't confine itself to raspberries. It punctures tender young rose canes and girdles them under the bark before laying its eggs.

DAMAGE: The insect is seldom seen, but you'll know the damage is there when you see a wilting cane tip. The adult borers lay their eggs one season. The larvae then burrow in and overwinter in the cane, emerging as adults the following spring.

SIGNS: The raspberry cane borer is mainly black with horns and long antennae. The cylindrical, legless larvae are white, reaching about ¾ inch long.

PREVENTION AND MANAGEMENT: The best treatment is to prune the cane a few inches below the wilted area. Since the life cycle of the borer is two years, prompt removal of wilted canes is important. When you see the insects, apply an organic or chemical insecticide effective against borers.

Common Insect, Animal & Disease Pests

Rose Slugs
Rose slugs are the larval stage of sawfly wasps. They are not actually slugs, but earned their name because they resemble slugs when curled up at rest. They should not be confused with leaf rollers.

DAMAGE: Rose slugs feed on leaf tissues and chew holes in the leaves, eventually leaving only the skeleton of the veins showing.

SIGNS: These pests look like small, pale green sluglike worms up to ¾ inch long, usually found on the undersides of leaves. Depending on the species of sawfly, the larvae may exude a slimy substance (like slugs), while others are hairy.

PREVENTION AND MANAGEMENT: For small outbreaks, use forceful water streams or hand pick slugs off leaves. For larger infestations, neem oil, insecticidal soap, and horticultural oil have proved effective. *Bacillus thuringiensis* will not work because these are wasp larvae, not butterfly or moth larvae. Most chemical insecticides also work on rose slugs.

Scales
Rose scales are an infrequent and generally low-level pest that can be caused by a variety of insects. They feed on plant tissue and form a crusty shell over their bodies for protection, giving them their name.

DAMAGE: The symptoms of rose scale are bumpy, discolored, and occasionally distorted canes, although leaves may be affected as well.

SIGNS: Female scales are nearly circular, flat, white, and about $\frac{1}{12}$ inch wide. Males are much smaller, with narrow and elongated shapes. These insects suck the sap from the plant

PREVENTION AND MANAGEMENT: The best treatment is to prune out the infected areas. Spray the bare canes with a lime-sulfur horticultural oil mix—the usual components in what is known as dormant spray—as you put the plants to bed for the winter and again in the spring to suffocate scales. Insecticidal soap can also help. Cut out and destroy any old, badly infested canes. Some ladybugs and parasitic wasps attack scales.

Spider Mites
Technically arachnids rather than insects, spider mites are minuscule pests that appear during hot, dry weather. They come up from the soil and appear first on the undersides of the lower leaves of a plant.

DAMAGE: Spider mites suck the juices out of the leaves, causing discoloration and leaf drop. These pests are especially troublesome for miniature roses because they grow so low to the ground.

SIGNS: Minute specks the size of pepper grains are hard to see unless you tap them off the plant onto a sheet of white paper, where they will start to crawl around.

PREVENTION AND MANAGEMENT: Washing the undersides of the rose leaves with a hose or watering wand is effective against spider mites but must be done repeatedly. Natural predators such as ladybugs and minute pirate bugs can also have good results. To be effective, chemical products must contain a miticide rather than simply an insecticide.

Thrips

Thrips (the term applies for both singular and plural) are small insects whose presence is hard to detect until the damage appears.

DAMAGE: Thrips symptoms appear as brown streaks or spots on rose petals, most evident on white or yellow blooms. Foliage may be flecked with yellow.

SIGNS: Tiny yellow or brown insects are seen when a deformed or streaked flower is pulled apart and shaken over a white paper.

PREVENTION AND MANAGEMENT: Severe thrips infestations can be fought with predator nematodes and predator mites as well as biological products containing the fungus *Beauveria bassiana*. As with other insect pests, most commercial insecticides are effective. In recent years, a particularly pernicious species known as chilli thrips has appeared in the southwestern United States. Unlike flower thrips, this species feeds on leaves and other plant tissue, and seems especially resistant to biological controls. Insecticides containing either acephate or imidacloprid as the active ingredient have proved most effective against chilli thrips.

Nibbling Pests

Animal pests, especially deer, rabbits, voles, and armadillos, often bedevil roses. Deer, a problem across the country, regard rose foliage and buds as prime delicacies.

DAMAGE: Canes and flowers show damage from chewing.

PREVENTION AND MANAGEMENT: Only two methods repel deer: a sturdy fence at least 8 feet high, and an aggressive guard dog. Other remedies, either homemade or commercial, have limited success. Homemade controls include deodorant soap, human hair, egg white or pepper sprays, and a host of others. Commercial repellent products for both deer and rabbits often contain predator urine, dried porcine or bovine blood, or foliage sprays with unpleasant tastes such as capsicum (pepper). These must be reapplied on a regular basis to maintain effectiveness. Rotate product use so deer don't become accustomed to just one repellent. Netting over a strong frame can also be used to keep out deer. Rabbits tend to nibble on roses during the winter. To protect plants, encircle rose bushes with netting or chicken wire; bury the lower few inches in the ground to prevent burrowing by voles and other critters.

Anthracnose

Often confused with black spot, spot anthracnose is a less virulent fungal disease promoted and spread by water on the foliage. Unlike black spot, the tiny ($1/8$ to $1/16$ inch) spots of purplish black seldom cause severe defoliation.

DAMAGE: Distinct dead spots appear on stems and leaves. Dead spots are often yellow first, then turn black. They have a water-spot appearance and are often depressed or sunken.

PREVENTION AND MANAGEMENT: Anthracnose is relatively easy to control. Mulch to limit disease spread. Avoid overhead watering. Properly space plants for good air circulation. At end-of-season cleanup, completely remove all plant material; keep it out of the compost to avoid overwintering disease. Most of the organic and chemical fungicides effective against black spot work equally well against anthracnose, including organic fungicides containing potassium bicarbonate such as GreenCure, endorsed by the American Rose Society.

Common Disease Pests

Black Spot

Black spot, the second most damaging rose disease (downy mildew is the most damaging), is caused by the fungus *Diplocarpon rosae*, with more than 200 known strains. It thrives in wet or humid areas of the country.

DAMAGE: Symptoms include dark rounded spots with feathered edges, along with yellowing of the leaves. Leaf drop is not rapid but persistent. If left untreated, black spot defoliates most rose plants by the end of the growing season. Defoliated plants cannot feed themselves, so they go into the winter much weaker than their strong and healthy brethren.

PREVENTION AND MANAGEMENT: Most home remedies for black spot include baking soda (sodium bicarbonate). Studies show a more effective organic fungicide is potassium bicarbonate, the principal ingredient in various commercial products, including GreenCure, endorsed by the American Rose Society. Both organic and chemical fungicides prevent rather than cure black spot. Apply regularly when the first leaves form on the plant. To cure an infestation, increase the frequency of application to every three to four days for two weeks to break the reproductive cycle of spore germination.

Crown Gall

Crown gall appears as a bumpy, woody, or corky growth on the crown of budded plants (hence the name) but may also appear on roots and canes. It is caused by a soil-borne bacteria through cuts or lesions in the epidermal layer.

DAMAGE: Galls weaken rose bushes, slow their growth, and turn leaves yellow.

PREVENTION AND MANAGEMENT: Once crown gall invades a plant there is no cure. Its growth and appearance can be curtailed by cutting off the galls, then treating the affected area with a spray of diluted chlorine bleach. Disinfect pruning shears after each cut by dipping them in a solution of 1 part chlorine bleach and 9 parts water. Healthy, vigorous plants are little affected by crown gall, but numerous galls cause more severe problems. For severe or repeated occurrences, preplanting dips such as Galltrol can help. Destroy severely affected plants.

Downy Mildew

Downy mildew, the most damaging rose disease, resembles neither down nor mildew. Instead, it is often confused with black spot. Downy lesions are usually less regular in shape than black spot markings and are often bounded by leaf veins on one side.

DAMAGE: Downy purple-black blotches appear on the upper sides of leaves, restricted by the leaf veins. The disease causes rapid defoliation of the plant, and it can quickly spread to neighboring bushes.

PREVENTION AND MANAGEMENT: Downy mildew is weather specific. It needs a humidity of at least 85 percent and temperatures below 80°F to develop, and can often be found on the West Coast. Most fungicides have little to no effect on preventing or eradicating downy mildew. Once conditions change, the disease disappears but it can do serious damage to a rose garden in the meantime. If you suspect the presence of downy mildew, contact a Consulting Rosarian ("Need Advice?" at www.ars.org) or other expert as quickly as possible. Downy mildew can be treated with specific fungicides such as Aliette or Subdue.

Powdery Mildew
Powdery mildew, a fungus, is easy to diagnose. It resembles white powder on new foliage and emerging buds. Germination is stimulated by warm days and cool nights.

DAMAGE: White patches on leaves look like someone dusted them with flour. Light infestations are ugly but generally harmless, while severe ones twist and stunt leaf growth and development.

PREVENTION AND MANAGEMENT: Recipes for homemade treatments abound. One widely available organic commercial product is E-Rase, a contact fungicide made from 97.5 percent jojoba oil. Neem oil has also been used successfully on powdery mildew, while several chemical fungicides are also very effective in controlling it. Promote good air circulation with proper spacing. Remove all affected leaves from the area.

Rose Rosette
Rose rosette disease is a viral disease spread by a minuscule mite. It cannot be prevented or cured.

DAMAGE: One symptom of RRD is a rampant and uncontrolled growth in the affected plant, often resembling a "witch's broom," but that alone isn't enough to confirm a diagnosis since some herbicides can cause this formation. Watch for excessive numbers of nonproductive canes that spring up in clusters on the bush with unusually soft and pliable red or green thorns that may stiffen later. Flowers may have abnormal coloring and fewer petals than normal. Buds may deform or convert to leaflike tissue.

PREVENTION AND MANAGEMENT: Plants diagnosed with RRD by a Consulting Rosarian or extension service specialist should be discarded. Infected plants usually die in one to two years. At present, the disease seems confined mainly to the Midwest, the South, and the eastern United States.

Rust
Rose rust is caused by several fungus species. Wind spreads the orange fungal spores, and moisture allows the spores to enter the leaf tissues. Eventually, spots develop directly on the upper sides of leaves.

DAMAGE: Orange to yellow-brown spots or pustules up to ¼ inch wide appear first on the undersides of rose leaves. If left untreated, rust deforms the leaves and causes leaf drop. Twigs may be attacked. Severely infected plants will be weakened by rust.

PREVENTION AND MANAGEMENT: Some rose varieties are particularly susceptible to rust and should be replaced if rust persists year after year. Neem oil can be effective; most chemical fungicides prevent rust. Remove and destroy affected leaves or twigs.

Pruning Roses

In regions with cold winters, most of the canes can die back to the ground. Fresh, new growth appears in spring. Remove old, dead wood.

Pruning terrifies most beginning gardeners and even rose growers

who wrongly believe that incorrect pruning stunts or kills a rose. However, pruning does not add or subtract vigor from a rose bush; it merely redirects it.

Roses pruned lightly, or not at all, still continue to grow and produce blooms. Roses that are pruned heavily—down to the ground after a severe winter kills all the canes—will grow and bloom, though later in the season.

Why prune?

So, why prune roses? Three basic reasons:

To encourage the plant to grow the type of blooms it was bred to grow. Gardeners do not ask a polyantha to grow and bloom like a climber, nor should they expect a rambler to grow and bloom like a hybrid tea. Choose rose varieties for specific purposes, then prune to fulfill those purposes.

To produce healthy roses. Resistance to diseases and other pests can be greatly reduced with proper pruning practices. Removing damaged and dead wood that can harbor insects or disease and opening crowded bushes to promote air circulation improves plant health and long-term performance.

To shape the bush into an attractive garden plant. Some rose varieties are sprawling and some are leggy. Some grow all their canes on one side of the plant, while others send them out into the lawn or into surrounding bushes. Your roses should grow where you want them to be, not where they are inclined to wander. Careful pruning corrects plant habit problems.

Pruning—cutting canes and leaves off roses—is nearly a year-round activity. In late winter or early spring, do the first pruning to cut out winter damage on last year's growth. Later in the spring, it's time to improve upon the original pruning by cutting out blind shoots and canes that show late dieback.

After each bloom cycle, remove spent blossoms to prepare the plant for its next bloom. In the fall, tender roses can be "headed back" to prevent them from being rocked by autumn winds and to apply winter protection. Experienced rose growers never let their pruning shears gather cobwebs.

Rose pruning basics

The basics of rose pruning are fairly simple and straightforward:

Use sharp bypass pruning shears. Loppers and saws of various sizes can be used for large canes or hard-to-reach places.

Make your pruning cut at a shallow (less than 45 degrees) angle approximately ¼ inch above a bud or leaf scar (the moon-shape mark left on the cane where a leaf has come off) with the slope away from the bud.

Sterilize your pruning shears frequently with a weak bleach solution or a commercial product.

Remove dead, diseased, very thin, and/or spindly canes from all types of roses.

To improve air circulation, which helps plant health and gives it room to grow, follow these three rules:

Prune to an outward-facing eye.

Open up the center of the bush.

Cut out crossing canes, or any canes touching each other.

However, some of these rules may not apply in all situations. For example, if a cane grows outward at a sharp angle, prune it to an inside eye. That allows the cane to grow inside toward the center of the bush to support new growth, gives the bush a pleasing shape, and keeps it within the bounds you set for it.

Rather than worrying about how to prune your roses properly, just do it. Keep a pruning log. List the cane lengths and diameters, number of canes left on the plant, and time of pruning. If the plant's habit and blooms fail to meet your expectations, prune it differently the following year or make corrections during this year's growing season.

TEST GARDEN TIP

Rejuvenate untamed roses

If you inherit roses left unpruned for many years, try this trick to get them back into a manageable shape and size. Prune half the bush moderately hard one year and the other half the following year. This way you get blooms both years while establishing a proper shape and size.

Far left: **Use a shallow (less than 45-degree) angle when removing old or new wood.**

Left: **Prune to an outward-facing eye so the new limb will grow in the direction you want.**

More Pruning Tips

Deadhead climbers and
remove any canes growing
in the wrong direction.

Don't worry about making a pruning mistake.

Roses easily adapt to the kinds of pruning cuts you make, and you learn from the ensuing growth how your cuts made the rose behave. Done properly, pruning improves performance.

Correctional pruning

Correctional pruning should be done throughout the growing season but is most needed in the weeks after the initial spring pruning. Late winter damage and other dieback or problems on canes can be removed at this time. By now, the plant will tell you where it wants to grow.

Weak or spindly shoots at the top of a cane accompanied by much stronger growth lower down are signs that you need to reprune lower. Blind shoots—canes with growing tips killed by the weather or by midges—should be pruned in spring. If the shoot is small, it can be pruned out completely; if it is more advanced and the wood has begun to harden, prune it back to a suitable bud.

Throughout the year, small twiggy shoots emerge on most plants, often low on the canes or in the middle of the bush where they can hide. Any shoot or cane without a growing tip terminating in a bud or bloom is the first to get black spot and should be cut out or pruned back.

Pruning for supportive canes

After pruning out winter-damaged canes, prune out weak or small canes, leaving supportive canes. Supportive canes feed the blooms and hold up blooms and their stems.

Small, thin canes produce small blooms. To get large blooms on a hybrid tea, for example, keep larger, healthy canes that can produce large stems. Seldom, if ever, does a cane larger in diameter grow from a smaller one. Some gardeners leave no cane smaller than their thumb (a real rule of thumb) on their first pruning of hybrid teas, knowing this ensures large flowers.

Many roses need physical support. Climbers and large shrubs need trellises or arbors to hold them up, old roses with thin canes need staking to keep them from flopping over, and even heavy bloomers like floribundas may need support to keep from collapsing during rainy periods. Pruning to inside eyes trains canes to grow in a direction that helps support the plant.

Give miniatures a haircut

Because of their small size and bushy habit, pruning miniatures in a traditional manner can be time consuming and stressful. If you grow them mostly for landscape color, consider the haircut method: grasp the canes with a gloved hand, pull them together into a bunch, and cut them all off at the same level.

How to prune climbers

Think of the long canes coming from the base of climbers (basal canes) as a rack or a skeleton on which blooms grow. To get as heavy a bloom as possible, let these canes grow to their full length and train them onto a supportive structure, spreading them out as much as possible.

A basal cane grown one year should bloom the following year on lateral canes growing from it. For repeat bloom, these lateral canes should be deadheaded in the summer. In the spring, laterals should be pruned according to the techniques mentioned above. After three to four years, when the laterals on a basal cane stop producing well, the basal cane should be completely removed.

Climbers and other long-caned roses are quite vigorous once established. New canes should be constantly growing from the base to replace old nonproductive ones. Basal canes that jut into walkways or grow in places you don't want them are better cut out completely than merely shortened.

Above left: **Prune at less than a 45-degree angle when making cuts above an outward-facing bud.**

Above center: **The thin, crossing, and dead limbs shown in this photo should be removed.**

Above right: **Prune a cane with low winter damage at ground level to promote new growth at its base.**

Deadheading & Seasonal Tips

Hybrid teas grow bigger single flowers when they are disbudded. Remove all but the bud at the terminal end of the stem by pinching or pruning.

Not all pruning involves cutting the canes.

Deadheading and disbudding blooms promote more and bigger flowers. Some pruning chores are best done at specific times of the growing season.

Deadheading

Deadheading is the term for removing spent blooms to promote the quickest possible rebloom. If not deadheaded, the calyxes—rounded portions just beneath the blooms—begin to form seeds. Seed production robs energy from bloom production, so prompt deadheading is important.

The rule for deadheading hybrid teas is to cut the stem back to the second leaf from the top having at least five leaflets. (In rose terminology, a leaf is the entire growth coming off a stem, while a leaflet is each of the individual portions.) However, this rule can be broken. The five-leaflet advice gives you a cane big enough to grow a new rose of sufficient size and quality, but you may deadhead higher or lower.

An alternate method of deadheading hybrid teas used by some rose growers in late summer or early fall is to simply snap off the bloom and calyx rather than cutting back the cane. This practice leaves more foliage for the bush to feed itself and contributes to better plant growth. The result is more blooms with shorter stems—something you may not want from hybrid teas.

Floribundas and other roses that bloom in sprays should be deadheaded anywhere below the entire cluster where the cane is big enough.

Shrubs produce flowers from the new growth, so deadhead only the flower and its short stem to encourage rebloom.

Disbudding

Disbudding, practiced throughout the year, is another way to make your roses do what you want. For large individual blooms on hybrid teas, grandifloras, or other types of roses, leave the terminal bud—the one that comes out first at the top of the stem—and remove all of the others as early as possible. This diverts all of the plant's energy to the terminal.

To achieve a uniform cluster on floribundas or other spray roses, do the opposite: remove the terminal as early as possible. This allows the other buds to develop into blooms at the same time and with sufficient space. Waiting until the terminal bud blooms and then taking it out results in a hole in the middle of the spray.

Seasonal pruning

Most roses need little or no pruning their first two to three years. Spend that time learning their growth and bloom habits. Knowing these, you'll be able to do a better pruning job when they mature. Pruning principles remain the same, but how they are specifically applied can change from one variety to the next, even within the same rose family.

Spring and new bush pruning

Appropriate and safe pruning times are different throughout the country, based on longtime weather patterns. Some areas rely on indicators such as "prune when the redbuds bloom" while others use specific dates such as Presidents' Day weekend as starting times.

A Consulting Rosarian ("Need Advice?" at www.ars.org) can suggest when to start, but there's no big hurry to remove winter protection and start pruning. Late pruning is safer than pruning too early.

Dried out or blackened canes are obvious signs of winter damage. The main indicator is the color of the pith in the center of the cane; it should be white to greenish white. The darker brown the pith, the more damage has occurred.

Modern bush roses such as hybrid teas, grandifloras, and floribundas should be pruned to at least very light brown pith, while Old Garden Roses, shrubs, and climbers can be left slightly darker. Monitor your plants and reprune as needed when growth begins to correct any errors.

After spring pruning, spray the remaining canes and the surrounding ground with a fungicide with an added surfactant/sticker-spreader because disease spores can live through winter.

Fall pruning

Pruning of any kind stimulates more growth. In the fall, you should cut fewer blooms for the house and leave them on shorter stems. Stop deadheading and let seed production take over. Forcing your plant to continue to bloom into cold weather, whenever that normally arrives in your area, places it at risk for severe damage from a hard freeze. As temperatures drop, the plants shut themselves down and move food from their leaves and stems into their roots.

There's one pruning exception: Cut tall modern roses—hybrid teas and grandifloras—down to about 4 feet tall to prevent them from whipping in the wind. This process is often called heading back.

TEST GARDEN TIP

Prune new growth first

When pruning after a hard winter, prune new growth first. These are the canes most apt to be damaged, and often must be taken out completely. If you cut out the old ones first, then find that the new ones are damaged or killed, you'll have to start from scratch with a new plant.

How to Deadhead a Shrub Rose

Many shrub roses are bred to cleanly drop their petals and the seedheads that form. But to improve the look of the rose and to keep it from expending energy creating a seedhead, follow these simple deadheading tips:

1 WHERE TO PRUNE
Look for the bare sepals left behind after the petals fall and the green seedheads that form below them. Prune at the base of the seedhead stem or just lop off the seedhead, being careful not to clip surrounding areas.

2 AFTER DEADHEADING
The new, red growth indicates where the next crop of flowers will come from.

Fall & Winter Maintenance

Stop deadheading roses in the fall. This lets the rose produce colorful hips and go dormant instead of putting its energy into flower production.

Far left: **Use a plastic collar around roses to hold layers of leaves and soil around the tender bases.**

Left: **A rose cone provides some winter protection from damaging winds and frost.**

ASK THE GARDEN DOCTOR

Can I use plastic to protect my roses?

ANSWER: No. Avoid wrapping a rose with plastic for the winter. Plastic heats up in winter sun, causing the rose to grow and making it more susceptible to winterkill when the temperature drops again.

Roses are tough. Many roses, including most shrub

and Old Garden Roses, require little or no winter protection. However, severely cold weather can kill the canes of most varieties. An even bigger danger is the death of the crown or bud union of a grafted plant such as a hybrid tea, since the desired variety dies, leaving just the rootstock. Tender roses such as hybrid teas and grandifloras benefit from winter protection in all but the warmest regions (Zones 9 and warmer).

Fall bed preparation

To prepare rose beds for winter, clean up and remove any leaves, petals, and other plant material on the ground so any diseases won't be carried into the following year. Refrain from pulling leaves off the bushes until after a hard frost when they can be snapped off easily. Removing them too early can tear the stems.

Stop fertilizing plants to discourage top growth. Any tall, free-standing plants should be pruned (also called "heading back") to about 4 feet to prevent them from whipping in the wind and disturbing the root structure.

Before applying winter protection, it's a good idea to spray the base of your plants with a lime-sulfur dormant oil to eliminate any insects that might try to overwinter there.

What to use for protection

The types and amounts of winter protection applied depend upon region, as well as location and microclimate.

The best protection for tender roses in the coldest areas of the United States is the "Minnesota Tip" method. Carefully dig up the roots on one side of a rose bush. On the opposite side, dig a 3½-foot trench about 12 to 14 inches deep. Prune stems to 3 feet and gently tie them together. Carefully tip the rose and the dug-up roots into the trench, being careful not to damage the graft union. Mound the entire trench and root area with 12 inches of soil, then cover the mound with 12 to 18 inches of straw or bags of dry leaves. In spring, remove the layers gradually as weather warms. Reset the rose in an upright position and water thoroughly.

For protection in other cold areas, rose cones, rigid foam cones, cylinders, or wire cages filled with leaves may be used to protect hybrid teas, grandifloras, and floribundas. Plants are trimmed to 1 or 2 feet tall to fit inside the structures.

If you live in USDA Zone 7 or warmer (see Zone map on page 103), place insulating material such as soil, compost, leaves, or grass clippings around the crowns and lower canes of your plants. In addition, 4 to 6 inches of soil or other organic material mounded on top of the crown provides enough protection.

Let plants breathe

The purpose of winter protection is to insulate, not incubate, your plants. Protective material should be porous enough to allow air to penetrate and moisture to evaporate.

Using soil to cover plant crowns (also called "hilling up") generally means you need to remove the soil in the spring. A much easier approach is to use an organic material such as oak leaves, well-aged manure, or compost that can be worked into the soil the following spring.

Check the USDA Zone map (page 103) and speak with a Consulting Rosarian about the type of protection appropriate for your area.

Rose Hardiness

Winter hardiness in roses is a difficult, if not impossible, quality to determine
for any given variety. Many variables go into hardiness issues:

How was the plant propagated—from a strong or weak bud?

How was the plant dug, stored, and shipped before purchase?

How well has the rose been treated during the growing season?

Is the rose located in a garden microclimate that is warmer or colder than the zone indicates?

Are there other stressful conditions, such as freeze-thaw cycles or drying winds?

It's difficult and economically unfeasible to do a scientifically valid hardiness test on modern rose varieties such as hybrid teas.

This leaves gardeners in very cold areas with three options:

Grow modern rose varieties on their own roots.

Plant roses known to be winter hardy, such as shrubs and Old Garden Roses.

Seek advice from a Consulting Rosarian about which roses seem to best weather the conditions in your region.

Roses for Cold Areas
If you live in a northern region, consider growing one of these hardy varieties with adequate winter protection suggested by a Consulting Rosarian in Minnesota:

HYBRID TEA
Elina
Hot Princess
Moonstone
Secret (*shown*)
Veterans' Honor

FLORIBUNDA
Eyepaint
Iceberg (*shown*)
Hannah Gordon
Playboy
Poulsen's Pearl

MINIATURE
Hot Tamale (*shown*)
Irresistible
Little Artist
Magic Carrousel

MINIFLORA
Butter Cream
Leading Lady
Memphis King (*shown*)
Tiffany Lynn

Roses for Hot Areas
Heat stress can be a problem for gardeners in hot areas. Water continually and heavily. Ask local Consulting Rosarians for advice about heat-tolerant varieties or use Earth-Kind roses listed on page 57. Consider this list from a Consulting Rosarian in Arizona, which contains three roses also good for northern climates: Hot Princess, Veterans' Honor, and Butter Cream.

HYBRID TEA
Gemini
Hot Princess
Let Freedom Ring
Marilyn Monroe
St. Patrick (*shown*)
Veterans' Honor

FLORIBUNDA
Fabulous! (*shown*)
Julia Child
Lavaglut
Sexy Rexy

MINIATURE
Baby Grand (*shown*)
Bees Knees
Fairhope
Miss Flippens

MINIFLORA
Butter Cream (*shown*)

The United States Department of Agriculture Plant Hardiness Zone Map

The **USDA** developed a map based on the lowest recorded temperatures across North America. To find your hardiness zone, match the color marking of your area to the key.

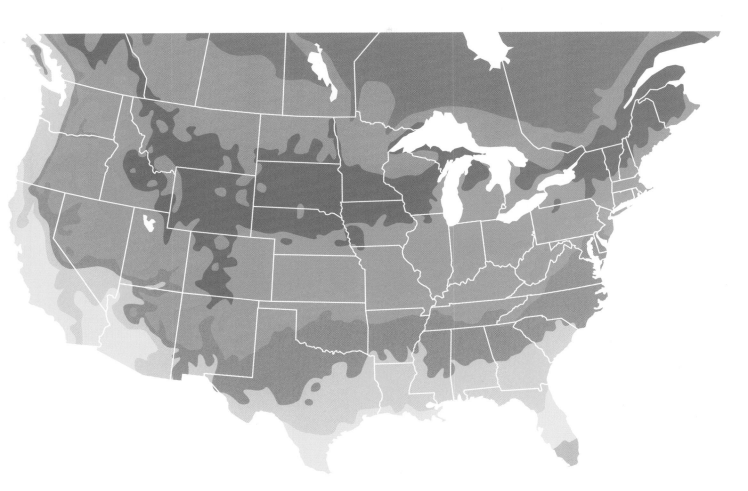

Range of Average Annual Minimum Temperatures for Each Zone

■ Zone 2: -50 to -40° F (-45 to -40°C)

■ Zone 3: -40 to -30° F (-40 to -35°C)

■ Zone 4: -30 to -20° F (-34 to -29°C)

■ Zone 5: -20 to -10° F (-29 to -23°C)

■ Zone 6: -10 to 0° F (-23 to -18°C)

■ Zone 7: 0 to 10° F (-18 to -12°C)

■ Zone 8: 10 to 20° F (-12 to -7°C)

■ Zone 9: 20 to 30° F (-7 to -1°C)

■ Zone 10: 30 to 40° F (-1 to 4°C)

ROSE CARE CALENDAR:
Northwest

Though the climate here is mild, gardeners often battle diseases caused by excess moisture and too many cool, sunless days. Place roses in as much sun as the yard offers, provide good air circulation that can be enchanced with lots of pruning, and choose varieties resistant to fungal diseases. If you desire perfection, be prepared to spray and otherwise coddle your plants.

JANUARY
Transplant roses as needed

Sharpen tools

FEBRUARY
Remove winter protection

Prune about Presidents' Day weekend in mild areas

Spray pruned roses with fungicide

MARCH
Purchase and plant bare-root roses

Start spray program when leaves appear

Weed throughout season as needed

APRIL
Improve initial pruning

Apply organic fertilizer, if using

Spray for insects as needed

MAY
Apply inorganic fertilizer, if using

Apply mulch

Prune blind shoots (stems with no flower buds) and twiggy growth

JUNE
Continue insect and disease control programs

Begin watering as needed

JULY
Water as needed

Deadhead as needed

Fertilize with inorganic fertilizer, fish emulsion, or alfalfa tea

AUGUST
Water as needed

Maintain insect and disease control programs

Deadhead as needed

SEPTEMBER
Water as needed

Begin lighter deadheading and cutting for bouquets

Fertilize lightly

OCTOBER
Maintain disease-control program

Stop fertilizing and deadheading

Order plants online or from nursery catalogs

NOVEMBER
Prune to shorten tall plants

Clean up beds

Spray canes and ground with dormant spray

DECEMBER
Apply winter protection

Transplant roses as needed

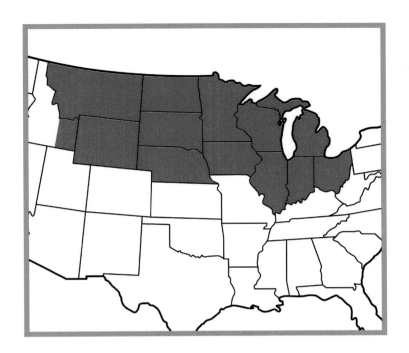

ROSE CARE CALENDAR:
Midwest & Plains

This region of extremes—with cold, windy winters and hot, humid summers—offers a relatively short window of time to enjoy growing roses, making them all the more precious. Grow own-root hybrid teas, grandifloras, and floribundas for better hardiness. Shrubs, species, and Old Garden Roses are good choices here. In the very coldest areas, winter protection is the most important chore you can provide for your roses.

JANUARY
Sharpen tools

Check winter protection

Order mail-order roses

FEBRUARY
Purchase spray materials

Check winter protection

MARCH
Water roses if there has been no snow cover and the ground is not frozen

APRIL
Remove winter protection after threat of killing frost is gone

Perform initial pruning

Apply fungicidal spray to pruned roses

Plant potted and bare-root roses if possible in your area

Transplant roses as needed

MAY
Start fungicidal spray program when leaves first appear

Fertilize with organic and inorganic fertilizer

Apply mulch

Improve on initial pruning

Spray for insects as needed

JUNE
Begin watering as needed

Begin weeding

Remove blind shoots and twiggy growth

JULY
Water

Fertilize

Apply fish emulsion or alfalfa tea to underperforming plants

Continue spray program

Deadhead as needed

AUGUST
Water as needed

Continue spray program

Deadhead as needed

SEPTEMBER
Deadhead lightly and cut roses on shorter stems

Stop fertilizing

Water as needed

OCTOBER
Stop pruning and deadheading

Acquire winter protection materials

Stop spraying

Clean up beds, removing any diseased leaves or stems

NOVEMBER
Cut tall roses back to accommodate winter protection program

Spray with a dormant spray

Apply winter protection, such as Minnesota Tip method, (*shown above and explained on page 101*)

DECEMBER
Read a good book about roses

ROSE CARE CALENDAR:
Northeast

Roses peak here in June, slow from heat in midsummer, then bounce back with more blooms during cooler fall temperatures. As in other northern climates, providing winter protection from cold and drying winds is one of the most important tasks facing rose gardeners in the Northeast.

JANUARY
Sharpen tools

Check for loss of winter protection

FEBRUARY
Purchase spray materials

Check winter protection

Water roses if there has been no snow cover

MARCH
Purchase potted roses when available

Remove winter protection depending upon USDA Zone

Prune roses

Spray pruned roses with fungicide

Transplant roses as needed

Water roses if there has been no snow cover

APRIL
Start fungicidal spray program when leaves first appear

Spray for insects as needed

Fertilize with organic fertilizer, if using

Apply mulch

MAY
Improve on initial pruning

Fertilize with inorganic fertilizer, if using

Begin watering as needed

JUNE
Weed as needed throughout the season

Prune blind shoots (stems with no flower buds) and twiggy growth

Continue spray program

JULY
Water as needed

Deadhead as needed

Treat spindly plants with fish emulsion or alfalfa tea

Fertilize with inorganic fertilizer, if using

Cut bouquets for the house

AUGUST
Continue spray program

Deadhead as needed

Water as needed

SEPTEMBER
Fertilize for the last time

Deadhead less

Cut blooms on shorter stems

Continue spray program

OCTOBER
Discontinue spraying and deadheading

Prune to shorten tall plants

Clean up ground

Order mail-order roses

NOVEMBER
Water

Spray with dormant spray

Apply winter protection

DECEMBER
Plan rose purchases for the next year

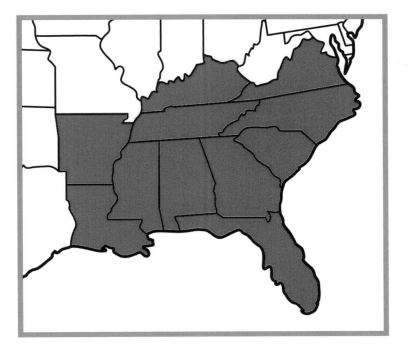

ROSE CARE CALENDAR:
Southeast

Roses bloom most of the year in these warm areas, although mountain regions experience a shorter season. Hot, humid conditions that promote diseases require gardeners to provide good air circulation and avoid overhead watering. Plan to use a fungicidal spray program to keep roses looking their best throughout the long growing season.

JANUARY
Prune in warmer areas

Spray pruned roses with a fungicide

Transplant roses if soil and weather permit

FEBRUARY
Prune, spray, and transplant in cooler areas

Purchase potted roses if available

MARCH
Prune, spray, and transplant in coldest areas

Apply mulch

Apply organic fertilizer

Water as needed

APRIL
Start fungicidal spraying when leaves first appear

Begin insecticidal spraying as needed

Improve on initial pruning

MAY
Weed as needed throughout season

Prune blind shoots (stems with no flower buds) and twiggy growth

Deadhead as needed

JUNE
Fertilize

Water as needed

Continue spray program

JULY
Apply fish emulsion or alfalfa tea

Deadhead as needed

Water as needed

AUGUST
Continue spray program

Water as needed

Fertilize

SEPTEMBER
Continue spraying, watering, and deadheading

Order mail-order roses

OCTOBER
Cease fertilizing in colder areas and prepare winter protection

Begin light deadheading and cutting on shorter stems

Maintain watering and spraying in warmer areas

NOVEMBER
Prune to shorten tall plants

Clean up ground

Spray with dormant spray

Apply winter protection in colder areas

DECEMBER
Sharpen tools

Review cultural practices and plant performance

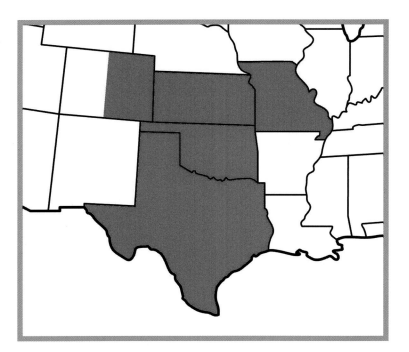

ROSE CARE CALENDAR:
South Central & Lower Midwest

Hot, hot, hot! Gardeners here focus on protecting roses during the summer. Buy heat-tolerant varieties and place roses where they get six to eight hours of sunshine in the morning hours while shielding them from harsher afternoon sun. Though roses like at least 1 inch of water per week, monitor soil moisture to prevent overwatering. In areas where temperatures drop in winter, some protection is still needed.

JANUARY
Sharpen tools

Begin pruning in warmer areas

FEBRUARY
Prune at appropriate time for your zone

Purchase roses

Plant potted and bare-root roses as weather warms

MARCH
Remove winter protection and prune in colder areas

Transplant roses as needed

Start fungicidal spray program when leaves first appear

APRIL
Improve on initial pruning

Spray for insects as needed

Fertilize with organic and inorganic fertilizers

Apply mulch

MAY
Begin watering in warmer areas

Weed throughout season as needed

Prune blind shoots (stems with no flower buds) and twiggy growth

JUNE
Continue spray program

Water as needed

Deadhead as needed

Cut bouquets for the house

JULY
Fertilize with liquid, organic, or inorganic fertilizer

Apply fish emulsion or alfalfa tea to underperforming plants

Water as needed

AUGUST
Continue spray program

Water as needed

Deadhead as needed

SEPTEMBER
Fertilize for the last time this year

Continue spray program

Water as needed

OCTOBER
Deadhead lightly and cut roses on shorter stems

Prepare winter protection, if needed

Order mail-order roses

NOVEMBER
Clean up beds

Prune to shorten tall plants

Apply dormant spray

Apply winter protection, if needed

DECEMBER
Transplant roses as needed if ground is workable

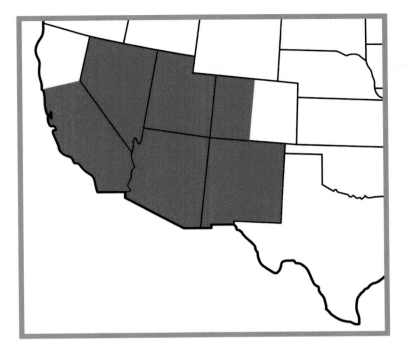

ROSE CARE CALENDAR:
Southwest & Southern California

Caring for roses in this temperate region is nearly a year-round activity. Roses love the nearly constant sunshine. Gardeners here should provide more consistent, deep watering and protective organic mulch than in some other parts of the country.

JANUARY
Prune roses

Spray pruned roses with fungicide

Plant bare-root roses

Purchase and plant potted roses

Transplant roses as needed

FEBRUARY
Start fungicidal spray program when leaves appear

Apply organic fertilizer

Apply inorganic fertilizer

Begin watering as needed

MARCH
Spray for insects as needed

Improve on initial pruning

Apply mulch

APRIL
Prune blind shoots (stems with no flower buds) and twiggy growth

Weed throughout season as needed

MAY
Continue spray programs

Continue watering, increasing frequency as weather warms

Deadhead as needed

JUNE
Fertilize with inorganic fertilizer

Treat wimpy plants with fish emulsion or alfalfa tea

Water

Cut bouquets for the house

JULY
Continue spray programs as needed

Deadhead as needed

Water

AUGUST
Fertilize with organic, inorganic, or liquid fertilizers

Water

Continue spray program as needed

Deadhead as needed

SEPTEMBER
Spray as needed

Water as needed

Deadhead as needed

OCTOBER
Stop deadheading

Stop fertilizing

Cut fewer bouquets on shorter stems

Order roses from mail-order nursery sources

NOVEMBER
Prune to shorten tall plants

Clean up beds

Apply dormant spray

DECEMBER
Transplant roses as needed

Sharpen tools

gallery of roses

Browse this showcase for the best of the best varieties in each rose family. There's a size, color, shape, and form to suit every garden.

p.114
HYBRID TEAS

Hybrid teas are the epitome of roses, with fragrance, form, and style. They take a bit more maintenance than other roses but reward with their beauty.

p.128
GRANDIFLORAS

Grandifloras combine the best qualities of two impressive rose families: big hybrid tea-style blooms that grow in large clusters like floribundas.

p.134
FLORIBUNDAS

Floribundas, with clusters of blooms that open nearly simultaneously, are like a bouquet on a single stem. As a bonus, they're vigorous repeat bloomers.

p.156
POLYANTHAS

The smaller flowers of polyanthas more than make up for their size with massive numbers of blooms. Group them together for a punch of color or a stunning hedge.

p.158
SHRUBS

All roses are technically shrubs, but the ones that fall into this diverse family are among the easiest to grow and maintain.

p.174
OLD GARDEN ROSES & SPECIES

Newer is not always better! Old Garden Roses and species varieties offer interesting forms, shapes, fragrance, and colors you won't find in other roses.

p.190
MINIATURES & MINIFLORAS

Got a small garden or merely a patio or balcony? One of these tiny treasures will fit easily into a container or another limited space.

p.208
CLIMBERS & RAMBLERS

Go vertical with one of these long-caned roses that can cover an arbor, pergola, or other structure with beautiful blooms.

The Best Roses

The 386 roses in this gallery are rated 7.5 or higher on a scale of 10

by the American Rose Society for 2010. They were grown and tested around the United States for two to three years by experienced rose growers and found to be significantly better than average.

ARS scoring system

The ARS's Roses in Review program annually evaluates roses in various categories. The number comes from judges around the country based on an average of the ratings for general garden use. Here's what they mean:

9.3–10: One of the best roses ever; seldom awarded

8.8–9.2: An outstanding rose; ranks in the top 1 percent

8.3–8.7: A very good to excellent rose; recommended without hesitation

7.8–8.2: A solid to very good rose; well above average

7.3–7.7: A little to somewhat above average rose

6.8–7.2: An average rose

6.1–6.7: A below average rose

0.0–6.0: Not recommended

The hybrid tea Tahitian Sunset was an All-America Rose Selections winner in 2006.

Awards key

Roses in the gallery have been listed with their awards. Here's what the abbreviations mean:

AARS: Since 1940, a yearly award from All-America Rose Selections, an arm of the commercial rose industry, to roses tested for at least two years and rated on a dozen criteria

ARS Members' Choice: American Rose Society Members' Choice Award, given yearly since 2004 to the highest scoring rose introduced in the previous five years

WFRS Hall of Fame: Given by the World Federation of Rose Societies, first awarded in 1976

GM: Gold Medal awarded in rose trials around the world

FA: Fragrance Award from rose trials around the world

AOE: ARS Award of Excellence for miniatures and minifloras, started in 1973

MHOF: ARS Miniature-Miniflora Hall of Fame, started in 1999

American Rose Society Members' Choice Awardees

This ARS honor goes to a rose introduced within the previous five years with the highest garden rating in Roses in Review. These are sure-fire garden winners.

2004: Knock Out, shrub (*left*)

2005: Gemini, hybrid tea

2006: Bees Knees, miniature

2007: Hot Cocoa, floribunda

2008: No award

2009: Julia Child, floribunda

2010: Home Run, shrub

World Rose Hall of Fame Winners

Looking for one of the best roses on the planet? Try a winner chosen by popular vote, currently every three years, by the member countries in the World Federation of Rose Societies.

1976: Peace, hybrid tea

1979: Queen Elizabeth, grandiflora

1981: Fragrant Cloud, hybrid tea

1983: Iceberg, floribunda

1985: Double Delight, hybrid tea

1988: Papa Meilland, hybrid tea

1991: Pascali, hybrid tea

1994: Just Joey, hybrid tea

1997: New Dawn, large-flowered climber

2000: Ingrid Bergman, hybrid tea

2003: Bonica, shrub

2006: Elina, hybrid tea, and Pierre de Ronsard, large-flowered climber

2009: Graham Thomas, shrub

Remember Me Roses

Shortly after September 11, 2001, Sue Casey of Portland, Oregon, decided to create three Remember Me rose gardens on or near the sites of each terrorist attack in New York City; Washington, D.C.; and Pennsylvania. A series of 11 Remember Me roses is planned to help to fund and support the gardens. Six roses are available to buy:

FIREFIGHTER A very fragrant red hybrid tea honors NYC firefighters.

FORTY HEROES (*above*) A yellow floribunda is named for the crew and passengers of Flight 93 that crashed in Pennsylvania.

SOARING SPIRITS A large-flowered climber with pink-and-white-striped blooms and golden stamens commemorates Twin Towers victims.

THE FINEST A creamy white hybrid tea honors the 23 NYPD officers who died.

PATRIOT DREAM (*above*) An orange-pink shrub rose honors the 59 crew and passengers of American Airlines Flight 77 that was crashed into the Pentagon.

WE SALUTE YOU An orange-pink hybrid tea with a spicy fragrance is named for the people in the Pentagon who lost their lives.

SURVIVOR This pink hybrid tea honors those who survived.

Future Remember Me roses will be named Flight 77, Port Authority Police, Flight 11, and Flight 175.

Fragrance Above All

To many gardeners, a rose is not a rose without fragrance. Because fragrance and a susceptibility to diseases often go hand in hand, many very fragrant varieties are rated lower than 7.5. But if fragrance is what you want, here are 10 olfactory delights.

CAPT. HARRY STEBBINGS Medium-pink blooms grace this disease-resistant hybrid tea, rated at 7.8.

FRAGRANT HOUR (*right*) Bronzy pink hybrid tea blooms rated 7.4 (slightly low) have great form and fragrance.

INTRIGUE This AARS-winning floribunda, rated only 7.1, has heavenly scented purple blooms in small sprays—and an affinity for black spot.

JUDE THE OBSCURE This creamy apricot David Austin rose may have the best fragrance of all, and it's rated at 8.0.

LAGERFELD Pale lavender blooms grow in large sprays on thin, nodding stems. This grandiflora has very good disease resistance but only a 6.9 rating.

PAROLE A German import whose name means "motto," the large, deep-pink hybrid tea has blooms with exceptional aroma, and it's rated 7.7.

PERFUME DELIGHT An AARS winner, this gorgeous medium-pink hybrid tea also tends to show black spot rather quickly, though it's rated 7.6.

RENAISSANCE This delicate pink hybrid tea from England has won two fragrance awards overseas but lacks a rating.

ROYAL HIGHNESS Light-pink blooms grow on a tall hybrid tea AARS winner that's rated 7.7.

VELVET FRAGRANCE Deep-velvety red hybrid tea blooms boast a super aroma and a rating of 7.8.

Hybrid Teas

Hybrid teas are the most popular family of roses in the United States—and perhaps the world. In the Rose Hall of Fame, created by the national rose societies from 41 countries, nearly 60 percent of the "World's Favorite Rose" awards have gone to hybrid teas.

Thanks to their large and often fragrant blooms on erect, manageable plants, hybrid teas remain the epitome of roses for many gardeners.

Their beauty continues to win fans and accolades even though they're generally the least hardy roses and require the most care to perform at their best.

For cutting, hybrid teas are ideal, especially when they're kept disbudded. You'll get a larger, more impressive cutting rose when you remove any side buds from each shoot, leaving only the center bud at the end to develop.

Anyone can grow hybrid teas, but gardeners in USDA Zone 7 and colder regions should provide adequate winter protection.

Gardeners in Zone 5 and colder areas should consider growing own-root roses for greater potential hardiness.

Because many factors, such as snow cover, wind, and temperature, are involved in the winter hardiness of roses, it's impossible to predict which hybrid teas will survive winter.

The bloom size and plant habit for hybrid teas vary greatly and depend on the varieties and where they're grown.

In the following gallery of hybrid teas, use the following general guides for size references:

BLOOM SIZE
SMALL: Less than 2 inches wide
MEDIUM: 2 to 5 inches wide
LARGE: More than 5 inches wide

PLANT SIZE
SHORT: Less than 4 feet tall
MEDIUM: 4 to 5½ feet tall
TALL: More than 5½ feet tall

UPRIGHT: Generally less than 2½ feet wide
BUSHY: 2½ to 4 feet wide
SPREADING: More than 4 feet wide

Bewitched
BLOOM SIZE, TYPE: Large, classic
FRAGRANCE: Moderate to heavy
GROWTH HABIT: Medium, bushy
DISEASE RESISTANCE: Good
AWARDS: AARS 1967
ARS RATING: 7.7
COMMENTS: This clear pink variety dates to 1967. The damask fragrance varies from moderate to heavy, depending on the weather.

Black Magic
BLOOM SIZE, TYPE: Medium, classic
FRAGRANCE: Light
GROWTH HABIT: Tall, bushy
DISEASE RESISTANCE: Good
ARS RATING: 7.7
COMMENTS: Originally a florist's variety, Black Magic made a successful transition to the garden. The deep-red blooms with near-black overtones are borne singly and are great for cutting.

Bride's Dream

BLOOM SIZE, TYPE: Medium, classic
FRAGRANCE: Light
GROWTH HABIT: Medium, bushy
DISEASE RESISTANCE: Good
ARS RATING: 8.1
COMMENTS: Beautiful light-pink blooms show nice form, developing primarily one to a stem. Plants grow with characteristic hybrid tea-size blooms and good disease resistance.

Brigadoon

BLOOM SIZE, TYPE: Large, classic
FRAGRANCE: Light
GROWTH HABIT: Medium, upright
DISEASE RESISTANCE: Good
AWARDS: AARS 1992
ARS RATING: 7.8
COMMENTS: Although classed as a pink blend, the petal edges of the distinctive blooms can be nearly red at times. They are borne generally in small clusters on clean, upright plants.

Chrysler Imperial

BLOOM SIZE, TYPE: Large, classic
FRAGRANCE: Heavy
GROWTH HABIT: Medium, bushy
DISEASE RESISTANCE: Fair
AWARDS: AARS 1953
ARS RATING: 7.8
COMMENTS: A classic red rose with exceptional fragrance, Chrysler Imperial is a good choice for dry areas. In any location, pruning promotes airflow that helps avoid disease problems.

Crystalline

BLOOM SIZE, TYPE: Large, classic
FRAGRANCE: Light
GROWTH HABIT: Medium, bushy
DISEASE RESISTANCE: Good
ARS RATING: 8.0
COMMENTS: The pure white flowers are borne both singly and in small sprays. This variety performs best in warm weather, which promotes blooms with excellent form.

Dainty Bess

BLOOM SIZE, TYPE: Medium, single
FRAGRANCE: Light
GROWTH HABIT: Medium, bushy
DISEASE RESISTANCE: Good
AWARDS: Gold Medal U.K.
ARS RATING: 8.5
COMMENTS: This winner, introduced in 1925, is the undisputed queen of the single hybrid teas. Light-pink blooms with low petals and prominent red stamens are borne in medium-size sprays.

Double Delight

BLOOM SIZE, TYPE: Large, classic
FRAGRANCE: Heavy
GROWTH HABIT: Medium, bushy
DISEASE RESISTANCE: Good
AWARDS: AARS 1977; GM Baden-Baden, Rome; WFRS Hall of Fame
ARS RATING: 8.4
COMMENTS: One of the most beautiful and fragrant hybrid teas. White blooms growing in small sprays show variable amounts of red edges.

Dublin

BLOOM SIZE, TYPE: Large, classic
FRAGRANCE: Heavy
GROWTH HABIT: Medium, upright
DISEASE RESISTANCE: Good
ARS RATING: 8.2
COMMENTS: Light-red blooms with smoky overtones and a raspberry fragrance are borne on vigorous, upright plants. Hot weather produces a redder color and enhances performance.

Electron

BLOOM SIZE, TYPE: Large, classic
FRAGRANCE: Heavy
GROWTH HABIT: Tall, spreading
DISEASE RESISTANCE: Good
AWARDS: AARS 1973; GM U.K., The Hague, Belfast
ARS RATING: 7.8
COMMENTS: A glorious garden rose! The only drawbacks are a spreading habit and vicious thorns. Blooms are intense deep-pink, very fragrant, and borne singly much of the time.

Elina

BLOOM SIZE, TYPE: Large, classic
FRAGRANCE: Slight
GROWTH HABIT: Tall, bushy
DISEASE RESISTANCE: Excellent
AWARDS: GM New Zealand; WFRS Hall of Fame
ARS RATING: 8.6
COMMENTS: A heavy bloomer with a quick repeat of creamy, light-yellow blooms, it is the highest-rated yellow hybrid tea on the market today.

Elizabeth Taylor

BLOOM SIZE, TYPE: Large, classic
FRAGRANCE: Slight
GROWTH HABIT: Tall, spreading
DISEASE RESISTANCE: Good
ARS RATING: 8.4
COMMENTS: Vigorous plants grow tall and wide. Elizabeth Taylor's medium-pink blooms with darker edges are borne singly or in small sprays. The best blooms are produced in warm weather.

Elle

BLOOM SIZE, TYPE: Large, classic
FRAGRANCE: Heavy
GROWTH HABIT: Medium, bushy
DISEASE RESISTANCE: Good
AWARDS: AARS 2005; GM Bagatelle; FA Tokyo
ARS RATING: 7.7
COMMENTS: Grow Elle for its very fragrant, soft pink blooms with golden yellow at their bases. The blooms grow larger in cool weather, which produces more intense colors.

Falling in Love

BLOOM SIZE, TYPE: Large, classic
FRAGRANCE: Medium
GROWTH HABIT: Medium, bushy
DISEASE RESISTANCE: Good
ARS RATING: 7.9
COMMENTS: Warm-pink blooms with lighter petal edges and a near-white underside make an intriguing combination. Abundant flowers carry a pleasing fragrance.

Firefighter

BLOOM SIZE, TYPE: Large, classic
FRAGRANCE: Heavy
GROWTH HABIT: Medium, bushy
DISEASE RESISTANCE: Good
AWARDS: GM Rome; FA Rome, Bagatelle, Geneva, Madrid, Monza, Severne
ARS RATING: 7.7
COMMENTS: A deep-red rose with great form and exceptional fragrance, Firefighter is the first in a series of "Remember Me" roses.

Folklore

BLOOM SIZE, TYPE: Medium, classic
FRAGRANCE: Medium
GROWTH HABIT: Tall, bushy
DISEASE RESISTANCE: Good
ARS RATING: 8.2
COMMENTS: Tall, vigorous plants that are slightly mildew prone bear orange-pink blooms with a golden yellow underside. A heavy bloomer with a good repeat, it needs disbudding since it tends to bloom in sprays.

Fragrant Cloud

BLOOM SIZE, TYPE: Large, classic
FRAGRANCE: Heavy
GROWTH HABIT: Medium, bushy
DISEASE RESISTANCE: Fair
AWARDS: WFRS Hall of Fame
ARS RATING: 8.1
COMMENTS: Arguably the most fragrant hybrid tea, this variety bears light-red, slightly orangey blooms in profusion. A must for any rose garden.

Frederic Mistral

BLOOM SIZE, TYPE: Large, classic
FRAGRANCE: Heavy
GROWTH HABIT: Medium, bushy
DISEASE RESISTANCE: Good
AWARDS: FA Belfast, Monza, Le Roeulx, Baden-Baden
ARS RATING: 7.9
COMMENTS: Light-pink blooms with deeper pink centers and petal undersides grace this rose. Extremely fragrant.

Garden Party

BLOOM SIZE, TYPE: Large, classic
FRAGRANCE: Light
GROWTH HABIT: Medium, upright
DISEASE RESISTANCE: Good
AWARDS: AARS 1960; GM Bagatelle
ARS RATING: 7.9
COMMENTS: This progeny of Peace has large creamy white blooms with touches of pink around the petals' edges. For 50 years, it's been a great performer in the garden.

Gemini

BLOOM SIZE, TYPE: Large, classic
FRAGRANCE: Light
GROWTH HABIT: Medium, upright
DISEASE RESISTANCE: Excellent
AWARDS: AARS 2000; ARS Members' Choice 2005
ARS RATING: 8.2
COMMENTS: Weather determines the intensity of pink markings on the light-pink blooms. The flowers of this extremely popular variety are produced mostly singly and are ideal for cutting.

Ingrid Bergman

BLOOM SIZE, TYPE: Large, classic
FRAGRANCE: Light
GROWTH HABIT: Medium, bushy
DISEASE RESISTANCE: Good
AWARDS: GM Belfast, Madrid, The Hague; WFRS Hall of Fame
ARS RATING: 7.8
COMMENTS: This vigorous, hardy variety hails from the Poulsen nursery in Denmark. Medium red blooms are very large, produced in abundance.

Just Joey

BLOOM SIZE, TYPE: Large, informal
FRAGRANCE: Heavy
GROWTH HABIT: Medium, spreading
DISEASE RESISTANCE: Good
AWARDS: GM U.K., WFRS Hall of Fame
ARS RATING: 7.9
COMMENTS: One of the few hybrid teas in this color, Just Joey has buff-amber blooms that carry a strong fragrance. Medium, somewhat spreading plants have good disease resistance.

Kardinal

BLOOM SIZE, TYPE: Medium, classic
FRAGRANCE: Light
GROWTH HABIT: Medium, upright
DISEASE RESISTANCE: Good
ARS RATING: 8.5
COMMENTS: Bred for use by florists, this rose also works well in a garden. The medium-red blooms, borne mostly singly, have incredible substance and are great for cutting.

Keepsake

BLOOM SIZE, TYPE: Large, classic
FRAGRANCE: Light
GROWTH HABIT: Medium, bushy
DISEASE RESISTANCE: Good
ARS RATING: 8.0
COMMENTS: Large, beautiful blooms in shades of pink make it a winner, particularly in cool weather. Plants are robust with good disease resistance.

Let Freedom Ring

BLOOM SIZE, TYPE: Large, classic
FRAGRANCE: None
GROWTH HABIT: Tall, bushy
DISEASE RESISTANCE: Good
ARS RATING: 7.9
COMMENTS: Bred by an American amateur hybridizer, Ernest Earman, this light-red variety bears classic shape blooms on tall, bushy plants.

Liebeszauber

BLOOM SIZE, TYPE: Large, classic
FRAGRANCE: Medium
GROWTH HABIT: Tall, spreading
DISEASE RESISTANCE: Excellent
AWARDS: FA, The Hague
ARS RATING: 8.0
COMMENTS: This extremely vigorous plant's name means "Love's Magic" in German. Large, deep red blooms are produced in large sprays, so constant disbudding is needed for best results.

Louise Estes

BLOOM SIZE, TYPE: Large, classic
FRAGRANCE: Medium
GROWTH HABIT: Medium, bushy
DISEASE RESISTANCE: Good
ARS RATING: 8.3
COMMENTS: With deep-pink blooms, lighter petal edges, and great classic form, this rose could be considered a warm-weather version of Keepsake. Plants are vigorous and disease resistant.

Love and Peace

BLOOM SIZE, TYPE: Large, classic
FRAGRANCE: Light
GROWTH HABIT: Medium, upright
DISEASE RESISTANCE: Good
AWARDS: AARS 2002
ARS RATING: 7.8
COMMENTS: An offspring of Peace, this lovely rose grows yellow blooms with splashes of orange, pink, and light red. Most blooms are borne one to a stem.

Lynn Anderson

BLOOM SIZE, TYPE: Large, classic
FRAGRANCE: Light
GROWTH HABIT: Tall, upright
DISEASE RESISTANCE: Fair
ARS RATING: 7.5
COMMENTS: Named for the country singer, Lynn Anderson grows small sprays of white to light-pink blooms with deep pink or cerise petal edges. Plants need black spot protection in rainy areas.

Marilyn Monroe

BLOOM SIZE, TYPE: Large, classic
FRAGRANCE: Light
GROWTH HABIT: Medium, bushy
DISEASE RESISTANCE: Excellent
ARS RATING: 7.9
COMMENTS: Large, soft apricot blooms with impeccable form and substance are borne mostly singly on robust, very thorny plants with great disease resistance.

Memorial Day

BLOOM SIZE, TYPE: Large, many petals
FRAGRANCE: Heavy
GROWTH HABIT: Medium, spreading
DISEASE RESISTANCE: Good
AWARDS: AARS 2004
ARS RATING: 7.7
COMMENTS: Large, soft pink blooms carry a heavy damask fragrance. Plants prefer warm weather for heavy and quick repeat bloom.

Midas Touch

BLOOM SIZE, TYPE: Large, classic
FRAGRANCE: Light
GROWTH HABIT: Medium, bushy
DISEASE RESISTANCE: Good
AWARDS: AARS 1994
ARS RATING: 7.5
COMMENTS: Solid yellow, unfading blooms open quickly. They are borne mostly one per stem on very disease-resistant plants.

Mister Lincoln

BLOOM SIZE, TYPE: Large, classic
FRAGRANCE: Heavy
GROWTH HABIT: Tall, bushy
DISEASE RESISTANCE: Fair
AWARDS: AARS 1965
ARS RATING: 8.3
COMMENTS: Velvety red blooms with incredible fragrance make this rose a must for any cutting garden. Plants are somewhat disease prone.

Moonstone

BLOOM SIZE, TYPE: Large, classic
FRAGRANCE: Light
GROWTH HABIT: Medium, upright
DISEASE RESISTANCE: Excellent
ARS RATING: 8.2
COMMENTS: Off-white blooms with pink petal edges and a pink center produce an attractive garden display. The flowers show great form but need warm weather to do well.

New Zealand

BLOOM SIZE, TYPE: Large, classic
FRAGRANCE: Heavy
GROWTH HABIT: Medium, bushy
DISEASE RESISTANCE: Excellent
AWARDS: GM New Zealand
ARS RATING: 7.9
COMMENTS: One of the few roses that combine excellent disease resistance with great fragrance, New Zealand's light-pink blooms do best in cool weather. Plants have good repeat bloom habits.

Olympiad

BLOOM SIZE, TYPE: Large, classic
FRAGRANCE: None
GROWTH HABIT: Medium, bushy
DISEASE RESISTANCE: Excellent
AWARDS: AARS 1994
ARS RATING: 8.6
COMMENTS: The best red hybrid tea for disease resistance, this variety, which commemorates the Los Angeles Olympics of 1984, regrettably has little to no scent. Plants produce classic blooms.

Opening Night

BLOOM SIZE, TYPE: Large, classic
FRAGRANCE: Light
GROWTH HABIT: Medium, bushy
DISEASE RESISTANCE: Good
AWARDS: AARS 1998
ARS RATING: 7.8
COMMENTS: Cooler weather brings out the best color—deep, vivid red. Blooms display great form and distinctive ruffled petal edges. Plants are very productive and have good disease resistance.

Peace

BLOOM SIZE, TYPE: Large, classic
FRAGRANCE: Light
GROWTH HABIT: Tall, spreading
DISEASE RESISTANCE: Excellent
AWARDS: AARS 1946; GM U.K., The Hague; WFRS Hall of Fame
ARS RATING: 8.1
COMMENTS: A 65-year-old winner. Blooms should be vibrant yellow and pink. If you can find a plant that resembles the original Peace, get it.

Perfect Moment

BLOOM SIZE, TYPE: Large, classic
FRAGRANCE: Light
GROWTH HABIT: Medium, bushy
DISEASE RESISTANCE: Fair
AWARDS: AARS 1991
ARS RATING: 7.8
COMMENTS: With yellow at the base of its petals and red at the edges, Perfect Moment makes an eye-catching addition to the garden.

Pristine

BLOOM SIZE, TYPE: Large, classic
FRAGRANCE: Light
GROWTH HABIT: Medium, bushy
DISEASE RESISTANCE: Good
AWARDS: FA U.K.
ARS RATING: 8.6
COMMENTS: Despite their tendency to open very quickly, Pristine's white blooms with delicate pink brushings are considered among the most beautiful. The bushes grow strong and vigorous.

Rosemary Harkness

BLOOM SIZE, TYPE: Large, informal
FRAGRANCE: Heavy
GROWTH HABIT: Medium, bushy
DISEASE RESISTANCE: Excellent
AWARDS: GM Belfast; FA Glasgow, Belfast
ARS RATING: 8.0
COMMENTS: This rose should be more widely known and grown. Blooms are a mix of orange, salmon, and pink. Great disease resistance.

St. Patrick

BLOOM SIZE, TYPE: Large, classic
FRAGRANCE: Light
GROWTH HABIT: Medium, bushy
DISEASE RESISTANCE: Good
AWARDS: AARS 1996
ARS RATING: 8.0
COMMENTS: Green-tinged buds open to yellow blooms with the faintest hints of green on strong, vigorous plants. St. Patrick performs exceptionally well in hot weather.

Savoy Hotel
BLOOM SIZE, TYPE: Large, classic
FRAGRANCE: Light
GROWTH HABIT: Tall, bushy
DISEASE RESISTANCE: Excellent
AWARDS: GM Dublin
ARS RATING: 7.8
COMMENTS: The quintessential cool-weather
hybrid tea, Savoy Hotel produces great quantities
of light pink, classical form blooms on tall,
disease-resistant plants.

Secret
BLOOM SIZE, TYPE: Large, classic
FRAGRANCE: Heavy
GROWTH HABIT: Medium, bushy
DISEASE RESISTANCE: Good
AWARDS: AARS 1994
ARS RATING: 7.9
COMMENTS: A great hybrid tea for a fragrance
garden, this offspring of Pristine shows deeper
pink brushings than its parent, with longer-lasting
blooms and strong plants.

Sheer Elegance
BLOOM SIZE, TYPE: Large, classic
FRAGRANCE: Light
GROWTH HABIT: Medium, bushy
DISEASE RESISTANCE: Good
AWARDS: AARS 1991
ARS RATING: 7.8
COMMENTS: Classic blooms of salmon pink that
hold their form make Sheer Elegance a must for
the cutting garden. The plant is of average size
for a hybrid tea, with good disease resistance.

Silver Jubilee
BLOOM SIZE, TYPE: Medium, classic
FRAGRANCE: Light
GROWTH HABIT: Tall, upright
DISEASE RESISTANCE: Excellent
AWARDS: GM U.K., Belfast
ARS RATING: 8.6
COMMENTS: Blooms that blend pink, salmon,
and amber are borne on exceptionally disease-
resistant plants. The flowers form sprays.
This variety does best in cool weather.

Stephens' Big Purple

BLOOM SIZE, TYPE: Medium, informal
FRAGRANCE: Heavy
GROWTH HABIT: Medium, upright
DISEASE RESISTANCE: Good
ARS RATING: 7.5
COMMENTS: The color of this very fragrant rose from New Zealand can vary from raspberry pink-purple to deep violet-purple. Most of the flowers are borne singly. Despite the many petals, the blooms still open well in cool weather.

Sunset Celebration

BLOOM SIZE, TYPE: Large, classic
FRAGRANCE: Light
GROWTH HABIT: Tall, bushy
DISEASE RESISTANCE: Excellent
AWARDS: AARS 1998; GM Belfast, The Hague
ARS RATING: 7.8
COMMENTS: This U.K. import was named for the 100th anniversary of *Sunset* magazine. Strong, very vigorous plants with great disease resistance produce profuse, well-formed buff-amber blooms.

Tahitian Sunset

BLOOM SIZE, TYPE: Large, classic
FRAGRANCE: Heavy
GROWTH HABIT: Medium, bushy
DISEASE RESISTANCE: Good
AWARDS: AARS 2006
ARS RATING: 7.7
COMMENTS: Strongly fragrant, blooms in a changing blend of pink and apricot blooms grow on vigorous, productive plants.

The McCartney Rose

BLOOM SIZE, TYPE: Large, classic
FRAGRANCE: Heavy
GROWTH HABIT: Medium, bushy
DISEASE RESISTANCE: Fair
AWARDS: GM & FA Le Roeulx, Monza, Paris; GM Geneva; FA Bagatelle, Madrid, Belfast, Durbanville
ARS RATING: 7.9
COMMENTS: Named for entertainer Paul McCartney, this rose has won the most trial awards. Medium-pink blooms are highly fragrant.

Tiffany

BLOOM SIZE, TYPE: Large, classic
FRAGRANCE: Heavy
GROWTH HABIT: Medium, upright
DISEASE RESISTANCE: Good
AWARDS: AARS 1955
ARS RATING: 7.9
COMMENTS: An oldie but a goodie, this classic bears light-pink blooms with yellow at the petals' base. The flowers are exceptionally fragrant but need warm weather to perform at their best.

Touch of Class

BLOOM SIZE, TYPE: Large, classic
FRAGRANCE: Light
GROWTH HABIT: Tall, bushy
DISEASE RESISTANCE: Good
AWARDS: AARS 1986
ARS RATING: 8.9
COMMENTS: One of ARS's highest-rated hybrid teas, Touch of Class bears soft, salmon-pink blooms that nearly always grow one per stem, making them ideal for cutting.

Veterans' Honor

BLOOM SIZE, TYPE: Large, classic
FRAGRANCE: Light
GROWTH HABIT: Medium, bushy
DISEASE RESISTANCE: Good
ARS RATING: 8.1
COMMENTS: Very large, solid red blooms with classic form are produced in abundance on strong, disease-resistant plants.

Voodoo

BLOOM SIZE, TYPE: Large, classic
FRAGRANCE: Moderate
GROWTH HABIT: Tall, upright
DISEASE RESISTANCE: Excellent
AWARDS: AARS 1986
ARS RATING: 7.5
COMMENTS: The blooms on this variety are basically orange but contain shades of amber, pink, and yellow depending upon the weather. Plants are exceptionally disease resistant.

Grandifloras

Grandifloras, at least ideally, are a perfect combination of hybrid teas and floribundas: plants with large blooms produced both individually and in sprays. Many varieties bear classic blooms while others have more informal flowers.

The first grandiflora, Queen Elizabeth, displays the prototype characteristics of this class: large, tall, rugged, disease-resistant plants that produce both sprays and one-per-stem blooms.

Grandifloras are consistent rebloomers, and can be disbudded and enjoyed as single blooms, similar to hybrid teas, or cut and brought into the house as complete bouquets, like floribundas.

Although the grandiflora class wasn't established until 1955, older varieties such as Buccaneer are called grandifloras today. That's because the American Rose Society, which is in charge of rose classification, often retroactively classifies older varieties once a new family has been approved. The grandiflora class is not recognized in Europe or other rose-growing countries outside the United States and Canada.

Tall, rugged roses such as Fragrant Plum or Gold Medal (the highest rated grandiflora) are ideal for the backgrounds of rose or mixed gardens. Shorter varieties, including Tournament of Roses, can be placed in the foreground. Pay attention to the size you select: Some grandifloras can reach 8 feet tall or more.

Fragrant varieties such as Maria Shriver and Melody Parfumée should be planted where they can be easily smelled and enjoyed.

BLOOM SIZE
SMALL: Less than 2 inches wide
MEDIUM: 2 to 5 inches wide
LARGE: More than 5 inches wide

PLANT SIZE
SHORT: Less than 4 feet tall
MEDIUM: 4 to 5½ feet tall
TALL: More than 5½ feet tall

PLANT HABIT
UPRIGHT: Generally less than 2½ feet wide
BUSHY: 2½ to 4 feet wide
SPREADING: More than 4 feet wide

About Face
BLOOM SIZE, TYPE: Large, informal
FRAGRANCE: Light
GROWTH HABIT: Tall, upright
DISEASE RESISTANCE: Good
AWARDS: AARS 2005
ARS RATING: 7.7
COMMENTS: The blooms of About Face are primarily orange, with shadings of pink and salmon. They are informal in shape and are borne mostly singly on strong, upright plants.

Candelabra
BLOOM SIZE, TYPE: Medium, classic
FRAGRANCE: Light
GROWTH HABIT: Medium, bushy
DISEASE RESISTANCE: Good
AWARDS: AARS 1999
ARS RATING: 7.6
COMMENTS: Candelabra, a moderate-size plant for a grandiflora, carries warm orange blooms that open to show beautiful golden stamens. Flowers are borne mostly in large, open clusters.

Caribbean

BLOOM SIZE, TYPE: Medium, classic
FRAGRANCE: Light
GROWTH HABIT: Medium, bushy
DISEASE RESISTANCE: Good
AWARDS: AARS 1994
ARS RATING: 7.6
COMMENTS: Apricot to orange blooms with yellow at the base of the petals and touches of pink make Caribbean's flowers especially attractive. They grow both singly and in clusters on plants of manageable size.

Cherry Parfait

BLOOM SIZE, TYPE: Large, informal
FRAGRANCE: Light
GROWTH HABIT: Short, bushy
DISEASE RESISTANCE: Good
AWARDS: AARS 2003, GM Buenos Aires
ARS RATING: 7.9
COMMENTS: White to light yellow blooms with cerise petal edges make Cherry Parfait an eye-catching rose. The flowers grow in medium-size clusters on short, compact plants.

Crimson Bouquet

BLOOM SIZE, TYPE: Large, classic
FRAGRANCE: Medium
GROWTH HABIT: Medium, bushy
DISEASE RESISTANCE: Excellent
AWARDS: AARS 2000
ARS RATING: 7.9
COMMENTS: Crimson Bouquet showcases large red blooms, held singly and in small clusters, on medium-size bushes that have great disease resistance.

Dream Come True

BLOOM SIZE, TYPE: Large, classic
FRAGRANCE: Light
GROWTH HABIT: Tall, upright
DISEASE RESISTANCE: Good
AWARDS: AARS 2008
ARS RATING: 7.5
COMMENTS: Hybridized by amateur John Pottschmidt, this variety has gorgeous yellow blooms shot with orange and cerise pink. They grow mostly singly on tall, robust plants.

Earth Song

BLOOM SIZE, TYPE: Large, informal
FRAGRANCE: Heavy
GROWTH HABIT: Medium, bushy
DISEASE RESISTANCE: Good
ARS RATING: 8.2
COMMENTS: This very hardy rose, part of the Griffith Buck series, produces medium- to deep-pink blooms that open quickly to show golden stamens. They are borne singly and in small sprays.

Fame!

BLOOM SIZE, TYPE: Large, classic
FRAGRANCE: Moderate
GROWTH HABIT: Tall, spreading
DISEASE RESISTANCE: Excellent
AWARDS: AARS 1998
ARS RATING: 8.1
COMMENTS: Hot-pink blooms with great classic form are borne in profusion, mostly singly, on large, vigorous, very disease-resistant plants.

Fragrant Plum

BLOOM SIZE, TYPE: Large, classic
FRAGRANCE: Heavy
GROWTH HABIT: Tall, bushy
DISEASE RESISTANCE: Good
ARS RATING: 7.7
COMMENTS: Very fragrant lavender blooms with deeper color petal edges make this a great rose for cutting. The flowers grow mostly in small sprays on tall, robust plants.

Gold Medal

BLOOM SIZE, TYPE: Large, classic
FRAGRANCE: Light
GROWTH HABIT: Tall, bushy
DISEASE RESISTANCE: Good
AWARDS: GM New Zealand
ARS RATING: 8.4
COMMENTS: This is the highest rated grandiflora. Gold Medal earns its name with deep golden blooms with pink petal edges that grow singly or in small sprays. Plants are tall and very productive.

Honey Dijon

BLOOM SIZE, TYPE: Large, classic
FRAGRANCE: Medium
GROWTH HABIT: Medium, bushy
DISEASE RESISTANCE: Good
ARS RATING: 7.5
COMMENTS: The unusual tan to mustard blooms exhibit good form and grow in sprays on strong plants. Honey Dijon was hybridized by amateur James Sproul.

Maria Shriver

BLOOM SIZE, TYPE: Large, classic
FRAGRANCE: Heavy
GROWTH HABIT: Medium, bushy
DISEASE RESISTANCE: Good
ARS RATING: 7.5
COMMENTS: Named for the former first lady of California, this variety has very fragrant, pure white blooms of classic form borne in medium to large sprays.

Melody Parfumée

BLOOM SIZE, TYPE: Large, classic
FRAGRANCE: Heavy
GROWTH HABIT: Medium, bushy
DISEASE RESISTANCE: Good
AWARDS: GM Baden-Baden, Bagatelle; FA Baden-Baden, Bagatelle
ARS RATING: 7.7
COMMENTS: Medium-lavender to purple blooms in large, loose sprays make this a very attractive garden rose. The flowers are exceptionally fragrant, and the plant is a fast repeat bloomer.

Octoberfest

BLOOM SIZE, TYPE: Medium, classic
FRAGRANCE: Medium
GROWTH HABIT: Tall, upright
DISEASE RESISTANCE: Excellent
ARS RATING: 7.5
COMMENTS: Classic orange blooms with yellow and pink overtones are carried on very upright, disease-resistant plants. The flowers form in well-arrayed sprays.

Prominent

BLOOM SIZE, TYPE: Medium, classic
FRAGRANCE: Light
GROWTH HABIT: Medium, bushy
DISEASE RESISTANCE: Good
AWARDS: AARS 1977
ARS RATING: 7.5
COMMENTS: Bright orange-red blooms with classic form are borne in small sprays on very healthy plants. Prominent is somewhat short for a grandiflora, but it's very productive with blooms.

Queen Elizabeth

BLOOM SIZE, TYPE: Large, informal
FRAGRANCE: Light
GROWTH HABIT: Tall, bushy
DISEASE RESISTANCE: Excellent
AWARDS: AARS 1955; GM U.K., The Hague; WFRS Hall of Fame
ARS RATING: 7.9
COMMENTS: Queen Elizabeth is the epitome of the grandiflora class, with very tall, robust plants and medium-pink blooms formed singly and in sprays. It does not like hard pruning; let it grow tall.

Radiant Perfume

BLOOM SIZE, TYPE: Large, classic
FRAGRANCE: Medium to heavy
GROWTH HABIT: Medium, bushy
DISEASE RESISTANCE: Good
ARS RATING: 7.5
COMMENTS: Solid yellow blooms with an enticing fragrance grace this variety. The flowers grow singly and in small sprays, opening quickly on robust plants.

Reba McIntyre

BLOOM SIZE, TYPE: Large, classic
FRAGRANCE: Light
GROWTH HABIT: Medium, bushy
DISEASE RESISTANCE: Good
AWARDS: GM New Zealand
ARS RATING: 7.7
COMMENTS: Named after the country singer, this New Zealand variety has red-orange blooms with a nice, light fragrance. They are carried singly and in sprays on tidy, compact plants.

Rejoice

BLOOM SIZE, TYPE: Medium, classic
FRAGRANCE: Medium
GROWTH HABIT: Medium, spreading
DISEASE RESISTANCE: Fair
ARS RATING: 8.0
COMMENTS: Rejoice, from amateur breeder Thomas McMillan, was the first rose to win a Gold Medal at the American Rose Society's trial grounds in Shreveport, Louisiana, in 1985. Soft-pink blooms with brushings of salmon and amber are borne in large sprays.

Strike It Rich

BLOOM SIZE, TYPE: Large, classic
FRAGRANCE: Heavy
GROWTH HABIT: Tall, bushy
DISEASE RESISTANCE: Good
AWARDS: AARS 2007
ARS RATING: 7.9
COMMENTS: Large sprays of golden yellow flowers with pink overtones are carried on tall, robust plants. This excellent rose is a solid garden performer.

Tournament of Roses

BLOOM SIZE, TYPE: Large, classic
FRAGRANCE: Light
GROWTH HABIT: Short, bushy
DISEASE RESISTANCE: Excellent
AWARDS: AARS 1989
ARS RATING: 8.2
COMMENTS: Beautiful blooms with deep-pink centers and lighter petal edges form in medium-size sprays. Plants grow only 3 to 4 feet tall with excellent disease resistance.

Wild Blue Yonder

BLOOM SIZE, TYPE: Large, informal
FRAGRANCE: Strong
GROWTH HABIT: Medium, bushy
DISEASE RESISTANCE: Good
AWARDS: AARS 2006
ARS RATING: 7.7
COMMENTS: Medium-purple, very fragrant blooms with reddish edges form in large clusters. It's one of several fine purple roses bred by Weeks Roses in recent years.

Floribundas

Floribundas are the quintessential spray rose. Created in the early 20th century as a cross between hybrid teas and polyanthas, these prolific bloomers came into their own about midcentury. Plants range from short to tall, bloom sizes vary from small polyantha-like flowers to virtual hybrid teas, and bloom forms are more variable than any other rose family, ranging from five-petal singles to many-petaled flowers.

To picture an ideal spray, imagine arranging roses or other flowers in a vase. You would give each bloom room to display itself without crowding the others, but leave no holes or gaps in the bouquet. You would place all the blooms at the same level, with a flat or slightly rounded top to the bouquet. Finally, you would arrange the stems so the bouquet was nearly round rather than lopsided or angular. This bouquet describes what an ideal floribunda spray should look like.

While hybrid teas are usually considered the best for cut roses, floribundas offer the same combination of colors, fragrances, and forms with just one or two stems rather than many. Varying sizes and heavy bloom habit make floribundas ideal for many landscape uses.

Consider growing single roses, with alluring stamens. Also beautiful are semidoubles (about 10 to 20 petals per flower) that quickly open to reveal their stamens as the blooms age.

Floribundas with an "excellent" rating for disease resistance are the easiest to care for, but the rest are also worth growing because of other stellar traits.

BLOOM SIZE
SMALL: Less than 2 inches wide
MEDIUM: 2 to 4 inches wide
LARGE: More than 4 inches wide

PLANT SIZE
SHORT: Smaller than 4 feet tall
MEDIUM: 4 to 5½ feet tall
TALL: More than 5½ feet tall

UPRIGHT: Generally less than 2½ feet wide
BUSHY: 2½ to 4 feet wide
SPREADING: More than 4 feet wide

Angel Face
BLOOM SIZE, TYPE: Large, classic
FRAGRANCE: Heavy
GROWTH HABIT: Medium, bushy
DISEASE RESISTANCE: Fair
AWARDS: AARS 1969; FA U.K.
ARS RATING: 7.7
COMMENTS: Angel Face is one of the most fragrant floribundas. Large, medium-purple blooms grow on strong plants.

Apricot Nectar
BLOOM SIZE, TYPE: Large, classic
FRAGRANCE: Heavy
GROWTH HABIT: Medium, bushy
DISEASE RESISTANCE: Good
AWARDS: AARS 1966
ARS RATING: 8.0
COMMENTS: This fragrant variety bears large, buff-apricot blooms on medium-size plants.

Bella Rosa

BLOOM SIZE, TYPE: Small, many petals
FRAGRANCE: Light
GROWTH HABIT: Short, bushy
DISEASE RESISTANCE: Excellent
AWARDS: GM Copenhagen, Baden-Baden
ARS RATING: 7.8
COMMENTS: Bella Rosa could well have been classed as a polyantha. Low-growing, disease-resistant plants carry small pink blooms borne in large clusters.

Betty Boop

BLOOM SIZE, TYPE: Medium, semidouble
FRAGRANCE: Medium
GROWTH HABIT: Medium, bushy
DISEASE RESISTANCE: Good
AWARDS: AARS 1999
ARS RATING: 8.0
COMMENTS: White blooms with cerise edges and yellow bases are carried in small sprays. This rose was named for the animated cartoon character.

Betty Prior

BLOOM SIZE, TYPE: Medium, single
FRAGRANCE: Light
GROWTH HABIT: Tall, bushy
DISEASE RESISTANCE: Fair
AWARDS: GM U.K.
ARS RATING: 8.2
COMMENTS: Large sprays of single medium-pink blooms are borne in profusion. The tall plants are somewhat prone to black spot.

Bill Warriner

BLOOM SIZE, TYPE: Medium, classic
FRAGRANCE: Light
GROWTH HABIT: Medium, bushy
DISEASE RESISTANCE: Good
ARS RATING: 7.8
COMMENTS: Salmon-pink blooms with classic form grace this variety, named for a longtime hybridizer at the Jackson & Perkins Company. Blooms open quickly to show attractive stamens.

Black Cherry

BLOOM SIZE, TYPE: Medium, classic
FRAGRANCE: Light
GROWTH HABIT: Medium, bushy
DISEASE RESISTANCE: Good
ARS RATING: 7.5
COMMENTS: Medium-size, manageable plants bear large clusters of solid red blooms with a light, fruity fragrance.

Blueberry Hill

BLOOM SIZE, TYPE: Large, semidouble
FRAGRANCE: Medium
GROWTH HABIT: Medium, spreading
DISEASE RESISTANCE: Good
ARS RATING: 7.8
COMMENTS: Large light-purple blooms set in medium-size sprays are nicely fragrant and open quickly to show their stamens.

Bolero

BLOOM SIZE, TYPE: Large, informal
FRAGRANCE: Medium
GROWTH HABIT: Medium, spreading
DISEASE RESISTANCE: Good
ARS RATING: 7.6
COMMENTS: A great garden plant. Medium-size sprays of large, fragrant white flowers are carried on somewhat spreading bushes.

Brass Band

BLOOM SIZE, TYPE: Medium, informal
FRAGRANCE: Light
GROWTH HABIT: Medium, upright
DISEASE RESISTANCE: Good
AWARDS: AARS 1995
ARS RATING: 7.9
COMMENTS: A real eye-catcher! Distinctive blooms of orange and yellow grow in medium-size sprays on strong, upright plants.

Burgundy Iceberg

BLOOM SIZE, TYPE: Medium, informal
FRAGRANCE: Light
GROWTH HABIT: Tall, spreading
DISEASE RESISTANCE: Fair
AWARDS: GM Australia
ARS RATING: 7.6
COMMENTS: Tall, somewhat gangly plants have deep-purple, low-petal-count blooms that form in large, loose sprays. It's a color sport of Brilliant Pink Iceberg, which is a sport of Pink Iceberg.

Cathedral

BLOOM SIZE, TYPE: Large, classic
FRAGRANCE: Light
GROWTH HABIT: Medium, bushy
DISEASE RESISTANCE: Good
AWARDS: AARS 1976; GM New Zealand
ARS RATING: 7.8
COMMENTS: Originally named Coventry Cathedral for the church destroyed in WWII, this variety has large yellow-orange blooms with hints of pink. Plants bear small, well-formed clusters of flowers.

Cherish

BLOOM SIZE, TYPE: Medium, classic
FRAGRANCE: Light
GROWTH HABIT: Tall, upright
DISEASE RESISTANCE: Good
AWARDS: AARS 1980
ARS RATING: 7.6
COMMENTS: Soft medium-pink blooms with classic form are borne both as singles and in small sprays on upright plants.

Chihuly

BLOOM SIZE, TYPE: Large, informal
FRAGRANCE: Light
GROWTH HABIT: Medium, bushy
DISEASE RESISTANCE: Good
ARS RATING: 7.5
COMMENTS: Named after the renowned glass artist Dale Chihuly, these large blooms are an eye-catching mix of reds and yellows, forming in medium-size sprays.

City of London

BLOOM SIZE, TYPE: Medium, semidouble
FRAGRANCE: Heavy
GROWTH HABIT: Tall, spreading
DISEASE RESISTANCE: Fair
AWARDS: GM Le Roeulx, Belfast, The Hague;
  FA The Hague
ARS RATING: 7.6
COMMENTS: Delicate pink blooms in large, well-arrayed sprays grace this award-winning rose. Long, floppy canes need pruning or support.

Class Act

BLOOM SIZE, TYPE: Large, informal
FRAGRANCE: Light
GROWTH HABIT: Medium, bushy
DISEASE RESISTANCE: Good
AWARDS: AARS 1989; GM New Zealand
ARS RATING: 7.8
COMMENTS: Strong plants with large white blooms that form in good size sprays offer great garden performance. Class Act does well in all areas of the country.

Day Breaker

BLOOM SIZE, TYPE: Medium, classic
FRAGRANCE: Medium
GROWTH HABIT: Medium, bushy
DISEASE RESISTANCE: Good
AWARDS: AARS 2004
ARS RATING: 7.9
COMMENTS: The perfect combination: fragrant, perfectly formed, classic blooms of yellow, amber, and pink form in large, well-arrayed sprays on this variety from England.

Dicky

BLOOM SIZE, TYPE: Medium, semidouble
FRAGRANCE: Light
GROWTH HABIT: Medium, spreading
DISEASE RESISTANCE: Fair
AWARDS: GM U.K.
ARS RATING: 8.3
COMMENTS: Beautiful salmon-pink blooms form in large clusters on this appealing variety. The canes are on the thin side and will need support in rainy areas.

Easy Going

BLOOM SIZE, TYPE: Large, informal
FRAGRANCE: Light
GROWTH HABIT: Medium, bushy
DISEASE RESISTANCE: Excellent
ARS RATING: 8.0
COMMENTS: This rose, a color sport of Livin' Easy, has the same attributes except for the yellow-amber bloom color. Large sprays of blooms are borne on very disease-resistant bushes.

Ebb Tide

BLOOM SIZE, TYPE: Medium, informal
FRAGRANCE: Heavy
GROWTH HABIT: Medium, upright
DISEASE RESISTANCE: Good
ARS RATING: 7.6
COMMENTS: Deep-purple, very fragrant flowers with good repeat bloom form in large sprays on medium-size plants.

Escapade

BLOOM SIZE, TYPE: Medium, semidouble
FRAGRANCE: Medium
GROWTH HABIT: Medium, bushy
DISEASE RESISTANCE: Good
AWARDS: GM Baden-Baden, Belfast
ARS RATING: 8.6
COMMENTS: Light silvery pink, fragrant blooms form in large, somewhat crowded sprays on strong, highly rated plants. A must for any garden.

Eureka

BLOOM SIZE, TYPE: Large, informal
FRAGRANCE: Light
GROWTH HABIT: Medium, bushy
DISEASE RESISTANCE: Good
AWARDS: AARS 2003
ARS RATING: 7.8
COMMENTS: This winner from Germany features sprays of large amber-yellow blooms and very glossy green foliage on medium-size plants.

Europeana

BLOOM SIZE, TYPE: Medium, informal
FRAGRANCE: Light
GROWTH HABIT: Medium, bushy
DISEASE RESISTANCE: Good
AWARDS: AARS 1968; GM The Hague
ARS RATING: 8.6
COMMENTS: One of the most widely grown floribundas, this variety performs well in all areas of the country. Its deep-red blooms grow in large sprays on strong, medium-size plants.

Eyepaint

BLOOM SIZE, TYPE: Small, single
FRAGRANCE: Light
GROWTH HABIT: Tall, spreading
DISEASE RESISTANCE: Excellent
AWARDS: Gold Medal Baden-Baden, Belfast
ARS RATING: 8.3
COMMENTS: More of a shrub than a floribunda, Eyepaint is a large, spreading plant that bears abundant single red blooms with white eyes and golden stamens. A stellar landscape rose.

Fabulous!

BLOOM SIZE, TYPE: Medium, informal
FRAGRANCE: Light
GROWTH HABIT: Medium, upright
DISEASE RESISTANCE: Good
AWARDS: GM Lyon
ARS RATING: 7.7
COMMENTS: Often called a white Sexy Rexy (one of its parents), this variety bears large, well-formed sprays of informal white blooms on upright, disease-resistant plants.

First Edition

BLOOM SIZE, TYPE: Small, classic
FRAGRANCE: Light
GROWTH HABIT: Medium, bushy
DISEASE RESISTANCE: Good
AWARDS: AARS 1977; GM Orleans
ARS RATING: 8.2
COMMENTS: Compact plants bear large clusters of small, classic blooms in shades of orange, amber, and pink.

First Kiss

BLOOM SIZE, TYPE: Medium, semidouble
FRAGRANCE: Light
GROWTH HABIT: Medium, bushy
DISEASE RESISTANCE: Good
ARS RATING: 8.2
COMMENTS: Very soft pink blooms are borne in large, somewhat crowded sprays on this popular variety. Plants have good disease resistance and quick repeat bloom.

Flirtatious

BLOOM SIZE, TYPE: Medium, informal
FRAGRANCE: Moderate
GROWTH HABIT: Medium, bushy
DISEASE RESISTANCE: Good
ARS RATING: 7.6
COMMENTS: Blooms start out light-yellow before fading to pale pink with yellow overtones as they age. They are borne in large sprays on bushy plants.

Fragrant Delight

BLOOM SIZE, TYPE: Medium, semidouble
FRAGRANCE: Heavy
GROWTH HABIT: Medium, spreading
DISEASE RESISTANCE: Excellent
AWARDS: FA U.K.
ARS RATING: 7.9
COMMENTS: These very fragrant flowers appear in an unusual shade of pink-amber in medium-size, somewhat irregular sprays. This highly disease-resistant variety should be more widely known and grown.

Francois Rabelais

BLOOM SIZE, TYPE: Medium, informal
FRAGRANCE: Light
GROWTH HABIT: Medium, spreading
DISEASE RESISTANCE: Good
ARS RATING: 7.5
COMMENTS: Large, vivid red old-fashioned blooms are the hallmark of this Romantica variety from Meilland of France. They are mildly fragrant and do well in warm weather.

French Lace

BLOOM SIZE, TYPE: Large, classic
FRAGRANCE: Medium
GROWTH HABIT: Medium, bushy
DISEASE RESISTANCE: Good
AWARDS: AARS 1982
ARS RATING: 8.1
COMMENTS: It's not quite a floribunda, not quite a hybrid tea. Fragrant creamy white, perfectly formed hybrid tea-type blooms form in small, crowded sprays on strong plants.

Gene Boerner

BLOOM SIZE, TYPE: Medium, classic
FRAGRANCE: Light
GROWTH HABIT: Medium, bushy
DISEASE RESISTANCE: Good
AWARDS: AARS 1969
ARS RATING: 8.3
COMMENTS: These compact plants, named for the longtime Jackson & Perkins hybridizer who popularized floribundas, bear loads of medium-pink blooms in large, well-formed sprays.

George Burns

BLOOM SIZE, TYPE: Medium, informal
FRAGRANCE: Medium
GROWTH HABIT: Short, bushy
DISEASE RESISTANCE: Good
ARS RATING: 7.7
COMMENTS: Get a real color blast from the red stripes on light-yellow blooms with deep-yellow eyes. This low-growing variety bears large blooms in small, irregular sprays.

Glad Tidings

BLOOM SIZE, TYPE: Medium, classic
FRAGRANCE: Light
GROWTH HABIT: Medium, bushy
DISEASE RESISTANCE: Good
AWARDS: GM Durbanville
ARS RATING: 8.1
COMMENTS: Tidy plants are good for landscape use. The medium-size, deep-red classic blooms form in well-arrayed sprays.

Golden Holstein

BLOOM SIZE, TYPE: Medium, semidouble
FRAGRANCE: Light
GROWTH HABIT: Medium, bushy
DISEASE RESISTANCE: Excellent
ARS RATING: 8.2
COMMENTS: Solid yellow blooms with gorgeous golden stamens characterize these strong, bushy plants. The sprays are large and somewhat irregular in size and shape.

Goldmarie

BLOOM SIZE, TYPE: Medium, informal
FRAGRANCE: Light
GROWTH HABIT: Short, bushy
DISEASE RESISTANCE: Good
AWARDS: GM The Hague
ARS RATING: 7.5
COMMENTS: Golden yellow blooms occasionally tinged with red grow in small sprays on disease-resistant, somewhat short plants.

Gruss an Aachen

BLOOM SIZE, TYPE: Medium, informal
FRAGRANCE: Light
GROWTH HABIT: Low, bushy
DISEASE RESISTANCE: Good
ARS RATING: 8.3
COMMENTS: This is the first floribunda, introduced in 1911. Short plants bear light, creamy-pink blooms in profusion. Nicely fragrant flowers have a heavily petaled, old-fashioned appearance.

Guy de Maupassant

BLOOM SIZE, TYPE: Medium, informal
FRAGRANCE: Heavy
GROWTH HABIT: Tall, bushy
DISEASE RESISTANCE: Good
ARS RATING: 7.7
COMMENTS: This very fragrant pink variety with many petals named after the 19th-century French writer bears medium-size sprays. It's one of the Meilland Romantica series.

H. C. Andersen
BLOOM SIZE, TYPE: Medium, informal
FRAGRANCE: Light
GROWTH HABIT: Medium, upright
DISEASE RESISTANCE: Good
ARS RATING: 8.0
COMMENTS: This tough, hardy variety from Denmark, named for storyteller Hans Christian Andersen, has deep red blooms in large but irregular sprays.

Hannah Gordon
BLOOM SIZE, TYPE: Large, informal
FRAGRANCE: Light
GROWTH HABIT: Tall, spreading
DISEASE RESISTANCE: Excellent
ARS RATING: 8.8
COMMENTS: The highest rated floribunda has large, light-pink blooms with deep cerise edges carried in large clusters on strong, thorny, spreading plants. It is sometimes sold as Nicole.

Honey Perfume
BLOOM SIZE, TYPE: Medium, classic
FRAGRANCE: Heavy
GROWTH HABIT: Medium, upright
DISEASE RESISTANCE: Good
AWARDS: AARS 2004
ARS RATING: 7.7
COMMENTS: Very fragrant amber-yellow blooms array themselves in small sprays. Tidy plants have good disease resistance.

Hot Cocoa
BLOOM SIZE, TYPE: Medium, informal
FRAGRANCE: Medium
GROWTH HABIT: Medium, spreading
DISEASE RESISTANCE: Excellent
AWARDS: AARS 2003; ARS Members' Choice 2007
ARS RATING: 7.9
COMMENTS: Intriguing, dusky red blooms are borne in medium-size clusters on very disease-resistant plants.

Iceberg

BLOOM SIZE, TYPE: Medium, semidouble
FRAGRANCE: Light
GROWTH HABIT: Tall, bushy
DISEASE RESISTANCE: Fair
AWARDS: GM U.K., Baden-Baden;
    WFRS Hall of Fame
ARS RATING: 8.7
COMMENTS: White semidouble blooms are borne
    in large, loose sprays on plants somewhat
    susceptible to blackspot.

International Herald Tribune

BLOOM SIZE, TYPE: Medium, semidouble
FRAGRANCE: Medium
GROWTH HABIT: Short, bushy
DISEASE RESISTANCE: Excellent
AWARDS: GM Geneva, Monza
ARS RATING: 7.9
COMMENTS: Masses of fragrant purple blooms
    with prominent gold stamens make this a winner
    in any garden. The relatively short and wide plants
    are ideal for low borders.

Irish Hope

BLOOM SIZE, TYPE: Large, informal
FRAGRANCE: Medium
GROWTH HABIT: Tall, bushy
DISEASE RESISTANCE: Excellent
ARS RATING: 7.7
COMMENTS: Medium to large, fragrant sprays
    of soft yellow, informal blooms grow on tall,
    slightly bushy plants.

Ivory Fashion

BLOOM SIZE, TYPE: Large, classic
FRAGRANCE: Medium
GROWTH HABIT: Medium, bushy
DISEASE RESISTANCE: Good
AWARDS: AARS 1959
ARS RATING: 8.3
COMMENTS: With a rating of 8.3 and an
    introduction more than 50 years ago, this rose
    must be good. Fragrant, large creamy white
    blooms are carried on rather short plants.

Johann Strauss

BLOOM SIZE, TYPE: Large, informal
FRAGRANCE: Light
GROWTH HABIT: Medium, bushy
DISEASE RESISTANCE: Good
ARS RATING: 7.8
COMMENTS: Soft pink blooms with yellow overtones grace this rose, named for the waltz composer, from Meilland of France. Lightly fragrant blooms are borne both singly and in small sprays.

Judy Garland

BLOOM SIZE, TYPE: Medium, classic
FRAGRANCE: Medium
GROWTH HABIT: Medium, bushy
DISEASE RESISTANCE: Good
ARS RATING: 7.6
COMMENTS: Judy Garland is an eye-catcher. Bright yellow flowers with orange to red petal edges have a light apple scent and are carried in small sprays on strong plants.

Julia Child

BLOOM SIZE, TYPE: Large, informal
FRAGRANCE: Light
GROWTH HABIT: Medium, bushy
DISEASE RESISTANCE: Excellent
AWARDS: AARS 2006; ARS Members' Choice 2009
ARS RATING: 8.1
COMMENTS: One of the most disease-resistant varieties to come from U.S. hybridizers in years. Julia Child bears large, solid yellow blooms that form in small sprays on medium-size plants.

Lavaglut

BLOOM SIZE, TYPE: Small, informal
FRAGRANCE: None
GROWTH HABIT: Medium, bushy
DISEASE RESISTANCE: Good
ARS RATING: 8.7
COMMENTS: Meet the top exhibition floribunda in the U.S. The name, German for "Lava Glow," aptly describes the small deep-red, pompon blooms that seem to last forever. Sprays are large and well formed on compact, medium-size plants.

Lime Sublime

BLOOM SIZE, TYPE: Medium, classic
FRAGRANCE: Light
GROWTH HABIT: Medium, bushy
DISEASE RESISTANCE: Good
ARS RATING: 7.6
COMMENTS: White with sublime shades of chartreuse, these classic blooms are borne in small sprays on tidy plants.

Little Darling

BLOOM SIZE, TYPE: Small, classic
FRAGRANCE: Light
GROWTH HABIT: Medium, spreading
DISEASE RESISTANCE: Good
ARS RATING: 8.2
COMMENTS: This variety, the parent of many miniatures, carries small classic pink blooms with yellow at the petal base and light pink on the edges. The blooms are borne in large sprays on large, vigorous plants that belie the name "little."

Livin' Easy

BLOOM SIZE, TYPE: Large, informal
FRAGRANCE: Light
GROWTH HABIT: Medium, bushy
DISEASE RESISTANCE: Excellent
AWARDS: AARS 1996; GM U.K.
ARS RATING: 8.1
COMMENTS: Extremely large sprays of orange blooms brushed with yellow grow on rugged, highly disease-resistant plants. This outstanding floribunda should be rated even higher.

Margaret Merril

BLOOM SIZE, TYPE: Large, classic
FRAGRANCE: Heavy
GROWTH HABIT: Tall, upright
DISEASE RESISTANCE: Good
AWARDS: GM Geneva, Monza, Rome, New Zealand; FA U.K., New Zealand, The Hague, Auckland
ARS RATING: 8.2
COMMENTS: Very fragrant white blooms are borne in medium-size sprays on tall, strong plants that hold up well.

Marina

BLOOM SIZE, TYPE: Medium, semidouble
FRAGRANCE: Medium
GROWTH HABIT: Medium, bushy
DISEASE RESISTANCE: Good
AWARDS: AARS 1981
ARS RATING: 7.5
COMMENTS: Bright, solid orange blooms with a yellow base have a nice fragrance and form in moderate-size sprays on bushy plants with dark, glossy foliage.

Marmalade Skies

BLOOM SIZE, TYPE: Medium, informal
FRAGRANCE: None
GROWTH HABIT: Medium, bushy
DISEASE RESISTANCE: Good
AWARDS: AARS 2001
ARS RATING: 7.8
COMMENTS: Vivid orange blooms call immediate attention to this variety, originally introduced as Tangerine Dream. The large blooms are carried in small to medium sprays on strong plants.

Moondance

BLOOM SIZE, TYPE: Large, classic
FRAGRANCE: Light
GROWTH HABIT: Tall, upright
DISEASE RESISTANCE: Good
AWARDS: AARS 2007
ARS RATING: 7.8
COMMENTS: Large, well-arrayed sprays of pure white blooms with mild fragrance grace this variety. This is a good, high-quality white floribunda.

Nearly Wild

BLOOM SIZE, TYPE: Medium, single
FRAGRANCE: Light
GROWTH HABIT: Short, bushy
DISEASE RESISTANCE: Good
ARS RATING: 7.8
COMMENTS: This golden oldie from 1941 has single pink blooms that resemble Betty Prior, except these have a white eye. They are carried in large clusters on short plants.

Our Lady of Guadalupe

BLOOM SIZE, TYPE: Medium, informal
FRAGRANCE: Light
GROWTH HABIT: Short, bushy
DISEASE RESISTANCE: Good
ARS RATING: 8.0
COMMENTS: Soft pink blooms arrayed in large clusters open quickly and fade to a very pleasing light pink on rather short, bushy plants.

Paprika

BLOOM SIZE, TYPE: Medium, single
FRAGRANCE: Light
GROWTH HABIT: Short, bushy
DISEASE RESISTANCE: Good
AWARDS: GM U.K., The Hague
ARS RATING: 8.1
COMMENTS: Single-petal, brick red flowers with prominent golden stamens are carried on short, spreading bushes.

Passionate Kisses

BLOOM SIZE, TYPE: Medium, informal
FRAGRANCE: Light
GROWTH HABIT: Medium, bushy
DISEASE RESISTANCE: Good
AWARDS: GM Bagatelle, Dublin
ARS RATING: 8.2
COMMENTS: Medium-pink blooms with silver pink on the undersides are borne in large sprays. Plants grow to moderate height.

Playboy

BLOOM SIZE, TYPE: Medium, single
FRAGRANCE: Light
GROWTH HABIT: Medium, bushy
DISEASE RESISTANCE: Good
ARS RATING: 8.5
COMMENTS: Vivid red-and-yellow single blooms that never fail to attract the eye characterize this rose. Cut some of the medium-size, well-formed sprays for bouquets.

Playgirl

BLOOM SIZE, TYPE: Medium, single
FRAGRANCE: Light
GROWTH HABIT: Short, bushy
DISEASE RESISTANCE: Excellent
ARS RATING: 8.4
COMMENTS: The offspring of Playboy and Angel
Face, Playgirl has deep-pink single blooms that
grow in large clusters on rather short plants.

Pleasure

BLOOM SIZE, TYPE: Large, informal
FRAGRANCE: Light
GROWTH HABIT: Medium, bushy
DISEASE RESISTANCE: Good
AWARDS: AARS 1990
ARS RATING: 8.0
COMMENTS: Loads of large medium-pink blooms in
small sprays hold their color well. Bushes produce
well in all climates.

Preference

BLOOM SIZE, TYPE: Medium, semidouble
FRAGRANCE: Light
GROWTH HABIT: Medium, bushy
DISEASE RESISTANCE: Good
ARS RATING: 7.7
COMMENTS: A rose preferred by many gardeners,
Preference has velvety, scarlet red blooms that
open quickly to show beautiful stamens. Flowers
are borne on tidy, compact plants.

Pretty Lady

BLOOM SIZE, TYPE: Large, informal
FRAGRANCE: Medium
GROWTH HABIT: Medium, upright
DISEASE RESISTANCE: Excellent
ARS RATING: 8.2
COMMENTS: Bred in the U.K by amateur hybridizer
Len Scrivens, this rose bears huge sprays of off-
white blooms with creamy white centers. Plants
are upright with good repeat bloom.

Priscilla Burton

BLOOM SIZE, TYPE: Large, semidouble
FRAGRANCE: Medium
GROWTH HABIT: Medium, bushy
DISEASE RESISTANCE: Good
AWARDS: GM U.K.
ARS RATING: 8.3
COMMENTS: Rose breeder Sam McGredy calls this a "hand painted" floribunda. Each light pink flower has slightly different markings of pink to deep red, depending on the weather.

Rainbow Sorbet

BLOOM SIZE, TYPE: Medium, semidouble
FRAGRANCE: Light
GROWTH HABIT: Medium, upright
DISEASE RESISTANCE: Good
AWARDS: AARS 2006
ARS RATING: 8.0
COMMENTS: Sometimes described as Playboy with more petals, this rose has yellow blooms with cerise petal edges. The large flowers form in medium-size clusters.

Regensberg

BLOOM SIZE, TYPE: Medium, classic
FRAGRANCE: Medium
GROWTH HABIT: Short, bushy
DISEASE RESISTANCE: Excellent
AWARDS: GM Baden-Baden
ARS RATING: 7.9
COMMENTS: The flowers of this so-called hand painted floribunda—because the markings are variable from bloom to bloom—are deep pink with silvery white undersides.

Royal Occasion

BLOOM SIZE, TYPE: Medium, informal
FRAGRANCE: Light
GROWTH HABIT: Medium, bushy
DISEASE RESISTANCE: Good
ARS RATING: 8.5
COMMENTS: Solid-red blooms with distinctive black petal edges grow in medium-size, well-formed sprays. Sometimes sold as Montana.

Sarabande

BLOOM SIZE, TYPE: Medium, semidouble
FRAGRANCE: Light
GROWTH HABIT: Medium, bushy
DISEASE RESISTANCE: Good
AWARDS: AARS 1960; GM Bagatelle, Geneva, Rome
ARS RATING: 8.0
COMMENTS: Vivid orange-red blooms with golden stamens maintain the popularity of this 1957 variety. The blooms grow in large, irregular sprays with nice fragrance.

Scentimental

BLOOM SIZE, TYPE: Large, informal
FRAGRANCE: Heavy
GROWTH HABIT: Medium, bushy
DISEASE RESISTANCE: Good
AWARDS: AARS 1997
ARS RATING: 7.7
COMMENTS: Large, very fragrant blooms are reminiscent of Old Garden Roses. Red-striped light pink blooms form in small, crowded sprays.

Sexy Rexy

BLOOM SIZE, TYPE: Medium, informal
FRAGRANCE: Light
GROWTH HABIT: Medium, upright
DISEASE RESISTANCE: Good
AWARDS: GM New Zealand, Orleans, Glasgow, Auckland
ARS RATING: 8.7
COMMENTS: Sexy Rexy bears large, perfectly formed sprays of light pink blooms. This floribunda is a must for any rose garden.

Sheila's Perfume

BLOOM SIZE, TYPE: Large, classic
FRAGRANCE: Heavy
GROWTH HABIT: Tall, upright
DISEASE RESISTANCE: Excellent
AWARDS: FA U.K., Glasgow
ARS RATING: 8.2
COMMENTS: This British import has large, classic yellow blooms with pink petal edges that resemble both hybrid teas and floribundas. Exceptionally fragrant, they're borne singly and in sprays.

Showbiz

BLOOM SIZE, TYPE: Medium, informal
FRAGRANCE: Light
GROWTH HABIT: Short, spreading
DISEASE RESISTANCE: Good
AWARDS: AARS 1985
ARS RATING: 8.3
COMMENTS: Loads of informal medium-red blossoms grow in large sprays on short, angular plants.

Simplicity

BLOOM SIZE, TYPE: Medium, semidouble
FRAGRANCE: Light
GROWTH HABIT: Medium, upright
DISEASE RESISTANCE: Good
AWARDS: GM New Zealand
ARS RATING: 7.6
COMMENTS: This upright, nearly thornless plant with small sprays of pink blooms is touted as a hedge plant but may not be the best choice. In many areas, it flowers well into fall.

Singin' in the Rain

BLOOM SIZE, TYPE: Small, classic
FRAGRANCE: Medium
GROWTH HABIT: Medium, bushy
DISEASE RESISTANCE: Good
AWARDS: AARS 1995; GM U.K.
ARS RATING: 7.7
COMMENTS: Small hybrid tea type blooms of buff-amber are attractive when fresh but do not age well. Plants bloom profusely.

Summer Fashion

BLOOM SIZE, TYPE: Large, classic
FRAGRANCE: Medium
GROWTH HABIT: Medium, upright
DISEASE RESISTANCE: Good
ARS RATING: 7.8
COMMENTS: Large, fragrant blooms—hybrid tea look-alikes—are carried in small sprays on strong plants. Yellow centers with pink petal edges remind admirers of the well-known Peace.

Sun Flare

BLOOM SIZE, TYPE: Medium, informal
FRAGRANCE: Light
GROWTH HABIT: Medium, bushy
DISEASE RESISTANCE: Excellent
AWARDS: AARS 1983; GM Japan
ARS RATING: 7.8
COMMENTS: Ruffled blooms of medium-yellow are carried in large sprays on this productive variety. The plant is very disease resistant and quite manageable in size.

Sunsprite

BLOOM SIZE, TYPE: Large, informal
FRAGRANCE: Heavy
GROWTH HABIT: Medium, bushy
DISEASE RESISTANCE: Excellent
AWARDS: GM Baden-Baden; FA U.K.
ARS RATING: 8.5
COMMENTS: A classic. Large, very fragrant, deep yellow blooms form medium-size, somewhat crowded sprays on strong plants that repeat bloom quickly.

Sweet Inspiration

BLOOM SIZE, TYPE: Large, semidouble
FRAGRANCE: Light
GROWTH HABIT: Medium, bushy
DISEASE RESISTANCE: Good
AWARDS: AARS 1993
ARS RATING: 7.7
COMMENTS: Soft medium-pink blooms with yellow at the petal base are borne in good-size sprays. Large flowers open to display gorgeous stamens.

Topsy Turvy

BLOOM SIZE, TYPE: Medium, semidouble
FRAGRANCE: Light
GROWTH HABIT: Short, bushy
DISEASE RESISTANCE: Good
ARS RATING: 7.6
COMMENTS: The blooms, scarlet red with a white underside, have an unusual habit of twisting sideways as they age, providing the name. Topsy Turvy makes a very decorative garden plant.

Trumpeter

BLOOM SIZE, TYPE: Medium, informal
FRAGRANCE: Light
GROWTH HABIT: Short, bushy
DISEASE RESISTANCE: Good
AWARDS: GM New Zealand
ARS RATING: 8.2
COMMENTS: Fiery orange-red blooms in large clusters grab the eye from a distance on Trumpeter, named to honor Louis Armstrong. Short plants have a heavy bloom and good repeat habit.

Tuscan Sun

BLOOM SIZE, TYPE: Medium, classic
FRAGRANCE: Light
GROWTH HABIT: Medium, upright
DISEASE RESISTANCE: Good
ARS RATING: 7.8
COMMENTS: Warm amber blooms blended with shades of orange, yellow, and pink make Tuscan Sun a stunner. The classic blooms form in good-size sprays.

Victorian Spice

BLOOM SIZE, TYPE: Medium, informal
FRAGRANCE: Heavy
GROWTH HABIT: Tall, bushy
DISEASE RESISTANCE: Good
AWARDS: Fragrance Award Paris, U.K., Glasgow
ARS RATING: 7.5
COMMENTS: Originally named L'Aimant for the Coty perfume, the blooms of this fragrant variety range from light pink to salmon pink, depending on the weather. They are borne in irregular sprays.

White Simplicity

BLOOM SIZE, TYPE: Medium, semidouble
FRAGRANCE: Light
GROWTH HABIT: Medium, upright
DISEASE RESISTANCE: Good
ARS RATING: 7.8
COMMENTS: An offspring rather than a sport of the original pink Simplicity, White Simplicity is rated even higher. Creamy white blooms show soft yellow centers.

Polyanthas

Polyanthas (Greek for "many petals") are typically short, bushy, extremely floriferous roses that are ideal for use in low borders, mass plantings, or container gardens. Their blooms may be single, semidouble, or double, and they have a wide range of colors.

The first polyanthas were bred in the 1870s, predating floribundas by nearly 40 years. Although there have been few new polyanthas in recent years, there are still plenty of good older varieties on the market.

An interesting characteristic of this family is its tendency to produce genetic mutations, called sports. More polyanthas have been created from sports than have roses in any other family.

Sports can be color mutations of the blooms (all other characteristics remain the same) or climbing mutations that produce long canes.

Many of the bush polyanthas have climbing forms. These large, mounding plants covered with blooms are ideal for many landscape uses, such as hedges, covering small trellises, or filling blank spaces in the garden.

The three top-rated polyanthas—Marie Pavie, Orange Morsdag (Morsdag means "Mother's Day" in Dutch), and Mrs. R. M. Finch—all have climbing sports. Orange Morsdag itself is a sport.

Five of the 21 Earth-Kind roses are polyanthas: La Marne, Mlle Cécile Brünner, Marie Daly, Perle d'Or, and The Fairy. That's a good indication of their garden value, since the designation is given only to roses with superior disease tolerance and outstanding landscape performance.

They may be oldies, but polyanthas are definitely goodies.

BLOOM SIZE
LARGE: More than 4 inches wide
MEDIUM: 2 to 4 inches wide
SMALL: Less than 2 inches wide

PLANT SIZE
TALL: More than 4 feet tall
MEDIUM: 2 to 4 feet tall
SHORT: Shorter than 2 feet tall

China Doll
BLOOM, SIZE, TYPE: Small, double
FRAGRANCE: Light
PLANT SIZE, HABIT: Short, bushy
DISEASE RESISTANCE: Good
ARS RATING: 8.1
COMMENTS: Soft porcelain pink blooms with yellow at their bases borne in large trusses grace this variety from 1946. The plant is very disease resistant, growing 1 to 2 feet tall. The canes of the climbing version reach up to 6 feet.

La Marne
BLOOM SIZE, TYPE: Medium, single
FRAGRANCE: Light
PLANT SIZE, HABIT: Tall, bushy
DISEASE RESISTANCE: Excellent
ARS RATING: 8.7
COMMENTS: Blush white single blooms with deep pink petal edges make this a popular variety. The blooms are carried in large, loose clusters on 6-foot plants, tall for a polyantha. La Marne is an Earth-Kind selection.

Mlle Cécile Brünner

BLOOM SIZE, TYPE: Medium, double
FRAGRANCE: Light
PLANT SIZE, HABIT: Medium, bushy
DISEASE RESISTANCE: Excellent
AWARDS: WFRS Old Rose Hall of Fame
ARS RATING: 8.4
COMMENTS: Often called Cécile Brünner, this rose dates from 1880. Light-pink blooms with yellow undertones are lightly fragrant, carried in large clusters. It's an Earth-Kind selection.

Marie Pavié

BLOOM SIZE, TYPE: Small, double
FRAGRANCE: Medium
PLANT SIZE, HABIT: Medium, bushy
DISEASE RESISTANCE: Good
ARS RATING: 8.9
COMMENTS: The bush form of this rose reaches 4 feet tall by 2 feet wide but its climbing sport grows much larger. Fragrant, white, pompon blooms with pink centers are borne in medium-size trusses.

Perle d'Or

BLOOM SIZE, TYPE: Small, double
FRAGRANCE: Heavy
PLANT SIZE, HABIT: Tall, bushy
DISEASE RESISTANCE: Excellent
ARS RATING: 8.5
COMMENTS: Very fragrant apricot peach blooms are carried in large clusters on nearly thornless plants reaching about 6 feet. The name is French for "gold pearl." A climbing version is available. It's an Earth-Kind selection.

The Fairy

BLOOM SIZE, TYPE: Medium, spreading
FRAGRANCE: Light
PLANT SIZE, HABIT: Small, double
DISEASE RESISTANCE: Good
ARS RATING: 8.7
COMMENTS: An Earth-Kind selection, The Fairy is one of the most popular roses in the world. Its small pompon blooms are clear pink, fading to near white. Spreading plants bear glossy green foliage. The climbing sport reaches 12 feet.

Shrubs

Shrubs are the largest and most diverse family in the rose world. The plants can range from short near-miniatures to tall and wide specimens. The blooms range from singles to the very double varieties with more than 40 petals. Gardeners should be particularly aware of the plant's size and habit before purchasing any shrub rose.

Many shrub roses have been labeled by their family or breeder so gardeners can easily recognize them.

Where appropriate, the gallery lists whether the rose belongs to one of the best known and most loved types: hybrid musk (plants 6 feet and taller with very good disease resistance); hybrid rugosa (bushes 5 to 7 feet tall with very good disease resistance); hybrid kordesii (large plants with blooms in shades of red and pink); Buck (hardy, medium-size shrubs); Austin (mostly very fragrant, very double blooms); Easy Elegance (bred for hardiness and disease resistance on their own roots); Earth-Kind (water-wise selections made by the Texas AgriLife Extension Service); and Knock Out (hardy, very disease resistant, short to medium size.)

You'll find little difference between large shrubs and climbers. Both need support and training to perform their best. Looking for a rose that will grow in the shade? Most large shrub varieties tolerate partial shade.

Many shrubs offer excellent disease resistance, so they require fewer chemical or organic controls. The petal counts and plant sizes of every shrub variety may vary depending upon climate.

BLOOM FORM

SINGLE: 5 to 8 petals
SEMIDOUBLE: 10 to 20 petals
DOUBLE: 20 to 40 petals
VERY DOUBLE: More than 40 petals

PLANT SIZE

SHORT: Up to 4 feet tall
MEDIUM: 4 to 7 feet tall
TALL: More than 7 feet tall

Abraham Darby

TYPE: Austin
BLOOM SIZE, TYPE: Large, very double
FRAGRANCE: Heavy
PLANT SIZE, HABIT: Tall, spreading
DISEASE RESISTANCE: Good
ARS RATING: 8.0
COMMENTS: Abraham Darby is arguably the best of the Austin roses. The large, fragrant blooms grow in small sprays in shades of pink, salmon, and amber. If you have room for it, get it!

Armada

BLOOM SIZE, TYPE: Small, double
FRAGRANCE: Light
PLANT SIZE, HABIT: Medium, spreading
DISEASE RESISTANCE: Excellent
ARS RATING: 8.4
COMMENTS: Extra-large sprays of pink blooms grow on extremely disease-resistant plants. The canes grow 6 to 7 feet long; add support to keep the heavy blooms from flopping over.

Ballerina

TYPE: Hybrid musk
BLOOM SIZE, TYPE: Small, single
FRAGRANCE: Light
PLANT SIZE, HABIT: Medium, spreading
DISEASE RESISTANCE: Excellent
ARS RATING: 8.7
COMMENTS: At peak bloom, huge sprays of small light-pink blooms cover the plant. The bush holds itself up well and can be maintained in a 5 x 5-foot space. A superb landscape rose.

Belinda's Dream

TYPE: Earth-Kind
BLOOM SIZE, TYPE: Medium, very double
FRAGRANCE: Medium
PLANT SIZE, HABIT: Medium, spreading
DISEASE RESISTANCE: Excellent
ARS RATING: 8.5
COMMENTS: Belinda's Dream, an Earth-Kind selection, needs warm weather to perform well. The pink blooms with many petals are borne in profusion on arching plants.

Belle Story

TYPE: Austin
BLOOM SIZE, TYPE: Large, double
FRAGRANCE: Medium
PLANT SIZE, HABIT: Medium, bushy
DISEASE RESISTANCE: Good
ARS RATING: 8.6
COMMENTS: Clear pink blooms with about 35 petals open to show amber centers and golden stamens. The name honors the first woman to serve as a nursing sister in Britain's Royal Navy in 1864.

Blanc Double de Coubert

TYPE: Hybrid rugosa
BLOOM SIZE, TYPE: Medium, semidouble
FRAGRANCE: Heavy
PLANT SIZE, HABIT: Medium, upright
DISEASE RESISTANCE: Excellent
ARS RATING: 8.3
COMMENTS: The French name means "Coubert's Double White." Strong upright plants bear very fragrant blooms. Deadhead for repeat bloom, as the hips form quickly.

Bonica

BLOOM SIZE, TYPE: Small, double
FRAGRANCE: None
PLANT SIZE, HABIT: Medium, spreading
DISEASE RESISTANCE: Good
AWARDS: AARS 1987; WFRS Hall of Fame
ARS RATING: 8.4
COMMENTS: Bonica bears large trusses of small, light to deep pink blooms. The plant is strong with a spreading habit so may need support.

Buff Beauty

TYPE: Hybrid musk
BLOOM SIZE, TYPE: Medium, informal
FRAGRANCE: Medium
PLANT SIZE, HABIT: Medium to tall, spreading
DISEASE RESISTANCE: Good
ARS RATING: 8.2
COMMENTS: Medium, fragrant buff or apricot pompon blooms are carried in small clusters on tall, wide plants.

Carefree Beauty

TYPE: Buck
BLOOM SIZE, TYPE: Large, semidouble
FRAGRANCE: Heavy
PLANT SIZE, HABIT: Medium, upright
DISEASE RESISTANCE: Excellent
ARS RATING: 8.6
COMMENTS: Carefree Beauty is the most widely grown Buck rose. Fragrant, pink blooms open to show their stamens. This hardy variety is an Earth-Kind selection.

Champlain

TYPE: Hybrid kordesii
BLOOM SIZE, TYPE: Medium, semidouble
FRAGRANCE: Light
PLANT SIZE, HABIT: Short, bushy
DISEASE RESISTANCE: Good
ARS RATING: 8.5
COMMENTS: Champlain, part of the Explorer series, can be kept to a size of 4 feet wide and tall. The semidouble red blooms are borne in small sprays. It's a tidy plant that performs well in cold areas.

Cherries 'n' Cream

BLOOM SIZE, TYPE: Medium, semidouble
FRAGRANCE: Medium
PLANT SIZE, HABIT: Medium, bushy
DISEASE RESISTANCE: Good
ARS RATING: 7.8
COMMENTS: Grow this rose for its clove-scented blooms, which are deep cerise pink with a white underside and touches of white around the petals' edges. They're produced in small sprays.

Cocktail

BLOOM SIZE, TYPE: Small, single
FRAGRANCE: Light
PLANT SIZE, HABIT: Tall, bushy
DISEASE RESISTANCE: Good
ARS RATING: 8.4
COMMENTS: Solid red single blooms with large yellow eyes are borne in loose clusters on this French import from 1957. Use Cocktail as a moderate-size shrub or train it as a small climber.

Cornelia

TYPE: Hybrid musk
BLOOM SIZE, TYPE: Medium, double
FRAGRANCE: Medium
PLANT SIZE, HABIT: Medium tall, bushy
DISEASE RESISTANCE: Good
ARS RATING: 8.7
COMMENTS: Deep-pink blooms with yellow shadings fade to light pink on this highly rated rose. Small pompon flowers are produced in large, irregular trusses on large, bushy plants.

Countess Celeste

BLOOM SIZE, TYPE: Medium, very double
FRAGRANCE: Medium
PLANT SIZE, HABIT: Short, bushy
DISEASE RESISTANCE: Excellent
ARS RATING: 7.9
COMMENTS: This low-growing plant from Poulsen's of Denmark could well be considered a floribunda. The very double coral-pink blooms grow in small clusters on bushes that remain shorter than 3 feet.

Country Dancer

TYPE: Buck
BLOOM SIZE, TYPE: Large, semidouble
FRAGRANCE: Medium
PLANT SIZE, HABIT: Medium, bushy
DISEASE RESISTANCE: Good
ARS RATING: 8.6
COMMENTS: Like most Buck roses, Country Dancer is a hardy, medium-size plant with very good disease resistance. The fragrant, large deep-pink blooms are carried in small clusters and singly.

Dortmund

TYPE: Hybrid kordesii
BLOOM SIZE, TYPE: Medium, single
FRAGRANCE: None
PLANT SIZE, HABIT: Tall, spreading
DISEASE RESISTANCE: Excellent
ARS RATING: 9.1
COMMENTS: The American Rose Society's highest rated shrub, this disease-free plant is covered with single red blossoms with white eyes and golden stamens. Support the 12-foot-long canes so the blooms cascade outward in a glorious display.

Double Knock Out

TYPE: Knock Out
BLOOM SIZE, TYPE: Medium, double
FRAGRANCE: Light
PLANT SIZE, HABIT: Short, bushy
DISEASE RESISTANCE: Excellent
ARS RATING: 8.2
COMMENTS: From the same cross that produced the original Knock Out, this variety has the same great disease resistance. The cherry red blooms, carried in clusters, have a classic rose form.

Felicia

TYPE: Hybrid musk
BLOOM SIZE, TYPE: Small, informal
FRAGRANCE: Heavy
PLANT SIZE, HABIT: Tall, bushy
DISEASE RESISTANCE: Excellent
ARS RATING: 8.5
COMMENTS: This hybrid musk bears a strong resemblance to its sister, Cornelia. The plant is larger and the light-pink blooms much more fragrant, growing in tight clusters of up to a dozen.

Flower Carpet

BLOOM SIZE, TYPE: Small, semidouble
FRAGRANCE: Light
PLANT SIZE, HABIT: Short, bushy
DISEASE RESISTANCE: Excellent
ARS RATING: 7.6
COMMENTS: The first in a family of low-growing plants, this disease-resistant variety has deep-pink blooms in small clusters. The plant grows about 2 to 3 feet tall and more than 3 feet wide.

Flower Girl

BLOOM SIZE, TYPE: Small, single
FRAGRANCE: Light
PLANT SIZE, HABIT: Medium, spreading
DISEASE RESISTANCE: Good
ARS RATING: 8.2
COMMENTS: Small, light-pink blooms that fade to white are borne in large clusters. With a size of 5 feet tall by 4 feet wide, this very floriferous shrub fits most any landscape.

Flutterbye

BLOOM SIZE, TYPE: Medium, single
FRAGRANCE: Medium
PLANT SIZE, HABIT: Tall, spreading
DISEASE RESISTANCE: Good
ARS RATING: 7.7
COMMENTS: Small single yellow flowers with shades of coral, orange, tangerine, and pink seem to dance in the sun like exotic butterflies. Spicy scented blooms are carried in large, somewhat irregular clusters.

Fred Loads

BLOOM SIZE, TYPE: Medium, single
FRAGRANCE: Light
PLANT SIZE, HABIT: Tall, upright
DISEASE RESISTANCE: Good
AWARDS: GM U.K.
ARS RATING: 8.5
COMMENTS: Brilliant orange blooms in large sprays, very sturdy canes, and a comparatively upright growth habit with canes about 10 feet long characterize this award winner.

Funny Face

TYPE: Easy Elegance
BLOOM SIZE, TYPE: Large, semidouble
FRAGRANCE: Light
PLANT SIZE, HABIT: Short, upright
DISEASE RESISTANCE: Good
ARS RATING: 7.7
COMMENTS: Small plants bear distinctive blooms of deep pink with white edges and yellow eyes. Part of the Easy Elegance series, Funny Face grows on its own root and deserves a wider audience.

Gartendirektor Otto Linne

BLOOM SIZE, TYPE: Small, double
FRAGRANCE: Light
PLANT SIZE, HABIT: Medium, spreading
DISEASE RESISTANCE: Excellent
ARS RATING: 8.8
COMMENTS: Large clusters of medium-pink blooms make this a very popular and highly rated variety. Introduced in 1934 and named for the first garden director in Hamburg, Germany, it is still going strong.

Golden Wings

BLOOM SIZE, TYPE: Large, single
FRAGRANCE: None
PLANT SIZE, HABIT: Medium, bushy
DISEASE RESISTANCE: Excellent
ARS RATING: 8.8
COMMENTS: The large light yellow single blooms with orange-red stamens dazzle in the light. Blooms form in sprays of three to five on strong, angular plants that grow about 5 feet tall and wide.

Grace

FAMILY: Austin
BLOOM SIZE, TYPE: Large, very double
FRAGRANCE: Heavy
PLANT SIZE, HABIT: Medium, spreading
DISEASE RESISTANCE: Excellent
ARS RATING: 8.0
COMMENTS: Plants grow about 4 feet tall and wide, with small sprays of fragrant warm buff-apricot blooms that fade to light yellow. Though Grace is not as well-known as many of Austin's yellow roses, it should be.

Graham Thomas

FAMILY: Austin
BLOOM SIZE, TYPE: Large, double
FRAGRANCE: Medium
PLANT SIZE, HABIT: Tall, spreading
DISEASE RESISTANCE: Good
AWARDS: WRS Hall of Fame 2009
ARS RATING: 8.2
COMMENTS: Named for the United Kingdom's preeminent rosarian, Graham Thomas boasts fragrant deep-yellow blooms growing in clusters on plants that can reach more than 12 feet tall.

Greetings

BLOOM SIZE, TYPE: Small, semidouble
FRAGRANCE: Light
PLANT SIZE, HABIT: Medium, upright
DISEASE RESISTANCE: Excellent
AWARDS: GM U.K.
ARS RATING: 8.1
COMMENTS: Greetings carries huge, crowded trusses of small red-purple blooms with white eyes. The plant is a heavy bloomer and a good repeater.

Heart 'n' Soul

BLOOM SIZE, TYPE: Medium, semidouble
FRAGRANCE: Light
PLANT SIZE, HABIT: Medium, bushy
DISEASE RESISTANCE: Good
ARS RATING: 7.7
COMMENTS: This French variety, with white blooms that have a wide and deep cerise edge, produces best in northern gardens. Flowers are borne in medium-size sprays on vigorous plants reaching about 5 feet tall.

Henry Hudson

TYPE: Hybrid rugosa
BLOOM SIZE, TYPE: Medium, semidouble
FRAGRANCE: Medium
PLANT SIZE, HABIT: Short, bushy
DISEASE RESISTANCE: Excellent
ARS RATING: 9.0
COMMENTS: A very hardy plant from Canada, this compact variety bears small sprays of large white blooms. Part of the Explorer Series, it's a great choice for super-cold gardens.

Heritage

TYPE: Austin
BLOOM SIZE, TYPE: Medium, double
FRAGRANCE: Heavy
PLANT SIZE, HABIT: Medium, spreading
DISEASE RESISTANCE: Good
ARS RATING: 8.4
COMMENTS: Very fragrant, medium-pink blooms in small sprays have a tendency to shatter quickly. The nearly thornless plant grows about 5 feet tall and 4 feet wide.

Home Run

BLOOM SIZE, TYPE: Medium, single
FRAGRANCE: None
PLANT SIZE, HABIT: Short, bushy
DISEASE RESISTANCE: Excellent
AWARDS: ARS Members' Choice 2010
ARS RATING: 8.1
COMMENTS: Knock Out is one parent of this low grower that has bright velvety red blooms with prominent yellow stamens produced in small sprays. Grow Home Run for disease resistance.

Hope for Humanity

BLOOM SIZE, TYPE: Small, semidouble
FRAGRANCE: Light
PLANT SIZE, HABIT: Tall, bushy
DISEASE RESISTANCE: Good
ARS RATING: 8.0
COMMENTS: Named to commemorate the 100th anniversary of the Canadian Red Cross, this very hardy plant, good for northern gardens, bears small clusters of deep-red, mildly fragrant flowers. It tolerates shade.

Jacqueline du Pré

BLOOM SIZE, TYPE: Large, semidouble
FRAGRANCE: Heavy
PLANT SIZE, HABIT: Medium, bushy
DISEASE RESISTANCE: Good
ARS RATING: 7.9
COMMENTS: Named for the late British cellist, this prolific-blooming variety carries very fragrant light-pink ruffled blooms with reddish pink stamens. Jacqueline du Pré grows about 5 feet tall and wide.

John Cabot

TYPE: Hybrid kordesii
BLOOM SIZE, TYPE: Large, semidouble
FRAGRANCE: Light
PLANT SIZE, HABIT: Medium, spreading
DISEASE RESISTANCE: Excellent
ARS RATING: 8.8
COMMENTS: Red blooms form in small clusters and open quickly to reveal their stamens despite the large number of petals. Massive plants grow about 10 feet wide and tall. John Cabot is a hardy member of the Explorer series.

John Davis

FAMILY: Hybrid kordesii
BLOOM SIZE, TYPE: Large, double
FRAGRANCE: Heavy
PLANT SIZE, HABIT: Medium, spreading
DISEASE RESISTANCE: Excellent
ARS RATING: 8.7
COMMENTS: If you're looking for a very fragrant, hardy shrub with medium-pink double blooms in large clusters, this is it. John Davis was an English explorer.

Kathleen

TYPE: Hybrid musk
BLOOM SIZE, TYPE: Small, single
FRAGRANCE: None
PLANT SIZE, HABIT: Tall, spreading
DISEASE RESISTANCE: Excellent
ARS RATING: 8.5
COMMENTS: One of the larger plants in the hybrid musk family, Kathleen grows canes that can reach 12 feet or longer, so it's best to support them on a structure. Small light-pink blooms are borne in very large sprays.

Knock Out

TYPE: Knock Out, Earth-Kind
BLOOM SIZE, TYPE: Medium, semidouble
FRAGRANCE: None
PLANT SIZE, HABIT: Medium, bushy
DISEASE RESISTANCE: Excellent
AWARDS: AARS 2000; ARS Members' Choice 2004
ARS RATING: 8.6
COMMENTS: Cerise red blooms grow in medium clusters on plants with unparalleled disease resistance. It's the top-selling rose in the world.

Lady Elsie May

BLOOM SIZE, TYPE: Medium, semidouble
FRAGRANCE: Light
PLANT SIZE, HABIT: Medium, bushy
DISEASE RESISTANCE: Excellent
AWARDS: AARS 2005
ARS RATING: 8.3
COMMENTS: Lady Elsie May, an import from Germany, grows orange-pink blooms borne in small clusters on compact plants.

Lavender Dream

BLOOM SIZE, TYPE: Small, semidouble
FRAGRANCE: Medium
PLANT SIZE, HABIT: Medium, bushy
DISEASE RESISTANCE: Good
ARS RATING: 8.3
COMMENTS: Light-pink blooms with lavender shadings adorn this variety from Holland. Blooms achieve better color in the shade. Plants grow about 6 feet wide and tall.

Leonard Dudley Braithwaite

TYPE: Austin
BLOOM SIZE, TYPE: Medium, very double
FRAGRANCE: Heavy
PLANT SIZE, HABIT: Tall, spreading
DISEASE RESISTANCE: Good
ARS RATING: 7.9
COMMENTS: With the largest and reddest blooms among the Austin roses, the rose named for David Austin's father-in-law is a glorious sight. Flowers often grow singly, making them ideal for cutting.

Linda Campbell

TYPE: Hybrid rugosa
BLOOM SIZE, TYPE: Medium, semidouble
FRAGRANCE: None
PLANT SIZE, HABIT: Tall, spreading
DISEASE RESISTANCE: Good
ARS RATING: 8.1
COMMENTS: Despite having a fragrant rugosa parent, this hardy rose has virtually no scent. The medium-red blooms are borne in tight sprays on canes that grow 6 feet or longer.

Lyda Rose

BLOOM SIZE, TYPE: Small, single
FRAGRANCE: Medium
PLANT SIZE, HABIT: Medium, bushy
DISEASE RESISTANCE: Excellent
ARS RATING: 8.9
COMMENTS: Beautiful small, white single blooms edged in lavender-pink cover medium to large bushes. The plant will tolerate shade but needs extra attention to keep it going.

Martha's Vineyard

BLOOM SIZE, TYPE: Small, semidouble
FRAGRANCE: Light
PLANT SIZE, HABIT: Short, bushy
DISEASE RESISTANCE: Good
ARS RATING: 8.3
COMMENTS: Profuse small bright-pink blooms cover this low-growing variety that grows about 4 feet wide and tall. Plants have good disease resistance and lend themselves well to low borders or mass plantings.

Mary Rose

TYPE: Austin
BLOOM SIZE, TYPE: Large, very double
FRAGRANCE: Medium
PLANT SIZE, HABIT: Medium, bushy
DISEASE RESISTANCE: Good
ARS RATING: 8.3
COMMENTS: Named after Henry VIII's warship that sank in the Battle of the Solent in 1545, this Austin rose has double, medium-pink blooms borne on medium-size plants. It will tolerate some shade.

Molineux

TYPE: Austin
BLOOM SIZE, TYPE: Large, very double
FRAGRANCE: Heavy
PLANT SIZE, HABIT: Medium, bushy
DISEASE RESISTANCE: Good
AWARDS: GM, FA U.K.
ARS RATING: 8.0
COMMENTS: Large deep-yellow, exceptionally fragrant blooms grow on this award-winning offspring of Graham Thomas.

Morden Blush
BLOOM SIZE, TYPE: Medium, double
FRAGRANCE: Light
PLANT SIZE, HABIT: Medium, bushy
DISEASE RESISTANCE: Good
ARS RATING: 8.0
COMMENTS: Morden Blush is one of the cold-hardy Parkland series roses bred at the Morden Research Station in Morden, Manitoba. It bears medium-pink double blooms that fade to light pink on the petal edges. Blooms are borne singly and in small sprays.

Morden Centennial
BLOOM SIZE, TYPE: Large, double
FRAGRANCE: Light
PLANT SIZE, HABIT: Medium, spreading
DISEASE RESISTANCE: Good
ARS RATING: 8.4
COMMENTS: This variety bears large hot pink blooms in small clusters and singly. Plants grow 6 feet tall and wide. A member of the Parkland series, this cold-hardy rose was bred at the Morden Research Station in Manitoba.

Oranges 'n' Lemons
BLOOM SIZE, TYPE: Medium, double
FRAGRANCE: Light
PLANT SIZE, HABIT: Medium, spreading
DISEASE RESISTANCE: Good
ARS RATING: 7.6
COMMENTS: Striking, distinctive orange blooms with yellow stripes form in crowded sprays. The plants bear long canes with clusters of flowers at the ends.

Outta the Blue
BLOOM SIZE, TYPE: Large, double
FRAGRANCE: Heavy
PLANT SIZE, HABIT: Medium, bushy
DISEASE RESISTANCE: Good
ARS RATING: 7.9
COMMENTS: Rich magenta blooms with yellow at their bases characterize this manageable plant that reaches about 5 feet tall and wide. Fragrant flowers form in small sprays.

Penelope

TYPE: Hybrid musk
BLOOM SIZE, TYPE: Medium, semidouble
FRAGRANCE: Heavy
PLANT SIZE, HABIT: Large, bushy
DISEASE RESISTANCE: Excellent
ARS RATING: 8.8
COMMENTS: As with most of the hybrid musks, this variety can grow in partial shade. The soft pink blooms show large clusters of stamens on moderately tall, bushy plants.

Pink Meidiland

BLOOM SIZE, TYPE: Small, single
FRAGRANCE: Light
PLANT SIZE, HABIT: Medium, bushy
DISEASE RESISTANCE: Good
ARS RATING: 8.6
COMMENTS: One of a series of prolific, disease-resistant shrubs from Meilland of France, this variety has single pink blooms with white eyes. They are borne in small sprays on bushes about 5 feet tall and wide.

Prairie Princess

TYPE: Buck
BLOOM SIZE, TYPE: Large, semidouble
FRAGRANCE: Light
PLANT SIZE, HABIT: Medium to tall, bushy
DISEASE RESISTANCE: Good
ARS RATING: 8.5
COMMENTS: Coral-pink blooms with prominent stamens adorn 6-foot-tall plants that in some areas grow equally wide. This very hardy rose from Iowa was used to breed Canadian roses.

Red Ribbons

BLOOM SIZE, TYPE: Small, semidouble
FRAGRANCE: None
PLANT SIZE, HABIT: Short, spreading
DISEASE RESISTANCE: Excellent
ARS RATING: 8.3
COMMENTS: A true groundcover rose, this German import has deep-red blooms with prominent stamens. Flowers form in small clusters on plants that grow about 2½ feet tall and 8 feet wide.

Robusta

BLOOM SIZE, TYPE: Large, single
FRAGRANCE: None
PLANT SIZE, HABIT: Tall, spreading
DISEASE RESISTANCE: Good
ARS RATING: 8.8
COMMENTS: Robust is an understatement for this variety. The plant grows 10 feet tall or higher, the sprays of single medium-red blooms are large, and the thorns are large and numerous. A heavy bloomer, it will create a sensation in any garden.

Sally Holmes

BLOOM SIZE, TYPE: Large, single
FRAGRANCE: Light
PLANT SIZE, HABIT: Tall, spreading
DISEASE RESISTANCE: Excellent
ARS RATING: 8.9
COMMENTS: This large, strong plant covers itself with huge sprays of large single blooms that start light pink and fade to white. The sprays are crowded unless they are continually disbudded, but their beauty is well worth the effort.

Sea Foam

TYPE: Earth-Kind
BLOOM SIZE, TYPE: Small, double
FRAGRANCE: Light
PLANT SIZE, HABIT: Medium, very spreading
DISEASE RESISTANCE: Excellent
ARS RATING: 8.2
COMMENTS: Sea Foam is a rampant, low-growing plant that can stretch to 12 feet and longer. It seldom grows taller than 2 feet. Covered with small white blooms, it's great for slopes or other problem areas in the landscape.

Sparrieshoop

BLOOM SIZE, TYPE: Large, single
FRAGRANCE: Medium
PLANT SIZE, HABIT: Tall, upright
DISEASE RESISTANCE: Good
ARS RATING: 8.2
COMMENTS: Named for a town in Germany, this tall plant has strong canes that hold themselves up well. Light-pink blooms with large, golden stamens form in medium to large clusters that are great for cutting.

Sunrise Sunset

TYPE: Easy Elegance
BLOOM SIZE, TYPE: Small, semidouble
FRAGRANCE: Light
PLANT SIZE, HABIT: Short, spreading
DISEASE RESISTANCE: Excellent
ARS RATING: 8.2
COMMENTS: Pink-blend blooms with yellow at their bases are borne on short, spreading, dense plants with great disease resistance, perfect for low borders. Colors change over time and vary with the temperature.

Westerland

BLOOM SIZE, TYPE: Large, double
FRAGRANCE: Heavy
PLANT SIZE, HABIT: Tall, spreading
DISEASE RESISTANCE: Good
ARS RATING: 8.2
COMMENTS: Beautiful, wonderfully fragrant golden apricot blooms are carried in medium to large clusters on plants that can reach 10 feet tall. The plant has good disease resistance and is a heavy bloomer if kept deadheaded.

White Meidiland

BLOOM SIZE, TYPE: Large, double
FRAGRANCE: Light
PLANT SIZE, HABIT: Medium, spreading
DISEASE RESISTANCE: Good
ARS RATING: 8.4
COMMENTS: Medium-size clusters of large white blooms are produced in great quantities on this medium-size plant.

William Baffin

TYPE: Hybrid kordesii
BLOOM SIZE, TYPE: Medium, semidouble
FRAGRANCE: Light
PLANT SIZE, HABIT: Large, bushy
DISEASE RESISTANCE: Excellent
ARS RATING: 8.9
COMMENTS: William Baffin, in the Canadian Explorer series, has deep-pink blooms with golden eyes that form in profusion. Hardy, disease-resistant plants reach 10 feet tall and 5 feet wide.

Once-Blooming Old Garden Roses

Please don't misunderstand Old Garden Roses. Many gardeners, and even rose growers, believe them all to be large, sprawling plants that only bloom once and are very disease prone. Such myths are persistent, but untrue.

It is true that some bloom only once. But they make up for that with a long bloom period of nearly two months, flower heavily, and are fairly disease resistant.

Hybrid gallicas are the exception to the general disease resistance of this rose family. They often show mildew on the new growth that forms after blooming is over.

Gardeners who don't have time to promptly deadhead roses appreciate once-blooming old roses. They don't need to be deadheaded as promptly because no amount of deadheading will promote more flowers.

Old Garden Roses include any variety that existed before 1867, when the first modern rose, a hybrid tea, was introduced, although new roses created from older varieties can still be considered "old."

The hundreds of Old Garden Roses today are the remainders of a family that once numbered into the thousands. They survived because of the hardiness of their plants, the beauty of their blooms, and perhaps most important, their heavenly fragrance.

The once-blooming Old Garden Roses profiled in this gallery—most rated higher than 8.0—still offer wonderful garden value today.

BLOOM TYPE
SINGLE: 5 to 8 petals
SEMIDOUBLE: 10 to 20 petals
DOUBLE: 20 to 45 petals
VERY DOUBLE: More than 45 petals

PLANT SIZE
SHORT: 3 feet tall and shorter
MEDIUM: 3 to 6 feet tall
TALL: More than 6 feet tall

Cabbage Rose
FAMILY: Centifolia
BLOOM SIZE, TYPE: Large, very double
FRAGRANCE: Heavy
PLANT SIZE, HABIT: Tall, spreading
DISEASE RESISTANCE: Good
ARS RATING: 8.3
COMMENTS: Large, very fragrant pink blooms packed with petals tend to nod and hang downward in an old-fashioned, romantic manner. The large plants need support.

Cardinal de Richelieu
FAMILY: Hybrid gallica
BLOOM SIZE, TYPE: Medium, very double
FRAGRANCE: Heavy
PLANT SIZE, HABIT: Medium, bushy
DISEASE RESISTANCE: Good
ARS RATING: 8.0
COMMENTS: Deep-purple blooms with outstanding fragrance form in medium-size sprays. This is a typical gallica: 3 to 5 feet tall with thin canes that sprawl if not supported.

Celestial

FAMILY: Alba
BLOOM SIZE, TYPE: Large, semidouble
FRAGRANCE: Heavy
PLANT SIZE, HABIT: Tall, spreading
DISEASE RESISTANCE: Excellent
ARS RATING: 8.5
COMMENTS: Light-pink blooms with prominent stamens are the hallmark of this variety. Like most albas, the bushy plants grow 6 to 8 feet tall.

Celsiana

FAMILY: Damask
BLOOM SIZE, TYPE: Large, semidouble
FRAGRANCE: Heavy
PLANT SIZE, HABIT: Medium, bushy
DISEASE RESISTANCE: Excellent
ARS RATING: 8.7
COMMENTS: Light-pink blooms with a strong fragrance make this one of the most popular damasks. Plants reach about 5 feet tall with thin canes that weigh down with the bloom.

Charles de Mills

FAMILY: Hybrid gallica
BLOOM SIZE, TYPE: Large, very double
FRAGRANCE: Heavy
PLANT SIZE, HABIT: Medium, bushy
DISEASE RESISTANCE: Good
ARS RATING: 8.4
COMMENTS: Large, deep-purple blooms that fade to a raspberry pink are borne profusely in small clusters on rather tall plants. This is one of the great hybrid gallica varieties.

Communis (Common Moss)

FAMILY: Moss
BLOOM SIZE, TYPE: Large, very double
FRAGRANCE: Heavy
PLANT SIZE, HABIT: Medium, bushy
DISEASE RESISTANCE: Good
ARS RATING: 8.3
COMMENTS: The moss family has the most varied plant habits of all the old roses. Communis reaches about 6 feet and carries pink blooms singly and in small clusters.

Complicata

FAMILY: Hybrid gallica
BLOOM SIZE, TYPE: Large, single
FRAGRANCE: Medium
PLANT SIZE, HABIT: Tall, spreading
DISEASE RESISTANCE: Good
ARS RATING: 8.8
COMMENTS: Pink blooms grown singly and in small sprays exhibit very pronounced stamens. Complicata is one of the few single-petal gallicas.

Crested Moss

FAMILY: Centifolia
BLOOM SIZE, TYPE: Large, double
FRAGRANCE: Heavy
PLANT SIZE, HABIT: Medium, bushy
DISEASE RESISTANCE: Good
ARS RATING: 8.7
COMMENTS: Though the name has "moss" in it, this is a centifolia, the family that spawned moss roses. Fragrant rosy pink blooms form in small clusters. As with Communis, it's also called Common Moss.

Fantin-Latour

FAMILY: Centifolia
BLOOM SIZE, TYPE: Large, double
FRAGRANCE: Medium
PLANT SIZE, HABIT: Medium, bushy
DISEASE RESISTANCE: Good
ARS RATING: 8.4
COMMENTS: Named for a French artist noted for his flower paintings, this rose bears warm pink blooms in medium-size clusters on vigorous, bushy plants up to 6 feet tall.

Félicité Parmentier

FAMILY: Alba
BLOOM SIZE, TYPE: Medium, very double
FRAGRANCE: Heavy
PLANT SIZE, HABIT: Medium, bushy
DISEASE RESISTANCE: Excellent
ARS RATING: 8.7
COMMENTS: A manageable size plant for an alba, this variety has soft pink, very double blooms that grow in small sprays.

Great Maiden's Blush

FAMILY: Alba
BLOOM SIZE, TYPE: Medium, double
FRAGRANCE: Heavy
PLANT SIZE, HABIT: Tall, bushy
DISEASE RESISTANCE: Excellent
ARS RATING: 8.1
COMMENTS: Up to a dozen white blooms with pink blush overtones form in large sprays. Bushes grow blue-green, very disease-resistant foliage.

Henri Martin

FAMILY: Moss
BLOOM SIZE, TYPE: Medium, semidouble
FRAGRANCE: Heavy
PLANT SIZE, HABIT: Medium, bushy
DISEASE RESISTANCE: Good
ARS RATING: 8.6
COMMENTS: Crimson-red blooms fade to deep pink on this lightly mossed variety. The flowers are borne in medium-size clusters on bushy, 6-foot-tall plants.

James Mason

FAMILY: Hybrid gallica
BLOOM SIZE, TYPE: Large, semidouble
FRAGRANCE: Medium
PLANT SIZE, HABIT: Tall, bushy
DISEASE RESISTANCE: Excellent
ARS RATING: 7.8
COMMENTS: A recent gallica introduced in 1982 and named for the British actor, this tall, rather sprawling plant bears large, deep-red blooms with very prominent golden stamens, singly or in small clusters.

Königin von Dänemark

FAMILY: Alba
BLOOM SIZE, TYPE: Medium, very double
FRAGRANCE: Heavy
PLANT SIZE, HABIT: Medium, bushy
DISEASE RESISTANCE: Excellent
ARS RATING: 8.6
COMMENTS: With the pinkest blooms of all the albas, the "Queen of Denmark" grows about 6 feet tall. Blooms have pale pink edges and are carried in small clusters.

La Ville de Bruxelles

FAMILY: Damask
BLOOM SIZE, TYPE: Medium, very double
FRAGRANCE: Heavy
PLANT SIZE, HABIT: Medium, bushy
DISEASE RESISTANCE: Excellent
ARS RATING: 8.5
COMMENTS: Salmon-pink flowers, heavily petaled and very fragrant, are borne in small sprays on disease-resistant plants up to 5 feet tall. Bruxelles is French for Brussels.

Léda

FAMILY: Damask
BLOOM SIZE, TYPE: Medium, double
FRAGRANCE: Medium
PLANT SIZE, HABIT: Short, bushy
DISEASE RESISTANCE: Good
ARS RATING: 8.3
COMMENTS: Sometimes called Painted Damask, this variety may rebloom, rare for a damask. White blooms with tinges of blush and crimson at the petals' edges grow on compact plants.

Mme Hardy

FAMILY: Damask
BLOOM SIZE, TYPE: Medium, very double
FRAGRANCE: Heavy
PLANT SIZE, HABIT: Tall, bushy
DISEASE RESISTANCE: Excellent
AWARDS: WFRS Old Rose Hall of Fame
ARS RATING: 8.9
COMMENTS: Pure white blooms with green button eyes are borne in medium-size sprays. Plants grow taller than 6 feet, so they welcome support. It's the premier damask.

Mme Plantier

FAMILY: Alba
BLOOM SIZE, TYPE: Medium, very double
FRAGRANCE: Heavy
PLANT SIZE, HABIT: Tall, spreading
DISEASE RESISTANCE: Good
ARS RATING: 8.8
COMMENTS: This alba has a centifolia habit, with long, arching canes up to 12 feet long. Creamy white blooms are borne in medium to large clusters on nearly thornless plants.

Mme Zöetmans

FAMILY: Damask
BLOOM SIZE, TYPE: Medium, very double
FRAGRANCE: Medium
PLANT SIZE, HABIT: Medium, bushy
DISEASE RESISTANCE: Excellent
ARS RATING: 8.7
COMMENTS: Often compared with Mme Hardy, this damask has smaller blooms that start light pink and fade to white. They grow singly and in small clusters on smaller plants about 5 feet tall.

Paul Ricault

FAMILY: Centifolia
BLOOM SIZE, TYPE: Large, double
FRAGRANCE: Heavy
PLANT SIZE, HABIT: Tall, spreading
DISEASE RESISTANCE: Good
ARS RATING: 7.6
COMMENTS: Deep-pink, intensely fragrant blooms with lots of petals are borne mostly singly on long-caned, arching plants. The flowers have an unusual, appealing, crepe-paper appearance.

Tuscany

FAMILY: Hybrid gallica
BLOOM SIZE, TYPE: Large, semidouble
FRAGRANCE: Heavy
PLANT SIZE, HABIT: Medium, bushy
DISEASE RESISTANCE: Good
ARS RATING: 8.5
COMMENTS: Velvety black-crimson blooms with stamens that leap out make this a very popular variety. Plants are typical of gallicas, with thin canes 4 to 5 feet long.

Veilchenblau

FAMILY: Hybrid multiflora
BLOOM SIZE, TYPE: Small, semidouble
FRAGRANCE: Medium
PLANT SIZE, HABIT: Tall, rambling
DISEASE RESISTANCE: Good
ARS RATING: 8.4
COMMENTS: The name means violet-blue in German. Consider it a rambler with canes 15 feet long. Large trusses of small violet blooms streaked with white grow on nearly thornless stems.

Reblooming Old Garden Roses

The world of roses underwent a major change in the early 19th century with the introduction of reblooming roses from China. Partially because of the country's moderate climate, French breeders were able to quickly cross and recross roses to develop hundreds of reblooming varieties, many bearing French names.

Crosbreeding led to a long list of reblooming families. Chinas, teas, and noisettes do particularly well in warm or hot weather and they're grown well and extensively in the southern United States. Bourbons, hybrid perpetuals, and portlands seem to do equally well in all parts of the country.

The reblooming habit of OGRs can't be compared with modern roses that repeat rapidly. These roses generally have an initial flush that's moderately heavy, followed by lighter, sporadic blooms for the rest of the growing season. To encourage a quicker rebloom, deadhead old flowers immediately.

Color behaves in interesting ways among reblooming Old Garden Roses. A hallmark of the noisette family is a palette of yellows: dark, light, creamy, orange, and more. Chinas have a delightful habit of blooms that deepen in color as they age.

Growth habits among these families vary wildly. The bourbons and noisettes can be considered small climbers and should either be supported or allowed to cascade. Hybrid perpetuals tend to grow tall on fairly sturdy plants. Teas, chinas, and portlands display a variety of growth habits.

BLOOM TYPE

SINGLE: 5 to 8 petals
SEMIDOUBLE: 10 to 20 petals
DOUBLE: 20 to 45 petals
VERY DOUBLE: More than 45 petals

PLANT SIZE

SHORT: Less than 3 feet tall
MEDIUM: 3 to 6 feet tall
TALL: More than 6 feet tall

Alister Stella Gray

FAMILY: Noisette
BLOOM SIZE, TYPE: Medium, double
FRAGRANCE: Medium
PLANT SIZE, HABIT: Tall, spreading
DISEASE RESISTANCE: Good
ARS RATING: 8.0
COMMENTS: Pale yellow flowers with amber centers borne in small clusters adorn the long (up to 15 feet) canes of this noisette.

Archduke Charles

FAMILY: China
BLOOM SIZE, TYPE: Medium, double
FRAGRANCE: Light
PLANT SIZE, HABIT: Medium to short, bushy
DISEASE RESISTANCE: Good
ARS RATING: 8.5
COMMENTS: The blooms start out rosy pink and turn crimson as they age. They are produced in small sprays on tidy plants that reach 5 to 6 feet tall in warm weather.

Autumn Damask

FAMILY: Damask
BLOOM SIZE, TYPE: Medium, double
FRAGRANCE: Medium
PLANT SIZE, HABIT: Medium, bushy
DISEASE RESISTANCE: Excellent
ARS RATING: 8.2
COMMENTS: Except for Léda, with its occasional late blossoms, this is the only reblooming damask. Warm pink blooms in small clusters grow on bushy plants with thin 5-foot canes.

Baronne Prévost

FAMILY: Hybrid perpetual
BLOOM SIZE, TYPE: Large, double
FRAGRANCE: Medium
PLANT SIZE, HABIT: Medium, upright
DISEASE RESISTANCE: Good
ARS RATING: 8.6
COMMENTS: Deep-pink blooms in small sprays adorn sturdy, productive plants with good rebloom. The flowers are carried in small sprays and have a moderate aroma.

Boule de Neige

FAMILY: Bourbon
BLOOM SIZE, TYPE: Medium, very double
FRAGRANCE: Medium
PLANT SIZE, HABIT: Tall, bushy
DISEASE RESISTANCE: Good
ARS RATING: 7.9
COMMENTS: The name, which means "snowball" in French, aptly describes the globular white blooms. They are moderately fragrant and borne in small sprays. Plants reach 6 to 10 feet.

Comte de Chambord

FAMILY: Portland
BLOOM SIZE, TYPE: Medium, very double
FRAGRANCE: Heavy
PLANT SIZE, HABIT: Medium, upright
DISEASE RESISTANCE: Good
ARS RATING: 8.3
COMMENTS: Perfect for the landscape, this variety grows very upright and no more than 2 to 3 feet wide. The very fragrant pink blooms grow in small sprays and repeat nicely.

Cramoisi Supérieur

FAMILY: China
BLOOM SIZE, TYPE: Small, double
FRAGRANCE: Medium
PLANT SIZE, HABIT: Medium, bushy
DISEASE RESISTANCE: Good
ARS RATING: 8.7
COMMENTS: Small crimson (*cramoisi* in French) blooms with a nice aroma grow in small to medium sprays. Medium-size, vigorous plants have a good repeat habit.

Duchesse de Brabant

FAMILY: Tea
BLOOM SIZE, TYPE: Large, double
FRAGRANCE: Heavy
PLANT SIZE, HABIT: Medium to tall, bushy
DISEASE RESISTANCE: Excellent
ARS RATING: 8.6
COMMENTS: A designated Earth-Kind variety, this rather tall tea rose has soft rosy pink blooms with yellow highlights borne in small sprays. Plants reach more than 8 feet tall in warm areas.

Gloire de Dijon

FAMILY: Climbing tea
BLOOM SIZE, TYPE: Large, very double
FRAGRANCE: Medium
PLANT SIZE, HABIT: Tall, spreading
DISEASE RESISTANCE: Good
AWARDS: WFRS Old Rose Hall of Fame
ARS RATING: 7.8
COMMENTS: Often wrongly sold as a noisette, this long-caned rose has buff pink blooms shaded with orange at the centers.

Jaune Desprez

FAMILY: Noisette
BLOOM SIZE, TYPE: Medium, double
FRAGRANCE: Medium
PLANT SIZE, HABIT: Tall, spreading
DISEASE RESISTANCE: Good
ARS RATING: 7.9
COMMENTS: Coppery yellow-pink blooms with a moderate fruity fragrance are borne in small sprays. This vigorous variety grows canes up to 20 feet long.

La Reine

FAMILY: Hybrid perpetual
BLOOM SIZE, TYPE: Large, very double
FRAGRANCE: Heavy
PLANT SIZE, HABIT: Moderate
DISEASE RESISTANCE: Good
ARS RATING: 8.0
COMMENTS: Large rosy pink blooms with good aroma grace "The Queen," an early member of the hybrid perpetual family from 1842. The bush is a manageable size of about 5 feet.

Louise Odier

FAMILY: Bourbon
BLOOM SIZE, TYPE: Medium, double
FRAGRANCE: Heavy
PLANT SIZE, HABIT: Tall, spreading
DISEASE RESISTANCE: Fair
ARS RATING: 8.4
COMMENTS: Think of this rose as a short climber that reaches 8 to 10 feet. Pink blooms are very fragrant, growing in small sprays. The bush is a heavy bloomer and a good repeater.

Mme Alfred Carrière

FAMILY: Noisette
BLOOM SIZE, TYPE: Medium, double
FRAGRANCE: Heavy
PLANT SIZE, HABIT: Tall, spreading
DISEASE RESISTANCE: Good
ARS RATING: 8.9
COMMENTS: A large climber-rambler for all intents, this light color noisette bears white blooms with hints of pink. Small sprays of blooms have a strong, fruity fragrance.

Mme Ernest Calvat

FAMILY: Bourbon
BLOOM SIZE, TYPE: Large, double
FRAGRANCE: Heavy
PLANT SIZE, HABIT: Medium-tall, spreading
DISEASE RESISTANCE: Good
ARS RATING: 8.1
COMMENTS: With canes to about 8 feet, this is rather short for a bourbon. The pink blooms are very fragrant and have a lighter shade on the outer petals. It's a good repeat bloomer.

Mme Isaac Pereire

FAMILY: Bourbon
BLOOM SIZE, TYPE: Large, very double
FRAGRANCE: Heavy
PLANT SIZE, HABIT: Medium tall, spreading
DISEASE RESISTANCE: Good
ARS RATING: 8.4
COMMENTS: Considered the most fragrant Old Garden Rose with intense raspberry aroma, its deep-pink blooms are cupped and quartered. Bushy plants grow to 8 feet and need support.

Mme Pierre Oger

FAMILY: Bourbon
BLOOM SIZE, TYPE: Very double
FRAGRANCE: Heavy
PLANT SIZE, HABIT: Large, spreading
DISEASE RESISTANCE: Good
ARS RATING: 8.0
COMMENTS: Very double, fragrant blooms have a rosy lilac underside and a pronounced globular form. This typical bourbon plant, about 8 feet tall, requires some disease protection.

Marchesa Boccella

FAMILY: Hybrid perpetual
BLOOM SIZE, TYPE: Large, very double
FRAGRANCE: Medium
PLANT SIZE, HABIT: Medium, upright
DISEASE RESISTANCE: Excellent
ARS RATING: 9.0
COMMENTS: The high rating for this rose is well deserved. Large pink blooms grow singly on stems that invite cutting. The 4-foot-tall upright plant has excellent disease resistance.

Marchioness of Lorne

FAMILY: Hybrid perpetual
BLOOM SIZE, TYPE: Large, double
FRAGRANCE: Heavy
PLANT SIZE, HABIT: Medium, upright
DISEASE RESISTANCE: Good
ARS RATING: 8.1
COMMENTS: Deep carmine-pink blooms with outstanding fragrance grow in small sprays on strong, upright plants with good repeat habits. It deserves a higher rating.

Mermaid

FAMILY: Hybrid bracteata
BLOOM SIZE, TYPE: Large, single
FRAGRANCE: Medium
PLANT SIZE, HABIT: Large, spreading
DISEASE RESISTANCE: Excellent
ARS RATING: 8.6
COMMENTS: This species hybrid grows with a
    rampant—20 foot—habit. The large blooms,
    borne mostly singly, are pale yellow with deep
    yellow centers and stamens.

Mrs B. R. Cant

FAMILY: Tea
BLOOM SIZE, TYPE: Large, double
FRAGRANCE: Medium
PLANT SIZE, HABIT: Tall, bushy
DISEASE RESISTANCE: Good
ARS RATING: 8.9
COMMENTS: A tea that grows more than 6 feet tall
    in warm areas, Mrs. B. R. Cant bears silvery pink
    blooms with buff undertones, borne singly and in
    small clusters.

Mutabilis

FAMILY: China
BLOOM SIZE, TYPE: Medium, single
FRAGRANCE: Light
PLANT SIZE, HABIT: Tall, bushy
DISEASE RESISTANCE: Excellent
ARS RATING: 8.9
COMMENTS: Single blooms start out buff
    yellow, darken to pink, and finally turn crimson,
    with all these colors appearing together on this
    large, spreading Earth-Kind selection.

Old Blush

FAMILY: China
BLOOM SIZE, TYPE: Medium, double
FRAGRANCE: Medium
PLANT SIZE, HABIT: Medium, bushy
DISEASE RESISTANCE: Good
AWARDS: Old Rose Hall of Fame
ARS RATING: 8.7
COMMENTS: Old Blush grows two-tone pink
    blooms in small clusters. Moderate-size plants
    can reach 6 feet in warm areas.

Reine des Violettes
FAMILY: Hybrid perpetual
BLOOM SIZE, TYPE: Large, very double
FRAGRANCE: Heavy
PLANT SIZE, HABIT: Tall, spreading
DISEASE RESISTANCE: Excellent
ARS RATING: 8.2
COMMENTS: Queen of the Violets has large purple blooms that are considered the bluest of all the old roses. The plant, which needs support, is tall and angular with relatively thin canes.

Rose de Rescht
FAMILY: Portland
BLOOM SIZE, TYPE: Medium, double
FRAGRANCE: Medium
PLANT SIZE, HABIT: Short, bushy
DISEASE RESISTANCE: Excellent
ARS RATING: 8.8
COMMENTS: Cerise-red pompon blooms grow singly or in small sprays on short, compact plants with very disease-resistant foliage. This is a perfect choice for a small garden or container.

Salet
FAMILY: Moss
BLOOM SIZE, TYPE: Large, double
FRAGRANCE: Medium
PLANT SIZE, HABIT: Medium, upright
DISEASE RESISTANCE: Good
ARS RATING: 8.2
COMMENTS: Salet has clear pink blooms with a lighter underside. They grow in small sprays with well-mossed sepals on plants that have a good rebloom habit.

Souvenir de la Malmaison
FAMILY: Bourbon
BLOOM SIZE, TYPE: Large, double
FRAGRANCE: Heavy
PLANT SIZE, HABIT: Short, bushy
DISEASE RESISTANCE: Excellent
AWARDS: Old Rose Hall of Fame
ARS RATING: 8.7
COMMENTS: Pale pink flowers with rosy centers are carried on plants that seldom grow taller than 3 feet. Very fragrant blooms are carried in small sprays.

Stanwell Perpetual

FAMILY: Hybrid spinosissima
BLOOM SIZE, TYPE: Medium, semidouble
FRAGRANCE: Heavy
PLANT SIZE, HABIT: Tall, very bushy
DISEASE RESISTANCE: Excellent
ARS RATING: 8.6
COMMENTS: The canes of this large, bushy plant are covered with hundreds of small thorns, and it seems never to be out of bloom. Soft pink flowers fade to white and have exceptional fragrance.

Variegata di Bologna

FAMILY: Bourbon
BLOOM SIZE, TYPE: Large, double
FRAGRANCE: Medium
PLANT SIZE, HABIT: Tall, spreading
DISEASE RESISTANCE: Good
ARS RATING: 8.0
COMMENTS: Fragrant, white blooms with red-purple stripes are borne singly and in small clusters. A typical bourbon plant, it grows as high as 8 feet tall.

Yolande d'Aragon

FAMILY: Portland
BLOOM SIZE, TYPE: Large, very double
FRAGRANCE: Heavy
PLANT SIZE, HABIT: Medium, bushy
DISEASE RESISTANCE: Good
ARS RATING: 8.4
COMMENTS: Heavily fragrant, distinctive, deep-pink blooms with small green eyes adorn strong plants. The flowers are produced singly and in small sprays.

Zéphirine Drouhin

FAMILY: Bourbon
BLOOM SIZE, TYPE: Medium, semidouble
FRAGRANCE: Medium
PLANT SIZE, HABIT: Tall, spreading
DISEASE RESISTANCE: Good
ARS RATING: 8.1
COMMENTS: The nearly thornless canes of this vigorous variety can grow more than 10 feet long. Profuse flowers are silvery pink with a nice fragrance.

Species

Species roses are wild roses that naturally interbred with each other. Most have single blooms, but a few have double and even very double flowers. Pink or white are the usual colors, but you'll also find some yellows and deep pinks to light reds.

Sadly, these beauties do not rebloom, but species roses are great for the garden because they offer more than just flowers. Interesting foliage, bark, thorns, and hips all add elements of shape and color. Grow *Rosa sericea pteracantha* for its showy red thorns and white spring flowers.

It's a misconception that all species roses are very large plants. Many have the size and habit of large shrubs, reaching about 6 to 10 feet tall by 4 to 5 feet wide, but some grow 1 or 2 feet shorter and narrower.

Some species roses grow in several forms. *R. banksiae*, for example, has six variations, each with different bloom colors and forms. The largest rose bush in the world is a banksiae, covering more than 8,000 square feet in Tombstone, Arizona.

Approximately a dozen species are native to North America. In the Southeast, you may encounter *R. palustris*, the swamp rose. The species known as the prairie rose, *R. blanda*, is native to the Midwest. From the Pacific Northwest to Alaska, the nootka rose, *R. nutkana*, grows wild.

Because few local nurseries sell species roses, check with mail-order sources.

FLOWER SIZE
SMALL: Less than 2 inches wide
MEDIUM: 2 to 4 inches wide wide
LARGE: More than 4 inches wide

PLANT SIZE
SHORT: Less than 2 feet tall
MEDIUM: 2 to 4 feet tall
TALL: More than 4 feet tall

Rosa banksiae lutea (Yellow Lady Banks' Rose)
BLOOM SIZE, TYPE: Small, double
FRAGRANCE: Light
PLANT SIZE, HABIT: Large, spreading
DISEASE RESISTANCE: Excellent
ARS RATING: 9.1
COMMENTS: Lady Banks' roses were named for the wife of British plantsman Sir Joseph Banks. Lutea has solid yellow double blooms borne in large clusters on plants good for warm-climate gardens.

Rosa gallica versicolor (*Rosa mundi*)
BLOOM SIZE, TYPE: Large, semidouble
FRAGRANCE: Moderate
PLANT SIZE, HABIT: Short, bushy
DISEASE RESISTANCE: Good
ARS RATING: 9.0
COMMENTS: The most popular striped species rose is a sport of *R. gallica officinalis*. White blooms are mottled with medium to deep pink. Nicely fragrant small clusters grace plants that seldom grow taller than 4 feet.

Rosa hugonis

BLOOM SIZE, TYPE: Medium, single
FRAGRANCE: Light
PLANT SIZE, HABIT: Medium, bushy
DISEASE RESISTANCE: Excellent
ARS RATING: 8.6
COMMENTS: Reportedly brought from China by a priest in the late 19th century, it's often sold as Father Hugo's rose. Solid-yellow single flowers grow on a thorny, disease-resistant plant about 9 feet tall. It produces deep scarlet hips in the fall.

Rosa macrantha

BLOOM, SIZE, TYPE: Large, single
FRAGRANCE: Light
PLANT SIZE, HABIT: Large, spreading
DISEASE RESISTANCE: Excellent
ARS RATING: 8.0
COMMENTS: This variety has large single delicate pink blooms that age to pure white. They are borne in small clusters on large, spreading thin-caned plants reaching 15 to 20 feet. Macrantha means "large flowered" in Latin.

Rosa rubrifolia (Rosa glauca)

BLOOM SIZE, TYPE: Small, single
FRAGRANCE: Light
PLANT SIZE, HABIT: Medium, bushy
DISEASE RESISTANCE: Excellent
ARS RATING: 8.8
COMMENTS: *Rosa rubrifolia* means "red leaves" but an earlier name is *R. glauca*, meaning "gray." Both refer to the blue-green foliage with pink overtones. Vivid pink single blooms with white eyes are carried in small clusters on nearly thornless bushes about 8 feet tall. Small bright red hips form in the fall.

Rosa rugosa

BLOOM SIZE, TYPE: Medium, single
FRAGRANCE: Light
PLANT SIZE, HABIT: Medium, bushy
DISEASE RESISTANCE: Excellent
ARS RATING: 9.1
COMMENTS: Purple-red single blooms up to 4 inches wide with golden yellow stamens make this an attractive landscape plant. Hardy plants reach about 6 feet tall. In the fall, large red hips form and the foliage turns yellow.

Miniatures

Perfect for containers, miniatures delight with their perfect imitations of hybrid teas and floribundas. They're generally hardy and produce profuse quantities of blooms throughout the growing season. Miniatures are good choices to edge borders or as accent specimens in mixed gardens or rose gardens.

These small wonders, like other modern roses, originated from wild Chinese roses. *Rosa chinensis minima* was brought to England in the early 1800s, but hybridizing with this miniature species didn't pick up until the 1930s.

For two decades European breeders dominated the market before American Ralph Moore created Centennial Miss in 1952.

It took a while for miniatures to catch on with the rose-buying public, but their beauty and ability to fit into small spaces have made them extremely popular. Another plus: They're generally hardier than hybrid tea roses.

Although large rose companies, such as Weeks Roses, Jackson & Perkins, and Conard-Pyle, often introduce new miniatures, most new varieties come from nursery growers and amateur breeders seeking new forms and colors.

For the best results, select a miniature rose from a nursery or catalog, not a supermarket.

Florist miniatures are designed as indoor plants to be discarded after they finish blooming.

Because the American Rose Society requires petite blooms for rose show judging, a bloom size between 1 to 2 inches is standard for miniatures.

PLANT SIZE
SHORT: Less than 1 foot tall
MEDIUM: 1 to 2½ feet tall
TALL: More than 2½ feet tall

PLANT HABIT
UPRIGHT: Less than 1 foot wide
BUSHY: 1 to 2½ feet wide
SPREADING: More than 2½ feet wide

Acey Deucy
BLOOM FORM: Classic
FRAGRANCE: Light
PLANT SIZE, HABIT: Medium, bushy
DISEASE RESISTANCE: Good
ARS RATING: 7.7
COMMENTS: Medium-red blooms that resemble small hybrid teas grow mostly singly on moderate-size plants.

Baby Grand
BLOOM FORM: Informal
FRAGRANCE: Light
PLANT SIZE, HABIT: Medium, bushy
DISEASE RESISTANCE: Excellent
ARS RATING: 8.6
COMMENTS: The multiple blooms that grow in small sprays lend Baby Grand the look of a dwarf Old Garden Rose. Flowers are slightly fragrant, borne on highly disease-resistant plants.

Baby Love

BLOOM FORM: Single
FRAGRANCE: Light
PLANT SIZE, HABIT: Tall, spreading
DISEASE RESISTANCE: Excellent
AWARDS: GM U.K
ARS RATING: 8.0
COMMENTS: Single buttercup yellow blooms grow mostly singly on large, bushy plants. Baby Love is revered for its superb disease resistance.

Bees Knees

BLOOM FORM: Classic
FRAGRANCE: Light
PLANT SIZE, HABIT: Medium, bushy
DISEASE RESISTANCE: Good
AWARDS: ARS Members' Choice Award 2006
ARS RATING: 8.0
COMMENTS: The blooms are a gorgeous combination of white with warm apricot centers and pink petal edges. Flowers are borne in large clusters.

Black Jade

BLOOM FORM: Classic
FRAGRANCE: Light
PLANT SIZE, HABIT: Medium, bushy
DISEASE RESISTANCE: Good
AWARDS: AOE 1985; MHOF 2006
ARS RATING: 8.0
COMMENTS: Probably the darkest rose of any type, Black Jade's deep-red blooms contrast with golden stamens. Flowers are borne mostly singly on medium-size plants.

Child's Play

BLOOM FORM: Classic
FRAGRANCE: Medium
PLANT SIZE, HABIT: Medium, upright
DISEASE RESISTANCE: Good
AWARDS: AARS & AOE 1993
ARS RATING: 8.0
COMMENTS: Porcelain white flowers with pink petal edges contrast beautifully with deep-green foliage. Blooms are borne singly or in small clusters.

Cinderella

BLOOM FORM: Informal
FRAGRANCE: Medium
PLANT SIZE, HABIT: Short
DISEASE RESISTANCE: Good
AWARDS: MHOF 2000
ARS RATING: 8.1
COMMENTS: This rose has been on the market for more than 50 years, primarily because the short plant covers itself with small white blooms. It's ideal for containers.

Crazy Dottie

BLOOM FORM: Single
FRAGRANCE: Light
PLANT SIZE, HABIT: Medium, bushy
DISEASE RESISTANCE: Good
ARS RATING: 8.0
COMMENTS: Named after a friend of the hybridizer, Crazy Dottie has eye-catching brilliant orange single blooms with copper-yellow centers. They're borne singly and in small sprays.

Cupcake

BLOOM FORM: Classic
FRAGRANCE: Light
PLANT SIZE, HABIT: Medium, bushy
DISEASE RESISTANCE: Excellent
AWARDS: AOE 1983; MHOF 2002
ARS RATING: 8.0
COMMENTS: Clear pink flowers with somewhat darker centers are carried in small clusters. Blooms are long-lasting as cut flowers, growing one per stem and in sprays.

Dancing Flame

BLOOM FORM: Classic
FRAGRANCE: Light
PLANT SIZE, HABIT: Medium, bushy
DISEASE RESISTANCE: Good
ARS RATING: 7.7
COMMENTS: The name suits the golden blooms with red edges. Flowers are carried mostly one per stem.

Giggles

BLOOM FORM: Classic
FRAGRANCE: Light
PLANT SIZE, HABIT: Tall, upright
DISEASE RESISTANCE: Light
ARS RATING: 8.8
COMMENTS: Soft coral-pink blooms with classic form boost the rating. The plant is on the tall side, with medium-green matte foliage.

Gizmo

BLOOM FORM: Single
FRAGRANCE: None
PLANT SIZE, HABIT: Medium, bushy
DISEASE RESISTANCE: Good
ARS RATING: 7.9
COMMENTS: Small brilliant orange-red blooms form in small clusters on this medium-size plant. It works well in the landscape, but don't count on it for cutting.

Gourmet Popcorn

BLOOM FORM: Informal
FRAGRANCE: Light
PLANT SIZE, HABIT: Medium, spreading
DISEASE RESISTANCE: Excellent
AWARDS: MHOF 2009
ARS RATING: 8.7
COMMENTS: Blooms resemble a bowl of popcorn with a dollop of butter in the centers of each popped kernel. The small blooms liberally cover low-growing, spreading plants.

Grace Seward

BLOOM FORM: Single
FRAGRANCE: Medium
PLANT SIZE, HABIT: Tall, bushy
DISEASE RESISTANCE: Good
ARS RATING: 8.2
COMMENTS: Named after a notable California rosarian, the pure white single flowers of Grace Deward sport very large golden stamens on plants with good repeat bloom.

Green Ice

BLOOM FORM: Double
FRAGRANCE: Light
PLANT SIZE, HABIT: Short, bushy
DISEASE RESISTANCE: Good
AWARDS: MHOF 2001
ARS RATING: 8.0
COMMENTS: Looking for something a little different for a container? Short, very floriferous plants produce small white blooms touched with pink and green as they develop.

Heartbreaker

BLOOM FORM: Classic
FRAGRANCE: Light
PLANT SIZE, HABIT: Medium, bushy
DISEASE RESISTANCE: Good
ARS RATING: 7.9
COMMENTS: White blooms suffused with pink in varying degrees form in small sprays. Disbudding will produce larger individual flowers.

Hot Tamale

BLOOM FORM: Classic
FRAGRANCE: Light
PLANT SIZE, HABIT: Medium, bushy
DISEASE RESISTANCE: Good
AWARDS: AOE 1994
ARS RATING: 8.3
COMMENTS: Golden yellow-orange blooms with glowing pink petal edges make this rose a standout in the garden. Bushy plants bear medium-green foliage.

Incognito

BLOOM FORM: Classic
FRAGRANCE: Light
PLANT SIZE, HABIT: Medium, upright
DISEASE RESISTANCE: Good
ARS RATING: 8.0
COMMENTS: Unusual, distinctive violet blooms overlaid with russet brown and a yellow underside are nicely set against the dark green semiglossy foliage.

Irresistible

BLOOM FORM: Classic
FRAGRANCE: Medium, spicy
PLANT SIZE, HABIT: Tall, upright
DISEASE RESISTANCE: Excellent
AWARDS: MHOF 2008
ARS RATING: 9.0
COMMENTS: One of the top-rated exhibition miniatures, this white beauty with the palest of pink centers also does well in the garden. Cut some for the spicy fragrance.

Jean Kenneally

BLOOM FORM: Classic
FRAGRANCE: Light
PLANT SIZE, HABIT: Tall, upright
DISEASE RESISTANCE: Excellent
AWARDS: AOE 1986; MHOF 2005
ARS RATING: 9.1
COMMENTS: This apricot-pink rose, with the highest ARS rating for a miniature, was named for a beloved California rosarian. Blooms grow mostly singly on long stems that are perfect for cutting.

Jeanne Lajoie

BLOOM FORM: Classic
FRAGRANCE: Medium
PLANT SIZE, HABIT: Tall, spreading
DISEASE RESISTANCE: Fair
AWARDS: AOE 1977; MHOF 2001
ARS RATING: 9.1
COMMENTS: The pink blooms on this climber are true miniatures, but the plant itself grows as a large, spreading mound with canes up to 12 feet long. It requires protection against black spot.

Kristin

BLOOM FORM: Classic
FRAGRANCE: Light
PLANT SIZE, HABIT: Medium, bushy
DISEASE RESISTANCE: Good
AWARDS: AOE 1993
ARS RATING: 8.1
COMMENTS: White blooms with yellow centers and deep cerise-pink edges are borne singly and in small clusters. A climbing form is available.

Lemon Drop

BLOOM FORM: Classic
FRAGRANCE: Light
PLANT SIZE, HABIT: Medium, bushy
DISEASE RESISTANCE: Excellent
ARS RATING: 7.8
COMMENTS: Solid yellow roses of any kind are relatively scarce, so this 1999 introduction is a good addition to the family. Blooms are carried in small sprays.

Little Artist

BLOOM FORM: Semidouble
FRAGRANCE: Light
PLANT SIZE, HABIT: Short to medium, bushy
DISEASE RESISTANCE: Good
ARS RATING: 8.4
COMMENTS: This "hand-painted" rose from breeder Sam McGredy grows red blooms with white eyes and deeper red brushings. Blooms are carried primarily in sprays.

Little Jackie

BLOOM FORM: Classic
FRAGRANCE: Moderate
PLANT SIZE, HABIT: Medium, upright
DISEASE RESISTANCE: Good
AWARDS: AOE 1984; MHOF 2003
ARS RATING: 7.9
COMMENTS: Red-orange flowers with yellow undersides grace this variety. The blooms are quite fragrant, borne on sturdy plants with semiglossy foliage.

Magic Carrousel

BLOOM FORM: Classic
FRAGRANCE: Light
PLANT SIZE, HABIT: Medium, bushy
DISEASE RESISTANCE: Good
AWARDS: AOE 1975; MHOF 1999
ARS RATING: 8.5
COMMENTS: Introduced in 1972, Magic Carrousel was one of the first miniatures with light-pink to white blooms with red edges. Small blooms grow mostly one per stem. A climbing form is available.

Millie Walters

BLOOM FORM: Classic
FRAGRANCE: Light
PLANT SIZE, HABIT: Short, bushy
DISEASE RESISTANCE: Good
ARS RATING: 8.4
COMMENTS: Deep coral-pink blooms grow singly and in small sprays on this plant. The rose is named for a former first lady of the American Rose Society.

Minnie Pearl

BLOOM FORM: Classic
FRAGRANCE: Light
PLANT SIZE, HABIT: Medium, bushy
DISEASE RESISTANCE: Excellent
AWARDS: MHOF 2004
ARS RATING: 9.0
COMMENTS: This highly rated variety named for the comedian and country-western singer bears light-pink blooms with deep pink undersides. Less intense heat produces better color.

My Sunshine

BLOOM FORM: Single
FRAGRANCE: Medium
PLANT SIZE, HABIT: Medium, bushy
DISEASE RESISTANCE: Excellent
ARS RATING: 8.5
COMMENTS: Large single solid yellow blooms bear a fairly pronounced fragrance. They grow singly and in small clusters on vigorous plants.

Neon Cowboy

BLOOM FORM: Single
FRAGRANCE: Light
PLANT SIZE, HABIT: Short, bushy
DISEASE RESISTANCE: Excellent
ARS RATING: 8.0
COMMENTS: Neon Cowboy has the habit of a short floribunda, with medium-size sprays on short plants. Red blooms are centered with large yellow eyes.

Party Girl

BLOOM FORM: Classic
FRAGRANCE: Medium, spicy
PLANT SIZE, HABIT: Short to medium, spreading
DISEASE RESISTANCE: Good
AWARDS: AOE 1981; MHOF 1999
ARS RATING: 8.2
COMMENTS: Plant this one close to the front door to enjoy the soft yellow-apricot flowers with lighter petal edges and a nice fragrance. Blooms grow singly and in small clusters.

Pierrine

BLOOM FORM: Classic
FRAGRANCE: Light
PLANT SIZE, HABIT: Medium, bushy
DISEASE RESISTANCE: Good
AWARDS: MHOF 2007
ARS RATING: 9.0
COMMENTS: Pierrine's large, coral-pink blooms have super exhibition form, accounting for the high rating. They're carried mostly one per stem.

Rainbow's End

BLOOM FORM: Classic
FRAGRANCE: None
PLANT SIZE, HABIT: Medium, bushy
DISEASE RESISTANCE: Good
AWARDS: AOE 1986; MHOF 2005
ARS RATING: 8.7
COMMENTS: A pot of gold edged with rubies describes this well-named variety, which also has a climbing form. Golden petals tipped with red are carried on free-flowering plants.

Red Cascade

BLOOM FORM: Informal
FRAGRANCE: None
PLANT SIZE, HABIT: Tall, spreading
DISEASE RESISTANCE: Good
AWARDS: AOE 1976; MHOF 2004
ARS RATING: 7.6
COMMENTS: Canes can reach 10 feet or longer on this climber. The lax canes can be either supported or left to flop as a groundcover. Solid-red blooms are borne mostly in small clusters.

Rise 'n' Shine

BLOOM FORM: Classic
FRAGRANCE: Medium
PLANT SIZE, HABIT: Medium, bushy
DISEASE RESISTANCE: Good
AWARDS: AOE 1978; MHOF 1999
ARS RATING: 8.4
COMMENTS: Ralph Moore bred many good yellow minis in his 101 years, and this is one of them. Solid-yellow blooms with good form and a nice fragrance are borne in profusion.

Roller Coaster

BLOOM FORM: Semidouble
FRAGRANCE: Light
PLANT SIZE, HABIT: Tall, spreading
DISEASE RESISTANCE: Good
ARS RATING: 8.2
COMMENTS: Yipes, stripes! Red stripes on white blooms with large clusters of stamens form in clusters. Canes reach 5 to 6 feet. In the fall, stop deadheading to encourage orange hips.

Ruby Pendant

BLOOM FORM: Classic
FRAGRANCE: Light
PLANT SIZE, HABIT: Medium, bushy
DISEASE RESISTANCE: Good
ARS RATING: 8.4
COMMENTS: Reddish purple flowers are borne mostly one per stem. Productive, vigorous plants grow with attractive reddish green foliage.

Ruby Ruby

BLOOM FORM: Classic
FRAGRANCE: Light
PLANT SIZE, HABIT: Medium, bushy
DISEASE RESISTANCE: Excellent
ARS RATING: 8.0
COMMENTS: This very floriferous compact plant is the type Europeans would call a patio rose. Solid-red blooms are borne in large sprays on vigorous, slightly spreading plants.

Scentsational

BLOOM FORM: Classic
FRAGRANCE: Heavy
PLANT SIZE, HABIT: Medium, upright
DISEASE RESISTANCE: Fair
ARS RATING: 7.6
COMMENTS: Nicely formed blooms in light purple with pink overtones carry one of the heaviest fragrances found in a miniature. Flowers grow singly and in medium-size clusters.

Simplex

BLOOM FORM: Single
FRAGRANCE: Light
PLANT SIZE, HABIT: Medium, bushy
DISEASE RESISTANCE: Excellent
ARS RATING: 8.4
COMMENTS: The five petals of this white rose do not overlap, as do most singles, but separate slightly to form a perfect star. Vigorous, bushy plants have dark green leathery foliage.

Small Miracle

BLOOM FORM: Classic
FRAGRANCE: Light
PLANT SIZE, HABIT: Medium, bushy
DISEASE RESISTANCE: Good
ARS RATING: 7.9
COMMENTS: Small white blooms are lightly fragrant, borne in small sprays on plants with dark green glossy foliage.

Snow Bride

BLOOM FORM: Classic
FRAGRANCE: Light
PLANT SIZE, HABIT: Medium, bushy
DISEASE RESISTANCE: Good
AWARDS: AOE 1983; MHOF 2003
ARS RATING: 8.5
COMMENTS: This variety from 1982 was *the* hot exhibition white miniature for many years. Perfectly formed blooms are borne mostly singly on vigorous plants.

Starina

BLOOM FORM: Classic
FRAGRANCE: Medium
PLANT SIZE, HABIT: Medium, bushy
DISEASE RESISTANCE: Excellent
AWARDS: GM, Japan; MHOF 1999
ARS RATING: 8.3
COMMENTS: Introduced in 1965, Starina was *the* miniature to emulate for many years. Orange-red blooms have good form and notable fragrance. Bushy plants are very disease resistant.

Sun Sprinkles

BLOOM FORM: Classic
FRAGRANCE: Light
PLANT SIZE, HABIT: Medium, bushy
DISEASE RESISTANCE: Excellent
AWARDS: AARS & AOE 2001
ARS RATING: 7.8
COMMENTS: This variety from Jackson & Perkins is one of very few miniatures to receive an AARS award. The deep-yellow blooms are borne in profusion, both singly and in small sprays, on compact, very disease-resistant plants.

Sweet Chariot

BLOOM FORM: Informal
FRAGRANCE: Heavy
PLANT SIZE, HABIT: Medium, spreading
DISEASE RESISTANCE: Good
ARS RATING: 8.4
COMMENTS: The blooms swing low on this short, spreading variety. The very double lavender-purple blooms are borne in large, very fragrant clusters. The bushes feature matte, medium-green foliage.

Sweet Diana

BLOOM FORM: Classic
FRAGRANCE: Light
PLANT SIZE, HABIT: Medium, bushy
DISEASE RESISTANCE: Good
AWARDS: AOE 2002
ARS RATING: 7.8
COMMENTS: Named by breeder Harm Saville for his granddaughter, this deep-yellow miniature grows small clusters of blooms on vigorous plants.

Minifloras

Minifloras are the newest family of roses. In 1999, the American Rose Society established the miniflora class at the request of hybridizers who said that they had to discard many promising seedlings simply because the blooms weren't small enough to be considered miniatures. After the class was created, existing larger miniatures were allowed to move into the miniflora category.

At first, breeders expected that minifloras would include both large classic bloom miniatures and short floribundas. However, the classic bloom miniatures dominate the category, with very few floribunda-type plants registered as minifloras.

Most miniflora breeding comes from rose exhibitors and small-scale hybridizers who exhibit the blooms at rose shows. Of the hundreds of miniflora varieties registered, only a handful come from the three biggest United States rose companies: Jackson & Perkins, Weeks Roses, and Conard-Pyle.

Virtually all miniflora blooms are 2 to 3 inches in diameter. The classic blooms of many resemble little hybrid teas. Since miniatures are in their bloodlines, what's "tall" for a miniflora is anything more than 4 feet.

Grow minifloras where you want to grow hybrid teas but just don't have enough room. Follow the same care instructions, providing plenty of sun, fertilizer, pest control, and winter protection. Repeat bloom is generally better than most of larger counterparts and they grow well on their own roots, making hardier bushes. Minifloras can produce dozens of blooms on a single bush.

PLANT SIZE
SHORT: Less than 2 feet tall
MEDIUM: 3 to 4 feet tall
TALL: More than 4 feet tall

PLANT HABIT
UPRIGHT: Less than 18 inches wide
BUSHY: 18 to 30 inches wide
SPREADING: More than 30 inches wide

Abby's Angel
BLOOM FORM: Classic
FRAGRANCE: Light
PLANT SIZE, HABIT: Tall, upright
DISEASE RESISTANCE: Good
ARS RATING: 7.7
COMMENTS: Red edges on deep yellow make Abby's Angel's blooms stunners. The flowers grow mostly one per stem on plants with dark-green, semiglossy foliage that reach 4 feet tall.

Amy Grant
BLOOM FORM: Classic
FRAGRANCE: Light
PLANT SIZE, HABIT: Short, upright
DISEASE RESISTANCE: Good
ARS RATING: 7.5
COMMENTS: Named for the gospel-country singer, Amy Grant has light-pink flowers that show a deep pink center. The plant is rather short for a miniflora. Foliage is dark green and glossy.

Autumn Splendor

BLOOM FORM: Classic
FRAGRANCE: Light
PLANT SIZE, HABIT: Medium, bushy
DISEASE RESISTANCE: Good
AWARDS: AOE 1999
ARS RATING: 8.1
COMMENTS: This variety includes the colors of fall foliage: yellow, gold, and orange, with slight touches of red. Blooms are carried singly and in small sprays on vigorous, productive plants.

Butter Cream

BLOOM FORM: Classic
FRAGRANCE: None
PLANT SIZE, HABIT: Medium, upright
DISEASE RESISTANCE: Good
ARS RATING: 7.8
COMMENTS: Soft-yellow petals with a deeper yellow reverse grow about 2 inches wide on plants with glossy green foliage and good disease resistance.

Conundrum

BLOOM FORM: Classic
FRAGRANCE: Light
PLANT SIZE, HABIT: Medium, bushy
DISEASE RESISTANCE: Good
ARS RATING: 7.7
COMMENTS: Warm yellow blooms with red edges are a hallmark of this rose from hybridizer Robbie Tucker. The flowers are borne singly on vigorous plants.

Dr John Dickman

BLOOM FORM: Classic
FRAGRANCE: Medium
PLANT SIZE, HABIT: Medium, upright
DISEASE RESISTANCE: Excellent
ARS RATING: 7.8
COMMENTS: Absolutely gorgeous lavender blooms with red edges grace this healthy, upright variety named for a long-time writer and columnist for the *American Rose* magazine.

Louisville Lady
BLOOM FORM: Classic
FRAGRANCE: Light
PLANT SIZE, HABIT: Medium, bushy
DISEASE RESISTANCE: Good
ARS RATING: 7.6
COMMENTS: Bright light-red blooms with a white underside have a long vase life as cut flowers. The plant has dark-green glossy foliage.

Memphis King
BLOOM FORM: Classic
FRAGRANCE: Light
PLANT SIZE, HABIT: Short to medium, bushy
DISEASE RESISTANCE: Good
ARS RATING: 7.7
COMMENTS: Probably named for Elvis, this variety bears solid red blooms on a rather short plant with medium-green semiglossy foliage.

Memphis Magic
BLOOM FORM: Classic
FRAGRANCE: Light
PLANT SIZE, HABIT: Medium, upright
DISEASE RESISTANCE: Good
ARS RATING: 7.6
COMMENTS: Deep-red blooms can be almost black, with a lighter red underside. Flowers are borne in small sprays on medium-size plants.

Olympic Gold
BLOOM FORM: Classic
FRAGRANCE: Light
PLANT SIZE, HABIT: Medium, bushy
DISEASE RESISTANCE: Good
ARS RATING: 7.7
COMMENTS: This rose dates from 1983, and has been reclassified from a miniature to a miniflora. The deep-yellow blooms are produced mostly one per stem on vigorous, bushy plants.

Overnight Scentsation

BLOOM FORM: Classic
FRAGRANCE: Heavy
PLANT SIZE, HABIT: Medium, bushy
DISEASE RESISTANCE: Good
ARS RATING: 7.5
COMMENTS: Grow this miniflora for its exceptional fragrance. Large medium-pink blooms grow mostly singly on vigorous plants with semiglossy medium- to dark-green foliage.

Peach Delight

BLOOM FORM: Classic
FRAGRANCE: Heavy
PLANT SIZE, HABIT: Medium, spreading
DISEASE RESISTANCE: Good
ARS RATING: 7.7
COMMENTS: Large, very fragrant deep apricot to peach beauties grow on arching, spreading plants with good disease resistance.

Rocky Top

BLOOM FORM: Classic
FRAGRANCE: Light
PLANT SIZE, HABIT: Medium, upright
DISEASE RESISTANCE: Good
ARS RATING: 7.6
COMMENTS: Named after a country-bluegrass song, these exhibition blooms vary from orange to coral pink depending upon the weather. The plants have dark green semiglossy foliage.

Sassy Cindy

BLOOM SIZE, TYPE: Medium, classic
FRAGRANCE: Light
PLANT SIZE, HABIT: Medium, upright
DISEASE RESISTANCE: Good
ARS RATING: 7.5
COMMENTS: Dark-green semiglossy foliage covers 3-foot plants. The exhibition-form blooms are an eye-catching deep red with a light yellow reverse, borne mostly one per stem.

Solar Flair

BLOOM FORM: Classic
FRAGRANCE: Light
PLANT SIZE, HABIT: Medium, bushy
DISEASE RESISTANCE: Good
ARS RATING: 7.5
COMMENTS: Yellow blooms with red petal edges add the flair to this sunny variety. The medium-size plants exhibit dark green, glossy foliage.

Spring's a Comin'

BLOOM FORM: Classic
FRAGRANCE: Medium
PLANT SIZE, HABIT: Medium, bushy
DISEASE RESISTANCE: Good
ARS RATING: 7.8
COMMENTS: If light pink is the color of spring, this rose qualifies. White blooms with delicate, light-pink edges are set off by dark-green, semiglossy foliage.

Tennessee Sunrise

BLOOM FORM: Classic
FRAGRANCE: Medium
PLANT SIZE, HABIT: Medium, upright
DISEASE RESISTANCE: Good
ARS RATING: 7.8
COMMENTS: Sunrise in Tennessee must be filled with blends of yellows, reds, and orange like the blooms on this miniflora. Medium-size plants have good disease resistance and dark green foliage.

Thanks to Sue

BLOOM SIZE, TYPE: Medium, classic
FRAGRANCE: Medium
PLANT SIZE, HABIT: Medium, spreading
DISEASE RESISTANCE: Good
ARS RATING: 7.7
COMMENTS: Semidouble blooms of solid amber to apricot fade to a soft peachy pink. The flowers, borne mostly singly, have a nice aroma. Plants grow to about 2 feet tall with medium-green foliage and a quick repeat bloom habit.

Tiffany Lite

BLOOM FORM: Classic
FRAGRANCE: Light
PLANT SIZE, HABIT: Tall, bushy
DISEASE RESISTANCE: Good
ARS RATING: 7.7
COMMENTS: This white sport of Tiffany Lynn produces double blooms in small sprays. Tiffany Lite has a mild fragrance.

Tiffany Lynn

BLOOM FORM: Classic
FRAGRANCE: Light
PLANT SIZE, HABIT: Tall, bushy
DISEASE RESISTANCE: Good
AWARDS: MHOF 2009
ARS RATING: 8.1
COMMENTS: Introduced in 1985, this lovely rose has light-pink petals suffused with deeper pink, especially at their edges.

Valentine's Day

BLOOM FORM: Informal
FRAGRANCE: Light
PLANT SIZE, HABIT: Large, spreading
DISEASE RESISTANCE: Excellent
ARS RATING: 7.5
COMMENTS: Valentine's Day, a climbing miniflora, bears deep-red blooms produced in small clusters on arching plants with canes reaching 10 feet.

Whirlaway

BLOOM FORM: Classic
FRAGRANCE: None
PLANT SIZE, HABIT: Tall, upright
DISEASE RESISTANCE: Good
ARS RATING: 7.7
COMMENTS: Whirlaway was the Triple Crown horse-racing winner in 1941. His namesake's pure white blooms are borne on tall plants with long stems that ideal for cutting.

Climbers & Ramblers

Large-flowered climbers and ramblers provide the most romantic looks in any rose garden: a bloom-laden archway welcoming guests. These vigorous and handy roses have numerous landscape uses. You can cover and partially hide sheds or adorn fences and pergolas. Long-caned roses also provide loads of cutting blooms for the house.

The American Rose Society in 1999 eliminated the classification name of "rambler" and replaced it with the more accurate "hybrid wichuriana" (for the history of ramblers, see page 9.)

However, the generic term rambler is still useful when describing very long-caned plants with small flowers and nonrecurrent blooms. Ramblers are useful in certain situations, but few are rated at 7.5 or above, partly because they're not grown frequently enough and rated.

The American Rose Society introduced the large-flowered climber classification in 1940. Most of the varieties here are large-flowered climbers except those marked otherwise.

Interestingly, some varieties do not grow large flowers, and none of them climb by attaching themselves naturally to structures. Use soft ties to manually attach the canes to supports.

Climbers can take two to three years to establish and produce blooms, so choose carefully. To get as heavy a bloom as possible, allow the canes at the base of the plant to grow to their full length and train them onto a structure, spreading them out.

BLOOM SIZE
> **SMALL:** 2 inches or smaller wide
> **MEDIUM:** 2 to 4 inches wide
> **LARGE:** More than 4 inches wide

BLOOM TYPE
> **SINGLE:** 5 to 8 petals
> **SEMIDOUBLE:** 9 to 20 petals
> **DOUBLE:** 21 to 45 petals
> **VERY DOUBLE:** More than 45 petals

CANE LENGTH
> **SHORT:** Less than 10 feet
> **MEDIUM:** 10 to 20 feet
> **LONG:** More than 20 feet

Albéric Barbier
BLOOM SIZE, TYPE: Small, double
FRAGRANCE: Medium
FAMILY, CANE LENGTH: Hybrid wichurana, long
DISEASE RESISTANCE: Good
ARS RATING: 8.0
COMMENTS: One of the few ramblers rated higher than 7.5, this rose has nicely fragrant, creamy white flowers with yellow eyes. They grow singly and in clusters.

Altissimo
BLOOM SIZE, TYPE: Large, single
FRAGRANCE: Light
CANE LENGTH: Medium
DISEASE RESISTANCE: Good
ARS RATING: 8.5
COMMENTS: Large deep-red blooms with golden stamens stand out in the garden. Looks like this make up for the lack of fragrance. Strong canes reach 10 to 12 feet.

America

BLOOM SIZE, TYPE: Medium, double
FRAGRANCE: Heavy
CANE LENGTH: Short to medium
DISEASE RESISTANCE: Good
AWARDS: AARS 1976
ARS RATING: 8.3
COMMENTS: The first climber to win an AARS award, America has been extremely popular since 1976. Very fragrant, medium-pink blooms are borne in small sprays.

American Pillar

BLOOM SIZE, TYPE: Small, single
FRAGRANCE: None
FAMILY, CANE LENGTH: Hybrid wichurana, medium
DISEASE RESISTANCE: Good
ARS RATING: 7.9
COMMENTS: Small carmine-pink blooms with white eyes are carried in large clusters on this old favorite. The plant is a heavy bloomer and will reach up to 20 feet.

Awakening

BLOOM SIZE, TYPE: Large, double
FRAGRANCE: Medium
CANE LENGTH: Medium
DISEASE RESISTANCE: Good
ARS RATING: 8.0
COMMENTS: This sport of New Dawn bears fragrant light-pink blooms with some salmon shading. Plants produce large flowers in small clusters.

Berries 'n' Cream

BLOOM SIZE, TYPE: Large, semidouble
FRAGRANCE: Medium
CANE LENGTH: Medium
DISEASE RESISTANCE: Good
ARS RATING: 7.8
COMMENTS: Are these blooms pink with white stripes or white with pink stripes? In either case, they blend nicely in large sprays on a medium-size plant. The variety originated in Denmark.

Blaze Improved

BLOOM SIZE, TYPE: Large, double
FRAGRANCE: Medium
CANE LENGTH: Medium
DISEASE RESISTANCE: Good
ARS RATING: 8.9
COMMENTS: Bred in the Czech Republic in 1935, this rose, also known as 'Demokracie' has better disease resistance than its parent. Blooms are borne in medium-size clusters on strong plants. It's a nice rose, but the rating is somewhat inflated.

Brite Eyes

BLOOM SIZE, TYPE: Medium, semidouble
FRAGRANCE: Light
CANE LENGTH: Short
DISEASE RESISTANCE: Excellent
ARS RATING: 7.9
COMMENTS: Medium-pink flowers with white eyes and golden stamens are borne in small clusters on this short climber. Because it's from the hybridizer of Knock Out, it's also very disease resistant.

Compassion

BLOOM SIZE, TYPE: Large, double
FRAGRANCE: Heavy
CANE LENGTH: Medium
DISEASE RESISTANCE: Excellent
AWARDS: GM Baden-Baden; FA ARS
ARS RATING: 8.5
COMMENTS: Very fragrant salmon-pink hybrid tea-type blooms grow in small clusters on very disease resistant plants.

Don Juan

BLOOM SIZE, TYPE: Large, double
FRAGRANCE: Heavy
CANE LENGTH: Medium
DISEASE RESISTANCE: Good
ARS RATING: 8.2
COMMENTS: Large velvety red blooms with heavy fragrance make this rose perfect for cut flowers. Plants reach 12 to 14 feet, so consider training the canes horizontally to reach the blooms easily.

Dream Weaver

BLOOM SIZE, TYPE: Medium, double
FRAGRANCE: Light
FAMILY, CANE LENGTH: Climbing floribunda, medium
DISEASE RESISTANCE: Good
ARS RATING: 7.9
COMMENTS: Coral-pink blooms form in large clusters on a medium-size climber. The flowers have a light rose fragrance. The foliage grows glossy green.

Dublin Bay

BLOOM SIZE, TYPE: Large, double
FRAGRANCE: Medium
CANE LENGTH: Medium
DISEASE RESISTANCE: Excellent
ARS RATING: 8.6
COMMENTS: This deep-red rose carries its blooms both in small sprays and singly. Although not as fragrant as Don Juan, it has better disease resistance and is another great climber for cutting.

Fourth of July

BLOOM SIZE, TYPE: Medium, semidouble
FRAGRANCE: Light
CANE LENGTH: Medium to short
DISEASE RESISTANCE: Good
AWARDS: AARS 1999
ARS RATING: 8.1
COMMENTS: Extremely attractive light-pink blooms with cerise stripes and golden stamens form in medium-size clusters.

Händel

BLOOM SIZE, TYPE: Large, double
FRAGRANCE: Light
CANE LENGTH: Short to medium
DISEASE RESISTANCE: Good
ARS RATING: 7.9
COMMENTS: This variety, introduced in 1965, was one of the first roses to feature light-pink blooms with deeper pink petal edges. Lightly fragrant blooms form in small sprays on plants with strong canes.

Harlekin

BLOOM SIZE, TYPE: Medium, double
FRAGRANCE: Medium
CANE LENGTH: Medium
DISEASE RESISTANCE: Good
ARS RATING: 8.1
COMMENTS: Creamy white blooms are striped with pink, sometimes on petal edges and sometimes throughout the bloom, depending on the weather. These very attractive flowers form in small clusters on plants that average about 10 feet.

High Society

BLOOM SIZE, TYPE: Large, double
FRAGRANCE: Medium
CANE LENGTH: Medium
DISEASE RESISTANCE: Good
ARS RATING: 7.5
COMMENTS: Fragrant magenta-pink blooms grow in large sprays on this vigorous recent introduction. The plant grows about 15 feet tall with a bloom color found on few roses of this type.

Joseph's Coat

BLOOM SIZE, TYPE: Medium, double
FRAGRANCE: Light
CANE LENGTH: Medium to short
DISEASE RESISTANCE: Good
AWARDS: GM Bagatelle
ARS RATING: 7.5
COMMENTS: This rose lives up to its name. Blooms grow in a blend of yellows, oranges, and reds, forming medium-size sprays.

New Dawn

BLOOM SIZE, TYPE: Medium, double
FRAGRANCE: Medium
CANE LENGTH: Medium to tall
DISEASE RESISTANCE: Good
AWARDS: WFRS Hall of Fame 1997
ARS RATING: 8.6
COMMENTS: New Dawn's soft pink blooms carry a moderate fragrance, forming singly and in small clusters. Although it's an Earth-Kind variety, it is susceptible to black spot in damp climates.

Newport Fairy

BLOOM SIZE, TYPE: Small, single
FRAGRANCE: Light
FAMILY, CANE LENGTH: Hybrid wichurana, medium to long
DISEASE RESISTANCE: Good
ARS RATING: 8.5
COMMENTS: The highest rated of the wichurana ramblers, this variety carries single light-pink blooms in very large sprays. Plants grow about 20 feet tall.

Night Owl

BLOOM SIZE, TYPE: Medium, single
FRAGRANCE: Medium
CANE LENGTH: Medium
DISEASE RESISTANCE: Good
ARS RATING: 7.8
COMMENTS: Single deep-purple blooms contrast stunningly with golden stamens. The moderately fragrant blooms are borne in large sprays on upright plants reaching about 14 feet.

Pearly Gates

BLOOM SIZE, TYPE: Large, double
FRAGRANCE: Heavy
CANE LENGTH: Medium
DISEASE RESISTANCE: Good
ARS RATING: 7.7
COMMENTS: A color sport of America, this sister variety bears large, fragrant blooms of soft pearl pink with slightly deeper pink centers.

Pierre de Ronsard

BLOOM SIZE, TYPE: Medium, very double
FRAGRANCE: Light
CANE LENGTH: Medium to tall
DISEASE RESISTANCE: Excellent
AWARDS: WFRS Hall of Fame 2006
ARS RATING: 8.2
COMMENTS: This rose, named after a 16th-century French poet, has creamy white flowers suffused with rich pink, carried in small clusters. In the United States, it's sold under the name Eden.

Polka

BLOOM SIZE, TYPE: Large, very double
FRAGRANCE: Medium
CANE LENGTH: Short to medium
DISEASE RESISTANCE: Good
ARS RATING: 7.8
COMMENTS: This multiple-petaled Romantica rose grows large flowers in shades of apricot and yellow. Small sprays form on strong plants reaching about 12 feet.

Ramblin' Red

BLOOM SIZE, TYPE: Large, double
FRAGRANCE: Light
CANE LENGTH: Short
DISEASE RESISTANCE: Excellent
ARS RATING: 7.8
COMMENTS: Solid cardinal red blooms grow in large sprays on this plant from the breeder of Knock Out. As disease resistance is the hallmark of William Radler's roses, it's very clean.

Rosarium Uetersen

BLOOM SIZE, TYPE: Large, very double
FRAGRANCE: Medium
CANE LENGTH: Short
DISEASE RESISTANCE: Excellent
ARS RATING: 8.5
COMMENTS: More a large shrub than a true climber, this rose from Germany grows about 8 feet tall and wide. Deep-pink, fragrant blooms grow in large clusters on disease-resistant plants.

Royal Sunset

BLOOM SIZE, TYPE: Large, semidouble
FRAGRANCE: Heavy
CANE LENGTH: Medium to long
DISEASE RESISTANCE: Good
ARS RATING: 8.9
COMMENTS: The highest rated ARS climber, this 50-year-old variety has gorgeous apricot-pink blooms that grow singly and in small clusters on pliable canes.

Social Climber

BLOOM SIZE, TYPE: Large, double
FRAGRANCE: Medium
CANE LENGTH: Short
DISEASE RESISTANCE: Good
ARS RATING: 7.7
COMMENTS: Social Climber grows only about 6 feet tall with strong branching canes and deep green foliage. The fragrant medium-pink blooms are borne singly and in small clusters.

Sombreuil

BLOOM SIZE, TYPE: Large, very double
FRAGRANCE: Heavy
CANE LENGTH: Medium
DISEASE RESISTANCE: Good
ARS RATING: 8.8
COMMENTS: Long classified as a climbing tea, this wonderfully fragrant rose is now a large-flowered climber. Many-petaled pure white blooms grow in small sprays on plants that tolerate shade.

Stairway to Heaven

BLOOM SIZE, TYPE: Medium, double
FRAGRANCE: Light
FAMILY, CANE LENGTH: Climbing floribunda, medium
DISEASE RESISTANCE: Good
ARS RATING: 7.5
COMMENTS: Classed as a climbing floribunda, this rose has medium-red blooms with a mild aroma. They form in small clusters on plants that reach 10 to 12 feet.

The Impressionist

BLOOM SIZE, TYPE: Large, very double
FRAGRANCE: Heavy
CANE LENGTH: Medium
DISEASE RESISTANCE: Good
ARS RATING: 8.0
COMMENTS: Varying hues of yellow, amber, and orange adorn this very double, very fragrant rose. Medium tall, bushy plants grow dark-green foliage.

Resources

The American Rose Society

To learn more about roses, join or consult the American Rose Society, the largest rose organization in the world and one of the largest plant societies in the United States. Most ARS members are home gardeners who enjoy growing roses and want to expand their knowledge.

Headquartered in Shreveport, Louisiana, the ARS includes some 11,000 members in more than 300 affiliated societies. For inspiration, visit the ARS American Rose Center gardens at 8877 Jefferson Paige Road.

The organization's 4-month trial membership program costs $10 and includes free advice from Consulting Rosarians; free or reduced admission at rose and botanical gardens; two issues of *American Rose* magazine; free online access to four quarterly publications devoted to miniatures and minifloras, rose arranging, rose exhibiting, and Old Garden and shrub roses; the *Handbook for Selecting Roses*, with numerical ratings for thousands of varieties, published every September; and discounts of up to 30 percent from ARS merchant partners. Go to www.ars.org.

The American Rose Society also offers free advice to all gardeners through the Consulting Rosarian program. To locate a Consulting Rosarian in your area, go to the "Need Advice?" tab at the top of the ARS home page. You may also submit specific questions at the bottom link on the left-hand column of the home page, "Ask a Question About Growing Roses."

American Rose Society, P.O. Box 30,000, Shreveport, LA 71130, 800-637-6534

Helpful publications

Combined Rose List Published yearly (about $25). Use it as a reference when shopping for roses at local nurseries. To order: www.combinedroselist.com; 330-296-2618.

Online resources

CanadianRoseSociety.org Information on hardy roses for cold climates.
RosariansCorner.net A free forum that discusses rose growing, rose varieties, and more.
GardenWeb.com Follow the links to "forums" and then to "roses."
HelpMeFind.com Find specific rose varieties, most with color images, indexed to a list of North American and overseas nurseries that carry them, plus website and other rose information.
Rose.org All-America Rose Selections, a nonprofit association of rose growers and introducers, offers regional information plus background on award-winning roses since 1938.
WorldRose.org The website of the World Federation of Rose Societies offers information on roses from around the world.

Roses by mail

Roses are available from many online sources, including these nurseries with wide selections:

CHAMBLEE'S ROSE NURSERY
10926 U.S. Hwy. 69 North, Tyler, TX 75706
903-882-5153, www.chambleeroses.com

COOL ROSES
888 Chase Road, West Palm Beach, FL 33415
561-684-2421, www.coolroses.com

DAVID AUSTIN ROSES
15059 State Hwy 64 West, Tyler TX 75704
800-328-8893; www.davidaustinroses.com

HEIRLOOM ROSES
24062 NE Riverside Drive, St. Paul, OR 97137
503-538-1576; www.heirloomroses.com

K & M ROSES
1260 Chicora River Road, Buckatunna, MS 39322
601-648-2908; www.kandmroses.com

PALATINE FRUIT & ROSES
2108 Four Mile Creek Road, RR# 3
Niagara-On-The-Lake, Ontario, Canada LoS 1Jo
905-468-8627; www.palatineroses.com

PICKERING NURSERIES
3043 County Road #2 RR#1
Port Hope, Ontario, Canada L1A 3V5
905-753-2155; www.pickeringnurseries.com

REGAN NURSERY
4268 Decoto Road, Fremont, CA 94555
510-797-3222. www.regannursery.com

ROGUE VALLEY ROSES
P.O. Box 116, Phoenix, OR 97535
541-535-1307; www.roguevalleyroses.com

ROSES UNLIMITED
363 N. Deerwood Drive, Laurens, SC 29360
864-682-7673; www.rosesunlimitedownroot.com

ROSEMANIA
4020 Trail Ridge Drive, Franklin, TN 37067
888-600-9665, www.rosemania.com

THE ANTIQUE ROSE EMPORIUM
Retail centers in Independence and San Antonio, TX
Order: 9300 Lueckemeyer Road, Brenham, TX 77833
800-441-0002; www.antiqueroseemporium.com

VINTAGE GARDENS
4130 Gravenstein Hwy. North, Sebastopol, CA 95472
707-829-2035; www.vintagegardens.com

WITHERSPOON ROSE CULTURE
3312 Watkins Road, Durham, NC 27707
800-643-0315; www.witherspoonrose.com

Rose gardens to visit

One of the best ways to learn about roses is to visit public rose gardens and botanical gardens. Most roses are at their peak in June, but you can gather valuable information in other months. For a more complete list, see www.ars.org.

BOERNER BOTANICAL GARDENS*
9400 Boerner Dr., Hales Corner, WI 53130
414-525-5650, www.boernerbotanicalgardens.org

BROOKLYN BOTANIC GARDEN*
1000 Washington Ave., Brooklyn, NY 11225
718-623-7200, www.bbg.org

CHICAGO BOTANIC GARDENS*
1000 Lake Cook Rd., Glencoe, IL 60022
847-835-5440, www.chicago-botanic.org

COLUMBUS PARK OF ROSES
3901 N. High St., Columbus, OH 43214
www.parkofroses.org

GARDEN OF ROSES OF LEGEND & ROMANCE
1680 Madison Ave., Wooster, OH 44691
330-263-3612; www.oardc.osu.edu/rosegarden

HERSHEY GARDENS*
170 Hotel Road, Hershey, PA 17033
717-534-3492, www.hersheygardens.org

INTERNATIONAL ROSE TEST GARDEN
400 SW Kingston Ave., Portland, OR 97201
503-227-7033 www.rosegardenstore.org

MSU HORTICULTURE GARDENS*
A-204E Plant & Soil Science, East Lansing, MI 48824
517-355-5191; www.hrt.msu.edu

NEW YORK BOTANICAL GARDEN*
Bronx River Parkway at Fordham Road
Bronx, NY 10458
718-817-8700, www.nybg.org

SAN JOSE HERITAGE ROSE GARDEN
Spring and Taylor streets, San Jose, CA
heritageroses.us

TYLER MUNICIPAL ROSE GARDEN
420 S. Rose Park Drive, Tyler, TX 75702
903-597-3130; www.texasrosefestival.com

THE HUNTINGTON BOTANICAL GARDENS
1151 Oxford Road, San Marino, CA 91108
626-405-2100, www.huntington.org

UNITED STATES NATIONAL ARBORETUM*
3501 New York Avenue NE, Washington, DC 20002
202-245-2726; www.usna.usda.gov

*Denotes free admission with an American Rose Society membership card.

Index

NOTE: Page references in **bold** denote a Gallery of Roses entry. Page references in *italics* denote rose photographs outside the Gallery of Roses.

A

Abby's Angel, **202**
About Face, **128**
Abraham Darby, *31, 32, 37,* **158**
Acey Deucy, **190**
Albéric Barbier, *23,* **208**
Albertine, *29*
Alister Stella Gray, *29,* **180**
All-America Rose Selections, *20,* 112, 216
Altissimo, *23, 28,* **208**
Amending soil, 74–75
America, *38,* **209**

American Beauty, *7*
American Pillar, *23, 29,* **209**
American Rose Society
   members' choice awardees, 113
   scoring system, 112
   visiting, 216
Amy Grant, **202**
Angel Face, *18, 21,* **134**
Animal pests, 91
Anthracnose, 91
Apothecary's Rose, *7*
Apricot Nectar, **134**
Archduke Charles, **180**
Armada, **158**
Augusta Luise, *21*
Autumn Damask, **181**
Autumn Splendor, **203**

Autumn Sunset, *22*
Awakening, **209**
Awards key, 112

B

Baby Grand, *39, 103,* **190**
Baby Love, **191**
Ballerina, **159**
Barbra Streisand, *21*
Bare-root roses, 76-78
Baronne Prévost, **181**
Bees Knees, *37, 103,* 113, **191**
Behold, *53*
Belinda's Dream, *32, 38, 57,* **159**
Bella Rosa, **135**
Belle Story, **159**
Berries 'n' Cream, **209**

Betty Boop, **135**
Betty Prior, *40*, **135**
Bewitched, *30*, **114**
Bill Warriner, **135**
Black Cherry, **136**
Black Jade, *18*, **191**
Black Magic, **114**
Black spot, 87, 92
Blanc Double de Coubert, *31*, **159**
Blaze Improved, **210**
Bloom habit, 19
Bloom shape, 19
Bloom size, 27
Blueberry Hill, **136**
Bolero, **136**
Bonica, *113*, **160**
Boule de Neige, **181**
Brass Band, *10*, **136**
Bredon, 31
Bride's Dream, **115**
Brigadoon, **115**
Brite Eyes, **210**
Buck roses, 32
Budded roses, 35
Buff Beauty, **160**
Burgundy Iceberg, **137**
Butter Cream, *103*, **203**
Buying roses, 40-43

C
Cabbage Rose, **174**
Caldwell Pink, 57
Calendars, regional care, 104–109
Candelabra, **128**
Cane borer, 88
Capt. Harry Stebbings, 113
Cardinal de Richelieu, **174**
Care and maintenance, 71–107
    amending soil, 74–75
    fall and winter, 100–101
    fertilizer use, 83–85
    mulch, 82–83
    pest and disease control, 86–93
    planting roses, 76–79
    pruning, 94–99
    regional care calendars, 104–109
    site preparation, 72–73
    watering, 80–81
Carefree Beauty, *32, 32, 35, 57*, **160**
Caribbean, **129**
Carpet of Color, *25*
Cathedral, **137**
Celestial, **175**
Celsiana, **175**

Champlain, **160**
Champneys' Pink Cluster, *6, 29, 37*
Charles Albanel, 33
Charles de Mills, *28*, **175**
Cherish, **137**
Cherries 'n' Cream, **161**
Cherry Parfait, **129**
Chihuly, **137**
Child's Play, **191**
China Doll, *28*, **156**
China roses, 7, 9
Chrysler Imperial, *21*, **115**
Chuckles, 22
Cinderella, **192**
City of London, **138**
Class Act, **138**
Clematis, pairing roses with, 62–63
Climbing Pinkie, 57
Climbing roses
    Earth-Kind cultivars, 57
    gallery of roses, 208–215
    growth habit, 23, 28
    history of, 9
    pruning, 96-97
    structures for, 54–55
    traits, 30
Cocktail, **161**
Cold areas, roses for, 103
Color, 17-19
Communis (Common Moss), **175**
Compassion, *34*, **210**
Complicata, *30*, **176**
Comte de Chambord, *29*, **181**
Constance Spry, *12, 62*
Consulting Rosarian, *17, 42, 99*, 216
Container roses, 58–59
Conundrum, **203**
Cornelia, **161**
Countess Celeste, **161**
Country Dancer, **162**
Cramoisi Supérieur, *9*, **182**
Crazy Dottie, **192**
Crested Moss, **176**
Crimson Bouquet, **129**
Crimson Glory, 21
Crown gall, 92
Crystalline, **115**
Cupcake, *19*, **192**
Cut roses, 60–61

D
Dainty Bess, **116**
Dancing Flame, **192**
David Austin English roses, 12–13, 32

David Thompson, 33
Day Breaker, **138**
Deadheading, 65, 98-99
Deer, 91
Design
    container roses, 58–59
    formal garden, 46–47
    garden plans, 62–69
    hedges, 53
    mass plantings, 52
    mixed garden, 48–49
    slopes and problem areas, 50–51
    structures for roses, 54–55
    water-wise garden, 56–57
Dicky, **138**
Disbudding, 98
Disease, 87, 91–93
Don Juan, *23*, **210**
Dortmund, *31, 31*, **162**
Double Delight, *21, 113*, **116**
Double Knock Out, *36*, **162**
Double rose form, 19
Downy mildew, 92
Dr Huey rootstock, *41*, 77
Dr John Dickman, *27*, **203**
Dr W. Van Fleet, 23
Drainage, 73, 75
Dream Come True, *28*, **129**
Dream Weaver, *23*, **211**
Drift roses, 13
Dublin, **116**
Dublin Bay, **211**
Ducher, 57
Duchesse de Brabant, *57*, **182**
Duchess of Portland, 29

E
Earth-Kind roses, 32, 56–57
Earth Song, *35*, **130**
Easy Elegance roses, 33, 64
Easy Going, **139**
Ebb Tide, **139**
Electron, **116**
Elina, *26, 35, 103, 113*, **117**
Elizabeth Taylor, **117**
Elle, **117**
Else Poulsen, 57
Entry gardens, 62–65
Escapade, *27*, **139**
Eureka, **139**
Europeana, **140**
Explorer roses, 33
Eyepaint, *35, 103*, **140**

F

Fabulous!, *103*, **140**
Fairhope, *103*
Falling in Love, **117**
Fall maintenance, 99–101
Fame!, *34*, **130**
Families, rose, 26-33
Fantin-Latour, **176**
Fashion, *10*
Feeding
  foliar, 85
  soil, 83
Felicia, *31*, **162**
Félicité Parmentier, **176**
Fertilizers, 83, 84–85
The Finest, *113*
Firefighter, *21*, *113*, **118**
First Edition, **141**
First Kiss, **141**
Flirtatious, **140**
Floribundas
  for cold and hot areas, *103*
  gallery of roses, 134–155
  growth habit, 27
  history of, *10*
  traits, 30
Flower Carpet Coral, *19*
Flower Carpet roses, *13, 23, 51, 64*, **163**
Flower Girl, **163**
Flutterbye, **163**
Foliar feeding, 85
Folklore, **118**
Formal garden, 46–47
Fortuniana rootstock, *41*, 77
Forty Heroes, *113*
Fourth of July, *30, 39*, **211**
Fragrance, 20–21, *113*
Fragrant Cloud, *21, 113*, **118**
Fragrant Delight, **141**
Fragrant Hour, *113*
Fragrant Plum, *21*, **130**
Francois Rabelais, **141**
Frederic Mistral, **118**
Fred Loads, **163**
French Lace, *30*, **142**
Fungicide, 87
Funny Face, **164**

G

Gallery of roses, 111–215
  awards, 112
  climbers and ramblers, 208–215
  floribundas, 134–155
  grandifloras, 128–133
  hybrid teas, 114–127
  miniatures, 190–201
  minifloras, 202–207
  Old Garden Roses
    once blooming, 174–179
    reblooming, 180–187
  polyanthas, 156–157
  scoring system, 112
  shrub roses, 158–173
  species roses, 188–189
Garden Party, **119**
Garden plans, 62–69
  arbor, 62-63
  circular, 66–67
  entry garden, 64–65
  romantic garden, 68–69
Gartendirektor Otto Linne, **164**
Gemini, *26, 36, 103, 113*, **119**
Gene Boerner, *10*, **142**
George Burns, **142**
Georgetown Tea, *57*
Giggles, *22*, **193**
Gizmo, **193**
Glad Tidings, **142**
Gloire de Dijon, **182**
Golden Holstein, **143**
Golden Wings, **164**
Goldmarie, **143**
Gold Medal, *39*, **130**
Gourmet Popcorn, *34*, **193**
Grace, **164**
Grace Seward, **193**
Graham Thomas, *32, 35, 113*, **165**
Granada, *21*
Grandifloras
  gallery of roses, 128–133
  growth habit, 28
  history of, *11*
  traits, 30
Grandma's Blessing, *33*
Great Maiden's Blush, **177**
Green Ice, **194**
Greetings, **165**
Groundcover roses, *13, 23, 25, 30, 51*
Gruss an Aachen, **143**
Guy de Maupassant, **143**

H

H. C. Andersen, **144**
Händel, **211**
Hannah Gordon, *103*, **144**
Hansa hybrid rugosa, *31, 34*
Hardiness Zones, 102-103
Harlekin, **212**
Heartbreaker, **194**
Heart 'n' Soul, **165**
Hedges, 25, 53
Henri Martin, **177**
Henry Hudson, **165**
Herbicides, 75
Heritage, **166**
High Society, **212**
History and development, 5–13
  first roses, 6–7
  modern roses, 8–9
  recent trends, 12–13
Home Run, *113*, **166**
Honey Dijon, **131**
Honey Perfume, **144**
Hope for Humanity, **166**
Hot areas,
  roses for, *103*
Hot Cocoa, *39, 95, 113*, **144**
Hot Princess, *103*
Hot Tamale, *35, 103*, **194**
Hybrid gallica roses, 29
Hybrid kordesii roses, 31
Hybrid moyesii roses, 31
Hybrid musk roses, 31
Hybrid rugosa roses, *13, 25, 31, 53*
Hybrid tea roses
  for cold and hot areas, *103*
  gallery of roses, 114–127
  growth habit, 23, 26
  traits, 30
Hybrid wichuriana roses, 29, 208

I

Iceberg, *103, 113*, **145**
The Impressionist, **215**
Incognito, **194**
Ingrid Bergmen, *26, 113*, **119**
Insecticide, 87
Integrated pest management, 86–87
International Herald Tribune, **145**
Intrigue, *113*
IPM, see Integrated pest management

Irish Elegance, 23
Irish Hope, **145**
Irresistible, *36*, *103*, **195**
Ivory Fashion, **145**

J

Jacqueline du Pré, **166**
James Alexander Gamble Award, 21
James Mason, *29*, **177**
Japanese beetle, 88
Jaune Desprez, **182**
Jean Giono, 33
Jean Kenneally, 22, **195**
Jeanne Lajoie, **195**
Jilly Jewel, 22
Johann Strauss, **146**
John Cabot, *33*, **167**
John Davis, **167**
Joseph's Coat, **212**
Jude the Obscure, 113
Judy Garland, **146**
Julia Child, *39*, *103*, *113*, **146**
Just Joey, *113*, **119**

K

Kardinal, *23*, **120**
Kathleen, **167**
Keepsake, **120**
Knock Out, *13*, *30*, *32*, *33*, *41*, *57*, *64*, *113*, **167**
Königin von Dänemark, *19*, **177**
Kristin, **195**

L

Lady Elsie May, **168**
La France, *8*, *9*
Lagerfeld, 113
La Marne, *9*, *57*, **156**
La Reine, **183**
Lavaglut, *37*, *103*, **146**
Lavender Dream, **168**
Lavender Lassie, 23
La Ville de Bruxelles, **178**
Layering, 51
Leading Lady, 103
Leafhopper, 88
Leaf roller, 89
Léda, **178**
Lemon Drop, **196**
Leonard Dudley Braithwaite, **168**
Let Freedom Ring, *103*, **120**
Liebeszauber, **120**
Lime Sublime, **147**
Linda Campbell, **168**

Little Artist, *103*, **196**
Little Darling, **147**
Little Jackie, **196**
Livin' Easy, *19*, *34*, **147**
Long-cane roses, see Climbing roses
Louise Estes, **121**
Louise Odier, **183**
Louisville Lady, **204**
Love and Peace, **121**
Lovely Fairy, 30
Lyda Rose, **169**
Lynn Anderson, **121**

M

Mme Alfred Carrière, **183**
Mme Antoine Mari, 57
Mme Ernest Calvat, **183**
Madame Ferdinand Jamin, 7
Mme Hardy, *36*, **178**
Mme Isaac Pereire, **184**
Mme Peirre Oger, **184**
Mme Plantier, **178**
Mme Zöetmans, **179**
Mlle Cécile Brünner, *37*, *57*, **157**
Magic Carrousel, *103*, **196**
Maintenance, see Care and maintenance
Marchesa Boccella, **184**
Marchioness of Lorne, **184**
Margaret Merril, *27*, **147**
Maria Shriver, **131**
Marie Daly, 57
Marie Pavié, **157**
Marilyn Monroe, *39*, *103*, **121**
Marina, **148**
Marmalade Skies, **148**
Martha's Vineyard, *53*, **169**
Mary Rose, **169**
Mass plantings, 52
Max Graf, 51
May Queen, 9
Melody Parfumée, *28*, *37*, **131**
Memorial Day, **122**
Memphis King, *103*, **204**
Memphis Magic, **204**
Mermaid, **185**
Midas Touch, **122**
Midge, 89
Midwest
    best roses for, 35
    rose care calendar, 105
Millie Walters, **197**
Miniature roses

for cold and hot areas, 103
gallery of roses, 190–201
growth habit, 22, 26
history of, 11
pruning, 97
Ralph Moore Rose Garden, 26
traits, 30
Miniflora roses
    for cold and hot areas, 103
    gallery of roses, 202–207
    growth habit, 27
    history of, 11
    traits, 30
Minnesota Tip method, 101
Minnie Pearl, **197**
Miss Flippens, 103
Mister Lincoln, *21*, **122**
Mites, 90
Mixed border, 48–49
Molineux, *20*, **169**
Moondance, **148**
Moonstone, *37*, *103*, **122**
Morden Blush, *33*, **170**
Morden Centennial, **170**
Morden roses, 33
Moss roses, 6
Mrs B. R. Cant, **185**
Mulch, 82–83
Multiflora rootstock, see *Rosa multiflora*
Musk rose, 31
Mutabilis, *38*, *57*, **185**
My Sunshine, *34*, **197**

N

Nearly Wild, **148**
Neon Cowboy, **197**
Nevada, 31
New Dawn, *9*, *9*, *36*, *56*, *57*, *62*, *68*, *113*, **212**
Newport Fairy, **213**
Newspaper, for grass and
    weed suppression, 75, 83
New Zealand, **123**
Night Owl, **213**
Noisette roses, 7, 29
Northeast
    best roses for, 36
    rose care calendar, 106
Northern Encore, 23-25
Northwest
    best roses for, 34
    rose care calendar, 104
Nozomi, 51

index

O

Octoberfest, *18*, **131**
Old Blush, **185**
Old Garden Roses, 28–29, *35*
    gallery of roses
        once blooming, 174–179
        reblooming, 180–187
    traits, 30
Olympiad, *34*, **123**
Olympic Gold, 27, **204**
Opening Night, **123**
Oranges 'n' Lemons, **170**
Our Lady of Guadalupe, **149**
Outta the Blue, **170**
Overnight Scentsation, **205**
Own-root roses, 41, 43

P

Papa Meilland, 21, 113
Paprika, **149**
Pâquerette, 9
Parole, 113
Parson's Pink China, 7, 29
Party Girl, **198**
Pascali, 113
Passionate Kisses, **149**
Patio rose, 25
Patriot Dream, *113*
Paul Ricault, **179**
Paul's Himalayan musk, *23*
Pax, 31
Peace, 113, **123**
Peach Delight, **205**
Pearly Gates, **213**
Penelope, **171**
Perfect Moment, **124**
Perfume Delight, 113
Perle d'Or, *57*, **157**
Pest and disease control, 86–93
Pierre de Ronsard, *23*, *37*, 113, **213**
Pierrine, **198**
Pillar rose, *23*, 25
Pink Knock Out, 22, *49*
Pink Meidiland, *30*, **171**
Pink Roamer, 9
Planting, 76–79
Playboy, *19*, 103, **149**
Playgirl, *38*, **150**
Pleasure, **150**
Polka, *33*, **214**
Polonaise, 32

Polyanthas
    gallery of roses, 156–157
    growth habit, 28
    history of, 9
    traits, 30
Portland roses, 29
Potted roses, 77, 79
Poulsen's Pearl, 103
Powdery mildew, 93
Prairie Princess, **171**
Preference, **150**
Pretty Lady, **150**
Priscilla Burton, **151**
Pristine, **124**
Prominent, **132**
Propagation, 51
Prospero, *12*
Pruning, 94–99

Q

Queen Elizabeth, *11*, 28, *36*, 113, **132**

R

Rabbits, 91
Radiant Perfume, **132**
Rainbow Knock Out, *13*, *33*
Rainbow's End, *26*, **198**
Rainbow Sorbet, **151**
Raised beds, 72, *73*, 75
Ramblers, 9, 25, 30, 208–215
Ramblin' Red, *25*, **214**
Raspberry cane borer, 89
Reba McIntyre, **132**
Red Cascade, **198**
Red Ribbons, 51, *51*, **171**
Regensberg, **151**
Reine des Violettes, **186**
Rejoice, **133**
Remember Me roses, 113
Renaissance, 113
Resources, 216–217
Rêve d'Or, *57*
Rise 'n' Shine, **199**
Robusta, *36*, **172**
Rocky Top, **205**
Rödhätte, *10*
Roller Coaster, **199**
Romantica roses, *33*, 66–67
Roots, 73
Rootstock, 41, 77
Rosa banksiae lutea, **188**
Rosa gallica versicolor, **188**
Rosa glauca, **188**

Rosa hugonis, **189**
Rosa macrantha, **189**
Rosa moschata, 31
Rosa multiflora rootstock, 41, 77
Rosa Mundi, **188**
Rosarium Uetersen, **214**
Rosa rugosa, **189**
Rosa rubrifolia, *49*, **189**
Rosa sericea pteracantha, *49*
Rosa wichuriana, 9
Rose de Rescht, *39*, **186**
Rose Hills fragrance award winners, 21
Rosemary Harkness, **124**
Rose rosette, 93
Rose slugs, 90
Rouge Royale, 21
Rouletii, 11
Royal Highness, 113
Royal Occasion, **151**
Royal Sunset, 28, *28*, *35*, **214**
Ruby Pendant, **199**
Ruby Ruby, *30*, **199**
Rugosa roses, *13*, 25, 31, 53
Rust, 93

S

St. Patrick, *19*, *38*, *53*, 103, **124**
Salet, **186**
Sally Holmes, *34*, *39*, **172**
Sarabande, **152**
Sassy Cindy, **205**
Savoy Hotel, **125**
Scales, 90
Scentimental, *18*, **152**
Scentsational, **200**
Sea Foam, *23*, *32*, *38*, 51, *57*, **172**
Secret, 21, *21*, 103, **125**
Selecting roses, 15–43
    basics for, 16–17
    buying roses, 40–43
    checklist, 17
    color, shape, and form, 18–19
    fragrant choices, 20–21
    by plant habit, 22–25
    regional choices, 34–39
    rose families, 26–29, 30
    shrub roses, 31–33
Semidouble rose, 19
Sexy Rexy, 103, **152**
Sheer Elegance, **125**
Sheila's Perfume, 21, **152**
Showbiz, **153**

Shrub roses
   deadheading, 99
   Earth-Kind cultivars, 57
   gallery of roses, 158–173
   traits, 22, 30
   varieties of, 12–13, 31–33
Silver Jubilee, **125**
Simplex, **200**
Simplicity, **153**
Singin' in the Rain, **153**
Site preparation, 72–73
Slopes, 50–51
Small Miracle, **200**
Snow Bride, **200**
Soaring Spirits, 113
Social Climber, **215**
Soil
   amending, 74–75
   drainage, 73, 75
   feeding, 83
   pH, 75
   potting, 77
Solar Flair, **206**
Sombreuil, **215**
South Central and Lower Midwest
   best roses for, 38
   rose care calendar, 108
Southeast
   best roses for, 37
   rose care calendar, 107
Southwest and Southern California
   best roses for, 39
   rose care calendar, 109
Souvenir de la Malmaison, **186**
Souvenir de St. Anne's, 57
Sparrieshoop, **172**
Species roses, 6, 30-31, 188–189
Spice, 57
Spider mites, 90
Sport, 25
Spring's a Comin', **206**
Stairway to Heaven, **215**
Standards, 23, 25, 30
Stanwell Perpetual, *34*, **187**
Starina, **201**
Stephens' Big Purple, **126**
Strike It Rich, *30*, **133**
Summer Fashion, **153**
Sun Flare, **154**
Sunlight requirements, 72–73
Sunrise Sunset, *33*, **173**
Sunset Celebration, **126**
Sun Sprinkles, *30*, **201**

Sunsprite, *21*, **154**
Survivor, 113
Sweet Chariot, *21*, **201**
Sweet Diana, **201**
Sweet Inspiration, **154**
Sweet Intoxication, *21*

T
Tahitian Sunset, *112*, **126**
Tennessee Sunrise, **206**
Thanks to Sue, **206**
The Fairy, *28, 57, 62*, **157**
The McCartney Rose, **126**
Thorns, snapping off, 61
Thrips, 91
Tiffany, *21*, **127**
Tiffany Lite, **207**
Tiffany Lynn, *103*, **207**
Tom Thumb, 11
Topsy Turvy, **154**
Touch of Class, *23*, **127**
Tournament of Roses, *19, 38*, **133**
Transplanting roses, 79
Tree roses, *23, 25, 30*
Trumpeter, *19*, **155**
Tuscan Sun, **155**
Tuscany, **179**

U
USDA Hardiness Zone map, 103

V
Valentine's Day, **207**
Variegata di Bologna, **187**
Veilchenblau, **179**
Velvet Fragrance, 113
Very double rose, 19
Veterans' Honor, *102*, **127**
Victorian Spice, **155**
Vogue, 10
Voluptuous!, *19*
Voodoo, **127**

W
Watering, 80–81
Water-wise garden, 56–57
We Salute You, 113
Westerland, **173**
Whirlaway, **207**
White Meidiland, *23*, **173**
White Simplicity, **155**
Wild Blue Yonder, *21*, **133**
William Baffin, **173**

Winter hardiness, 102
Winter protection, 59, 101
World Rose Hall of Fame winners, 113

Y
Yellow Lady Banks' Rose, **188**
Yolande d'Aragon, **187**

Z
Zéphirine Drouhin, **187**

Looking for more
gardening inspiration?

See what the experts at
Better Homes & Gardens have to offer.

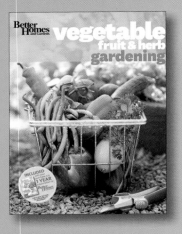

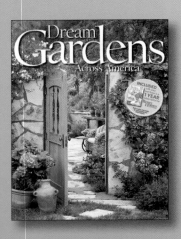

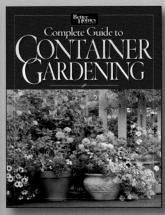

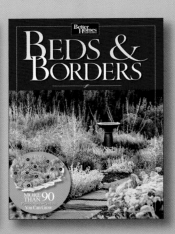

Available where all great books are sold.